SOPHOCLES

Plate I

Sophocles as an Elderly Man

From a Herm in the British Museum

SOPHOCLES

Poet and Dramatist

By

WILLIAM NICKERSON BATES, Ph.D.

Professor of the Greek Language and Literature Emeritus
University of Pennsylvania

•

Fellow of the American Academy of Arts and Sciences

A Perpetua Book

A. S. Barnes & Company, Inc.

New York

Perpetua Edition 1961

UNIVERSITY OF PENNSYLVANIA PRESS

Manufactured in the United States of America

To my former teachers

William Watson Goodwin

John Henry Wright

Frederick De Forest Allen

Charles Rockwell Lanman

in grateful remembrance

this book is dedicated

CONTENTS

ILLUSTRATIONS

PLATES

FIGURES

PREFACE

In writing this book the author has had in mind especially that large company of American readers who are deeply interested in Greek literature, but who do not read Greek easily. For such readers a translation however good is not enough. They want more information about the writer and his work, and above all they want to know the evidence upon which statements about him are based. Such information the author has undertaken to supply, giving at the foot of the page the ancient authority for all statements in the text, and adding references to the more important modern authorities where it seemed desirable to do so. It is hoped that this feature will, without overburdening the reader with unnecessary footnotes, make the book useful to students of Sophocles generally. A list of the Sophocles papyri has been added as an Appendix.

It has been thought well to include in the book a number of illustrations taken from Greek vase-paintings in order to make clearer the ancient conception of certain scenes. Some of the drawings were directly inspired by the play which they are introduced to illustrate. In other cases the artist was influenced by the same source from which the dramatist drew. Thus the illustration for the *Ichneutae* is taken from a vase painted long before the play was written, when the artist was inspired by the Homeric *Hymn to Hermes;* but it gives a good idea of how the ancient Greek pictured to himself the story of the infant Hermes and the stolen cattle.

In making his translations the author has used, except in a very few places, the text of the Oxford edition of the plays by A. C. Pearson; and for his discussion of the lost plays the text of the monumental edition of the fragments by the same scholar, adding such new material as has been brought to light since the publication of that work. As usual the iambic trimeter lines of the Greek have been rendered in blank verse in English; for the more complicated lyric rhythms the author has used simple verse forms without rhyme. Familiar proper names have been spelled in the way in which they usually appear in English literature.

Sophocles has had the great good fortune in modern times to be admired and appreciated in a much higher degree than his two famous contemporaries. This has been especially true in England, where scholars in a long line have labored, correcting and expounding the text of the dramas, and repeatedly editing them. Interest in him today is attested by such books as Heinrich Weinstock's *Sophokles* (Berlin, 1931) and Karl Reinhardt's *Sophokles* (Frankfurt a. M., 1933) in Germany; and by T. B. L. Webster's *Introduction to Sophocles* (Oxford, 1936) in England; as well as by Max Pohlenz's *Griechische Tragoedie* (Berlin, 1930) and J. E. Harry's *Greek Tragedy* (New York, 1933), all brought out during the last ten years. To these should be added numerous articles about him in learned publications issued in all countries, all showing that a keen interest in the great dramatist still exists.

In American colleges at the present time Sophocles is much read in English translation, especially by students specializing in the field of English literature. Plumptre's verse translation is the one generally used. Jebb's fine prose version seems not to be as well known as it should be.

The author wishes to acknowledge his indebtedness to all who have helped him in the book. To the British Museum, the *Journal of Hellenic Studies*, and the Archaeological Institute of America for permission to reproduce illustrations; to the Louvre for permitting a drawing of a vase to be made; to the libraries of Harvard, Columbia, and Princeton Universities and to the Library of Congress for books; to Dr. Sterling Dow for the squeeze of an inscription; to Dr. Charles W. Burr, Dr. J. M. Paton, Dr. T. H. Westbrook, and other friends for their assistance; and particularly to his colleagues at the University of Pennsylvania, Professor H. Lamar Crosby and Mr. Edwin C. Tappert, and to Professor Robert E. Dengler of Pennsylvania State College, who have read proof-sheets of the book.

Philadelphia,
February 22, 1940

W. N. B.

CHAPTER I

THE LIFE OF SOPHOCLES

SOURCES

IN WRITING an account of the life of any man it is essential first of all to know what the sources are from which information about him may be derived. Then, when these sources have been examined and compared, it will be possible to set forth with some degree of exactness the probable incidents in his career. This is all the more necessary when the subject of the biography lived in ancient times, for the letters and other first-hand documents available for the life of a man of the modern world are lacking for antiquity.

For Sophocles our most important source is an anonymous *Life* (Σοφοκλέους γένος καὶ βίος) found in the thirteenth-century manuscript of the plays in Paris[1] and in some other less important manuscripts. It is lacking in the more famous Florentine codex of the eleventh century (Codex Laurentianus xxxii, 9). When it was composed can only be conjectured, but some of the sources from which the compiler drew may be inferred from his text. Thus he mentions a certain Istrus no less than seven times. Little is known about this man. He came from Callatis, a town in Thrace on the Euxine Sea, and published a book on tragedy (περὶ τραγῳδίας).[2] The references in the *Life* are presumably to that work. Nothing is known about his date.[3]

Then there are three references to Satyrus, the peripatetic,

[1] Codex Parisinus 2712. Other manuscripts which have it are Marcianus 468; Vindobonensis 281; Abbat. Florentinus 152; Ambrosianus L 39 super.; Parisinus 2794; Jenensis B 7; and Parisinus 2711.

[2] See Pauly-Wissowa, *Real-Encyclopädie*, s. v. Istros.

[3] See Susemihl, *Geschichte der griech. Lit. in der Alexandrinerzeit*, I, p. 512.

who lived in the second, or possibly third, century B.C. and wrote a biographical work apparently of some length. Considerable portions of his account of the life of Euripides have been recovered from a papyrus found at Oxyrhynchus (No. 1176), from which it is learned that his Sixth Book was devoted to the lives of the three great tragic poets, Aeschylus, Sophocles, and Euripides.[1] There can be no doubt that this is the work from which the author of the *Life* was drawing.

He mentions also several other writers whom he used directly or indirectly. Thus Hieronymus of Rhodes, a peripatetic philosopher and writer of literary history, is referred to as an authority for the piety of Sophocles. This man lived in the third century B.C. and is known to have published a work entitled *περὶ ποιητῶν* and another *περὶ τραγῳδοποιῶν*.[2] The latter is presumably the book to which reference is made.

Neanthes of Cyzicus, about whom little is known, is mentioned once along with Istrus for his account of the death of Sophocles. He was the author of a book about famous men (*περὶ ἐνδόξων ἀνδρῶν*).

Carystius of Pergamum, who lived in the latter half of the second century B.C., is quoted as the authority for the victories of Sophocles. He wrote *περὶ χορῶν* and also *περὶ διδασκαλιῶν*.[3] The latter work is probably the one referred to.

There are two references to the great authority on music, Aristoxenus of Tarentum, whose book *περὶ τραγῳδοποιῶν* is presumably the one to which the writer is referring, though it is possible that he may have been drawing from another work of his entitled *περὶ τραγικῆς ὀρχήσεως*.

The great scholar Aristophanes of Byzantium is mentioned twice. He is known to have edited the plays of Sophocles with critical notes on the text, and to have added prefatory notices, or

[1] The contents of the book are given thus at the end: *Σατύρου Βίων Ἀναγραφῆς ϛʹ Αἰσχύλου, Σοφοκλέους, Εὐριπίδου.* See *Oxyrhynchus Papyri*, IX, p. 168.

[2] Pauly-Wissowa, *op. cit.*, s. v. Hieronymos.

[3] See Athenaeus, VI, 235e.

hypotheses as they are called, to them. Such notices as have come down to us in the manuscripts probably go back to him more or less directly. Two actually bear his name, one in prose prefixed to the *Antigone*,[1] and another in verse preceding the *Oedipus Tyrannus*. He is quoted as authority for the statement that there were 130 plays attributed to Sophocles, but that seventeen were spurious.

Lobon[2] of Argos, who was reputed to have attributed to more famous writers lines of his own composition, is quoted as the authority for the inscription on the tomb of the poet.

It is thus seen that the author of this *Life* went back directly or indirectly to a number of sources. He makes no mention of Philochorus, who wrote a work in five books on the plots of Sophocles (περὶ τῶν Σοφοκλέους μύθων),[3] as well as another on tragedy;[4] but there is no way of ascertaining whether these works were known to him or not.

When we ask who the author of the biography was we are equally in the dark. It might be supposed that the indefatigable Didymus was the real compiler. He is known to have written a commentary on the plays of Sophocles, and the most important of the extant scholia may be traced back to him; but there is not sufficient evidence to attribute to him this *Life*.

There is a short and much condensed account of Sophocles in the *Lexicon* of Suidas which gives us a few additional facts. It differs from the *Life* in regard to the poet's date and the number of his victories.

In addition to these two accounts there are scattered through the literature numerous references to the great dramatist which give some further information about him. The passages were collected long ago and may be found in the Jahn-Michaelis

[1] Ἀριστοφάνους γραμματικοῦ ὑπόθεσις Ἀντιγόνης.

[2] It should be noted that Λόβων is really a conjecture of Bergk. The manuscripts have the meaningless λαβών.

[3] See Suidas, s. v. Φιλόχορος.

[4] Scholium to Euripides, *Hecuba*, l. 3. Φιλόχορος . . . ἐν τῷ περὶ τραγῳδιῶν συγγράμματι.

edition of the *Electra*.[1] Since that book was published a few other facts have come to light in inscriptions and papyri; and there are some incidental bits of information, such as his acquaintance with Herodotus, to be gathered from the plays themselves.

LIFE

Sophocles was born at Colonus, a deme located about a mile north of the Acropolis and now within the limits of the city of Athens, probably in the year 497 B.C.[2] The anonymous *Life*, to be sure, gives a date two years later; but as it is in error in comparing his date with those of Aeschylus and Euripides, and other evidence is available, the statement may be rejected without hesitation His father was named Sophillus, and the writer of the *Life* declares that he was neither a carpenter, nor a bronze-worker, nor a maker of knives, as certain writers had stated, though he may have owned slaves who were engaged in such work. The son had the usual education of a boy in a well-to-do family of the fifth century B.C. and is said to have won prizes in wrestling and music. He studied under the distinguished musician Lampros. As a boy he took part in the celebration of the great naval victory over the Persians at Salamis, leading a chorus in singing a paean to the music of the lyre. This incident is evidence for the position of his family in Athens.

[1] *In usum scholarum*, 3d edition, Bonn, 1882.

[2] Sophocles was still living when Euripides died in 406 B.C., but he had died before the performance of the *Frogs* of Aristophanes at the Lenaea in 405. His death, therefore, occurred in the latter part of 406 or early in 405. This date, the archonship of Callias, in the third year of the ninety-third Olympiad, is also given by the Parian Marble (line 78) and by the Hypothesis to the *Oedipus at Colonus* and may be regarded as certain. The Parian Marble also gives his age at the time of his death. The figures on the stone have usually been read as 91, but F. Jacoby in his edition of the inscription (Berlin, 1904) reads them 𐅄ΔΔΔΔII, that is 92. In line 72, however, it says that the dramatist was twenty-eight years old in the archonship of Apsephion, that is in the year 469–68. It might be added that Diodorus Siculus (XIII, 103, 4) says that he was ninety when he died; and in the *Macrobii* (24) which has come down under the name of Lucian it is stated that he was ninety-five.

During his young manhood Aeschylus, who was a generation older, was the all-important figure on the tragic stage.[1] It would be natural, therefore, that the youthful Sophocles should be influenced by him. The outer form of tragedy had already been well developed by the older poet, but Sophocles saw that improvements might be made in it. He added a third actor,[2] and enlarged the chorus from twelve to fifteen members. These were important developments. The possibility of having three speaking actors on the stage at one time greatly increased the dramatist's means of producing an effective scene. He may have gone a step further and used a fourth actor in the *Oedipus at Colonus*.[3] Another important innovation of his consisted in making the tetralogy, or group of three tragedies and a satyr drama with which the tragic poets competed, to consist of plays on unrelated subjects, instead of having all of them concerned with different parts of one great theme.[4] He also improved the stage properties[5] and introduced the white shoes of the chorus and actors and, according to Satyrus,[6] the curved staff. Furthermore, because of his weak voice,[7] he discontinued the practice of a dramatist acting in his own plays; although he is said to have played ball in his *Nausicaa*, wearing the mask of Nausicaa,[8] and to have played the lyre in the performance of his *Thamyras*.[9]

Sophocles won his first tragic victory in the year 468 B.C., when he was twenty-eight years old, with a tetralogy which

[1] The word "stage" is used throughout the book in accordance with modern usage. There was no elevated stage in the Greek theatre of the fifth century B.C.

[2] *Vita*, 4; also Aristotle, *Poet.* p. 1449a 19; Diogenes Laertius, III, 56; *Vita Aesch.* 14, quoting Dicaearchus; Scholia to Demosthenes, XVIII, 267 and XIX, 200.

[3] See p. 72.

[4] Suidas, s. v. Σοφοκλῆς . . . . δρᾶμα πρὸς δρᾶμα, ἀλλὰ μὴ τετραλογίαν.

[5] Aristotle, *Poet.* p. 1449a 19 says that Sophocles introduced scene painting, but that may go back to Aeschylus. See Haigh, *Attic Theatre*, ed. 2, p. 207.

[6] *Vita*, 6.

[7] *Vita*, 4.

[8] See p. 240.

[9] *Vita*, 5; Athenaeus, I, p. 20 f.

included the *Triptolemus*.[1] The youthful poet was competing against the mighty Aeschylus, and the feeling among the spectators ran so high that according to Plutarch[2] the archon did not select the ten judges who were to decide the winner of the contest by lot, which was the usual way, but when the board of ten generals entered the theatre to perform their customary libations, he appointed them as judges. Their reputation was sufficient to insure an impartial decision, which was in favor of the younger dramatist.

Sophocles is known to have been in competition with Euripides for the first time in 438 B.C. when he won first place, and Euripides came second with plays which included the *Alcestis*.[3] In 431 B.C. he was awarded second place[4] when Euphorion, the son of Aeschylus, came first, and Euripides with a tetralogy which included the *Medea* came third. He competed against the various tragic poets of the day including his son Iophon.[5] Suidas[6] says that he won the tragic prize twenty-four times; the *Life* says twenty times, quoting Carystius as its authority, and adding that he came second many times and was never third.[7] An inscription dating from the middle of the third century B.C. gives the number of his victories as eighteen,[8] presumably those won at the Great Dionysia.[9] If the number given by Suidas is correct the six other victories were won at the Lenaea.[10]

[1] Parian Marble, l. 78; Plutarch, *Cimon*, VIII, 9; Pliny, *Nat. Hist.* XVIII, 65.

[2] *Cimon*, VIII, 9. Plutarch's further statement that Aeschylus took the decision so much to heart that he went to Sicily and died there cannot be correct, for the death of Aeschylus occurred twelve years later.

[3] Hypothesis to *Alcestis*.

[4] Hypothesis to *Medea*.

[5] *Vita*, 19.

[6] S. v. Σοφοκλῆς.

[7] *Vita*, 8.

[8] *I. G.* II, 977a.....Σοφ]οκλῆς ΔΠΙΙΙ. Cp. *Rhein. Mus.* XXXIV, p. 298. Diodorus Siculus, XIII, 103, 4 gives the same number.

[9] He may have won at the Great Dionysia in the spring of 447 B.C. A fragment of the list of victors for the year 448–47 recently found in the Agora reads, according to Mr. Eugene Schweigert, to whom I am indebted for it:

[Ἴω]ν Λαμπτρε: ἐχορήγε
[Σοφο]κλῆς ἐδίδασκεν
[ὑποκριτὴς Ἡρ]ακλείδης

Sophocles was a very prolific writer. According to Suidas he wrote 123 plays.[1] The writer of the *Life* quotes Aristophanes of Byzantium as authority for the statement that there were 130 plays attributed to him of which seventeen were spurious. Bergk's suggestion[2] that for ιζ′ (17) we should read ζ′ (7) is a natural correction to make both statements agree. Seven tragedies have come down to modern times: the *Ajax*, the *Antigone*, the *Oedipus Tyrannus*, the *Oedipus at Colonus*, the *Electra*, the *Philoctetes*, and the *Trachiniae*. In addition there are well-authenticated titles of 110 more. These will be discussed later. Five plays are quoted with alternative titles. They are: Ἀτρεὺς ἢ Μυκηναῖαι, Μάντεις ἢ Πολύιδος, Ναυσικάα ἢ Πλύντριαι, Ὀδυσσεὺς ἀκανθοπλὴξ ἢ Νίπτρα, and Πανδώρα ἢ Σφυροκόποι. Some others should probably be added to this list. Altogether 132 different titles are known, but when the spurious plays and those with alternative titles are deducted[3] the number will not be far from that given by Suidas.[4]

Heraclides is known to have been the victorious actor also in 449 B.C. See *I. G.* II, 2325, Frag. *p*, and Wilhelm, *Urkunden Dram. Aufführungen*, p. 138.

[10] Plutarch, *Moralia*, p. 497a comments on the fact that the fathers of Sophocles and Euripides did not know of their sons' victories.

[1] Suidas, however, knew that some people put the number higher.

[2] *Sophocles*, p. xxxix.

[3] It has been conjectured that Sophocles wrote a tragedy entitled *Alcmaeon or Alphesiboea*, because the Roman poet Attius wrote an *Alphesiboea* which may have been the same as his *Alcmaeon*; but it cannot be proved that he was following Sophocles. Sometimes a play is wrongly quoted by the name of one of its chief characters. Thus there are lines attributed to an *Hippodameia* (Frag. 472), not otherwise known, which may have come from the *Oenomaus*. Again there is a reference to the *Talos* (Frag. 161) which should probably be to the *Daedalus*. We have one line from a *Cerberus* (Frag. 224) which probably came from the *Heracles*; and one from a *Pelias* which should probably be assigned to one of the two plays entitled *Tyro*, or possibly to the *Peleus*. Fragment 851, in which the speaker was evidently Alcestis, led Welcker (*Die griechischen Tragödien*, I, pp. 344 ff.) to the conclusion that the line came from an *Alcestis* by Sophocles, although it is expressly stated in the Hypothesis to the *Alcestis* of Euripides that neither Aeschylus nor Sophocles used the myth. In the Hypothesis to the *Ajax* there is a reference to an Ἑλένης Ἁρπαγή which is probably a mistake, although Welcker (*op. cit.*, I, pp. 158 ff.) thought it an alternative title for the *Deïphobus*. A scholium on line 496 of the *Knights* of Aristophanes mentions an *Iolaus* by Sophocles, not otherwise known. We have also certain corrupt references which have been

Sophocles was evidently a man of a very kindly disposition, for he was universally beloved.[1] His family life so far as we know was happy, though our information about it is rather scanty. He married at least once. By Nicostrate he had a son Iophon who won a reputation as a tragic poet; and he is said to have had a son by Theoris of Sicyon, named Ariston.[2] Suidas mentions three other sons—Leosthenes, Stephanos and Meneclides—of whom nothing more is known. The poet is said to have been especially fond of Ariston's son, the younger Sophocles, who also was a dramatist and is said by Suidas to have composed forty plays of which seven won first prize. He likewise had a reputation as a writer of elegies. The dramatic tradition seems to have continued in the family for several generations, for in the third century B.C. there was a third Sophocles, reputed to be a descendant of the great dramatist, who won fame as a tragic and a lyric poet. Fifteen plays by him were known. A story has come down that Iophon brought his father into court in his extreme old age charging him with senility, but that he failed to convince the judges and the poet was acquitted. If this tale is true it would seem to show a lack of confidence between father and son at that time.[3]

The esteem in which the people of Athens held him is testified to not only by his numerous victories in the theatre, but also by

---

thought to indicate an *Oeneus* (see below p. 244), though the writer may have had in mind the play of the same name by Euripides. There are also very doubtful references to an *Orithyia* (see Welcker, *op. cit.*, I, pp. 298 f.) and to the peculiar title *Xoenephoroi*.

[4] The fact that 123 is not divisible by 4 is not necessarily an argument against the correctness of this number. The *Oedipus at Colonus* was brought out after the poet's death, and the satyr drama which was to have accompanied it as the fourth member of the tetralogy may never have been written.

[1] See e.g., the *Life*, 7, where it is said of him . . . . τοῦ ἤθους τοσαύτη γέγονε χάρις ὥστε πάντη καὶ πρὸς ἁπάντων αὐτὸν στέργεσθαι. And Aristophanes (*Frogs*, 82) makes Dionysus say of him εὔκολος μὲν ἐνθάδ', εὔκολος δ' ἐκεῖ. The fact that he was called a "bee" (μέλιττα) may be regarded as further evidence of the kindly feeling of the people towards him.

[2] *Vita*, 13. The existence of Theoris has been doubted. See Christ-Schmid, *Geschichte der griech. Lit.* 6th ed. I. p. 314.

[3] See p. 59.

his election to high public office. Thus he was chairman of the Hellenotamiae, or board of ten officials who had charge of the collection of the tribute from the dependent cities, in the year 443–442 B.C. as is known from a fragment of the tribute list for that year.[1] In 440 he was elected one of the ten generals to take charge of the Samian War—an appointment said to have been brought about by the success of his *Antigone*.[2] Pericles was one of his colleagues.[3] There is some evidence that he was also general at a later time, for Plutarch in his *Life of Nicias* (XV, 2) tells a story to the effect that at a certain meeting of the board of generals Sophocles was asked his opinion first because he was the oldest, but declined to give it saying that although he was the oldest Nicias was the senior.[4] Nicias was not a member of the board at the time of the Samian War.

This friendly feeling towards him on the part of the Athenian people was reciprocated by the poet. He was devoted to Athens. The author of the *Life* comments on the fact that although many kings sent for him he was unwilling to leave his native land.[5] In this respect he differed from Aeschylus and Pindar, both of whom visited Hiero, tyrant of Syracuse; and from Euripides who died while staying at the court of Archelaus, king of Macedonia.

[1] *I. G.* I², 202. See Tod, *Greek Historical Inscriptions*, No. 46. It reads Σ]οφοκλῆς Κολώ[νηθεν Ἑλληνοταμί]ας ἦν.

[2] Argumentum I to the *Antigone* ll. 15 f.; also Suidas. s. v. Μέλισσος. Cp. *Vita*, 9. See p. 73.

[3] A scholium to Aristides (III, p. 485, Dindorf) gives the names of eight of these generals on the authority of Androtion as follows: Socrates of Anagyrus, Sophocles the poet, Andocides, Creon, Pericles, Glaucon, Callistratus, and Xenophon of Melite.

[4] ἐγὼ, φάναι, παλαιότατός εἰμι, σὺ δὲ πρεσβύτατος. In a corrupt passage in the *Life* (9) it is stated that the Athenians elected him general when he was sixty-nine (ξθ′) years old. Some late manuscripts give the figures as sixty-five (ξε′). In *An Introduction to Sophocles*, pp. 11 f. and 181 f., T. B. L. Webster summarizes the unsatisfactory evidence for a third generalship. The Sophocles who was one of the ten Probouloi in 413 B.C. was probably not the poet. See Cope, *Rhetoric of Aristotle*, Vol. I, p. 263.

[5] 10. οὕτω δὲ φιλαθηναιότατος ἦν ὥστε πολλῶν βασιλέων μεταπεμπομένων αὐτὸν οὐκ ἠθέλησε τὴν πατρίδα καταλιπεῖν.

Sophocles was noted for his piety.[1] He was especially associated with deities of healing and was a priest of one of them, called in the *Life* Alcon.[2] The name should, perhaps, be corrected to Amynos[3] who is known to have had a sanctuary on the west slope of the Acropolis. According to Philostratus[4] a paean of his in honor of Asclepius was sung at Athens; and three small pieces of a poem by him in honor of that god and bearing his name were actually found near the entrance to the temple of Asclepius south of the Acropolis.[5] He is also said to have founded a shrine of Heracles.[6] After his death he was honored as a hero by the Athenians under the name of Dexion,[7] and offerings were made to him each year.[8]

Athens was not a large city during the fifth century B.C. and Sophocles no doubt knew personally all the literary men of note living there in his time, but his friendship with Herodotus seems to have been especially close. Plutarch[9] has preserved the beginning of an ode to the historian written by the poet when he was fifty-five years old. There are also certain passages in the extant tragedies which appear to be references to the history of Herodotus. Thus in the *Oedipus at Colonus*, ll. 337–341 the dramatist makes Oedipus compare the conduct of his children with that of the people of Egypt, where the men remain indoors and ply the loom and the women attend to outside duties. Here the dramatist seems to have in mind Chapter 35 of the Second

[1] In the *Life*, 12, on the authority of Hieronymus he is called θεοφιλὴς ὡς οὐκ ἄλλος, and in a scholium on the *Electra*, 831, he is spoken of as εἷς τῶν θεοσεβεστάτων.

[2] *Vita*, 12. This is a correction by Meineke of the corrupt manuscript reading ἄλωνος. See scholium on Apollonius Rhodius, *Argonautica*, I, 97.

[3] So A. Körte, *Athenische Mittheil.* XXI, pp. 311 ff., on the evidence of an inscription.

[4] *Apollonius*, III, 17.

[5] See Wilhelm, *Beiträge zur griech. Inschriftkunde*, 1909, pp. 102 ff.

[6] *Vita*, 12. ἱερὸν ἱδρύσατο Μηνυτοῦ Ἡρακλέους.

[7] *Etymologicum Magnum*, s. v. Δεξίων.

[8] *Vita*, 17.

[9] *Moralia*, p. 785 b (*An seni sit res pub. ger.* III, 5). The words are:

Ὠιδὴν Ἡροδότῳ τεῦξεν Σοφοκλῆς ἐτέων ὢν
πέντ' ἐπὶ πεντήκοντα.

Book of Herodotus in which the historian is describing the manners and customs of the Egyptians. Again in the *Electra*, ll. 417–423, where Chrysothemis in relating the dream of Clytaemnestra in which the sceptre of Agamemnon planted in the ground sends forth a great branch which shades the whole land, the poet may have been thinking of the dream of Astyages about his daughter Mandane as told in Book I, Chapter 108. Various other passages have been pointed out in which the poet may have been indebted to the historian.[1]

The story that he put on mourning on hearing of the death of Euripides and brought in his chorus and actors uncrowned at the *proagon*[2] is good evidence that his relations with the younger dramatist were not unfriendly.[3]

Sophocles died, as we have seen, some time after Euripides and before the performance of the *Frogs* of Aristophanes at the Lenaea in January 405, B.C., at the great age of ninety-one. Several stories are told about the cause of his death, no one of which is altogether satisfactory. Thus he is said to have choked on an unripe grape; or to have died from overexertion while giving a public reading of his *Antigone*; or to have died from joy when proclaimed victor after reading the play.[4] Perhaps we should not look for any other cause than his advanced age, for, in his own words,

A little stroke puts aged bodies to sleep.[5]

He died, as he had lived, happily. The words of Phrynichus in his comedy of the *Muses*, brought out at the same time as the *Frogs* of Aristophanes, well describes the great dramatist's

[1] This subject is discussed at length by J. Rasch in *Commentationes Philologae Jenenses*, Vol. X, Part 2. He has assembled all the passages which may with more or less probability be traced to Herodotus.

[2] *Vita Eurip.* ll. 67 ff. λέγουσι δὲ καὶ Σοφοκλέα ἀκούσαντα ὅτι ἐτελεύτησεν αὐτὸν μὲν ἱματίῳ φαιῷ προελθεῖν, τὸν δὲ χορὸν καὶ τοὺς ὑποκριτὰς ἀστεφανώτους εἰσαγαγεῖν ἐν τῷ προαγῶνι καὶ δακρῦσαι τὸν δῆμον.

[3] For his acquaintance with the tragic poet Ion of Chios and his influence upon the latter's style of tragedy see T. B. L. Webster, *Hermes*, LXXI, 1936, pp. 263 ff.

[4] *Vita*, 14.

[5] *Oed. Tyr.*, 961.

career. "Happy Sophocles," he says, "who died after a long life, fortunate, clever, who composed many beautiful tragedies and died happily without having experienced any evil."[1] The sentiment expressed in the old Greek saying, "Call no man happy until he is dead"—a sentiment which he occasionally expresses in his tragedies,[2] and which is sometimes referred to as his philosophy of life—can hardly be said to apply to him.

He was buried in his ancestral tomb on the road to Decelea, eleven stadia or about a mile and a half from the city walls. At that time Lysander, the Spartan, was besieging Athens, but permitted the burial to take place as soon as he learned that it was Sophocles who had died. The figure of a siren is said to have surmounted the tomb.[3]

FAME

Of the fame of Sophocles both in antiquity and in modern times much might be written. He won it early in his career and retained it throughout his life. The number of his tragic victories alone is proof of that. In the centuries after his death Euripides surpassed him in popularity, but both poets had readers even in distant parts of the ancient world.[4] Incidentally Polemon's pleasant designation of him[5] as the "tragic Homer" and of Homer as the "epic Sophocles" may be cited as a significant tribute to his fame. Papyrus fragments of his plays are, to be sure, less numerous than those of Euripides, but the fact that his little-known dramas such as the *Ichneutae*[6] and the *Eury-*

[1] The lines are preserved in Hypothesis II to the *Oedipus at Colonus*. They read:

> μάκαρ Σοφοκλέης, ὃς πολὺν χρόνον βιοὺς
> ἀπέθανεν, εὐδαίμων ἀνὴρ καὶ δεξιός,
> πολλὰς ποιήσας καὶ καλὰς τραγῳδίας,
> καλῶς δ' ἐτελεύτησ', οὐδὲν ὑπομείνας κακόν.

[2] E.g., *Oed. Tyr.* 1528 ff.; *Trach.* 1 ff.; Frag. 646.

[3] *Vita*, 15.

[4] Plutarch, *Moralia*, p. 328 f (*de Alex. Mag. Fortuna*, I, 5) says that the sons of Persians, Sousianians, and Gedrousians sang the tragedies of Sophocles and Euripides. See Tarn, *The Greeks in Bactria and India*, pp. 94 and 382.

[5] Diog. Laert. IV, 20; also Suidas, s. v. Πολέμων.

[6] See p. 211.

pylus were being read and studied in the second century A.D. shows that his reputation had not greatly declined. Among modern readers he has found hosts of warm admirers, so that he has in a way won back the position among dramatists which he held in Athens in the fifth century B.C.

PORTRAITS

Portraits of Sophocles are by no means rare. Bernoulli[1] records forty-three, most of them life-size marble heads, which give a good idea of the features of the dramatist; and there are several others which may be identified with less certainty. A life-size statue in the Lateran Museum is usually regarded as his best portrait.[2] It represents him in his prime, standing with his mantle wrapped around him, while on the ground beside him rests a circular box holding rolls of manuscript. This may be a copy of the famous portrait statue of him made of bronze which Lycurgus set up in the theatre at Athens in the fourth century B.C. The fine, intellectual face accords well with what might be expected of the poet. A herm in the British Museum (PLATE I) shows him as an older man. In the Painted Colonnade at Athens there was a painting representing him playing the lyre.[3]

[1] *Griech. Ikonographie*, I, pp. 123 ff.

[2] It might be noted that T. Reinach, *Jour. of Hel. Studies*, XLII, pp. 50 ff. doubts the identification.

[3] *Vita*, 5.

CHAPTER II

THE DRAMATIC ART OF SOPHOCLES

HIS PLOTS

IN A study of the dramatic art of Sophocles[1] the nature of his plots and their construction call for our first consideration, for plot according to Aristotle[2] is the very soul of tragedy. For his sources he turned chiefly to the old Greek epics[3], as was usual with the tragic poets of his time, and particularly to the poems of the Trojan Cycle. The plots of forty-three of his plays, or about thirty-eight per cent of his known titles, may be traced to that source. Exact figures cannot be given for all the others because so little is known about some of them, but other poems of the Epic Cycle furnished him with subjects for approximately fifteen more, Attic legends for eleven, Theban for twelve, Argive for twenty-one, while the plots of the remaining plays were taken from various other sources. They show great variety and were sometimes based on very slight mythological material, such as the plot of the *Oedipus at Colonus*. In general he seems to have followed the old stories rather closely,[4] though he did not hesitate to alter them occasionally for dramatic effect. Thus the bringing of Neoptolemus to Lemnos in the *Philoctetes* seems to have been an invention of his; and the prominence given to

[1] For a good discussion of this subject see C. R. Post, *Harv. Stud. in Class. Philol.*, XXIII, pp. 71 ff. and XXXIII, pp. 1 ff.

[2] *Poet.*, p. 1450a 38 *ἀρχὴ μὲν οὖν καὶ οἷον ψυχὴ ὁ μῦθος τῆς τραγῳδίας.*

[3] Athenaeus, VII, p. 277 e says *ἔχαιρε Σοφοκλῆς τῷ ἐπικῷ κύκλῳ, ὡς καὶ ὅλα δράματα ποιῆσαι κατακολουθῶν τῇ ἐν τούτῳ μυθοποιίᾳ.*

[4] This is in accord with Aristotle's dictum, *Poet.*, p. 1453b 22 f. *τοὺς μὲν οὖν παρειλημμένους μύθους λύειν οὐκ ἔστιν*, though he grants that certain liberties may be permitted, *Poet.*, p. 1451b 23 f. *ὥστ' οὐ πάντως ἂν εἴη ζητητέον τῶν παραδεδομένων μύθων, περὶ οὓς αἱ τραγῳδίαι εἰσίν, ἀντέχεσθαι.*

Electra in the *Electra* is a modification of the earlier story as we find it in Aeschylus. These variations from the accepted traditions seem to have been greater and more frequent in his satyr dramas than in his tragedies, as will be noted later.

In the construction of his plots Sophocles shows his mastery of the technique of the drama.[1] In this he is unsurpassed. He develops his story step by step in such a way as to hold the attention and arouse the sympathy of his audience whether it consist of spectators in the theatre or a solitary reader in his study. He is especially happy in his recognition scenes (ἀναγνωρίσεις). The most famous of these is found in the *Oedipus Tyrannus* where it occurs at the same time as the "reversal of fortune" (περιπέτεια) and thus exemplifies Aristotle's ideal.[2] All this will be made clear in our discussion of the separate plays. Nothing could, however, show better his genius as a dramatist than this treatment of the plot in the *Oedipus at Colonus*. The story of the death of Oedipus in itself offered little material to work with, and yet he made a great tragedy out of it.

But it would be a mistake to imagine that Sophocles always maintained the same high standard in his plots and in the composition of his tragedies that we find in the extant plays. In fact there is evidence from antiquity that this was not the case. Thus in the *Moralia* of Plutarch[3] his unevenness (ἀνωμαλία) is mentioned as something which might be criticized; and a similar observation is made by the author of the treatise *On the Sublime*.

In all but one of the extant tragedies, as will be seen later, there is one outstanding character. This has led to a suggestion on the part of some writers that the dramatist may have composed some of his tragedies with a particular actor in mind. The

[1] The author of the *Life* says (21) οἶδε δὲ καιρὸν συμμετρῆσαι καὶ πράγματα, ὥστε ἐκ μικροῦ ἡμιστιχίου ἢ λέξεως μιᾶς ὅλον ἠθοποιεῖν πρόσωπον.

[2] *Poet.*, p. 1452a 32 καλλίστη δὲ ἀναγνώρισις, ὅταν ἅμα περιπέτειαι γίνωνται, οἷαν ἔχει ἐν τῷ Οἰδίποδι.

[3] P. 45 b (*De Audiendo*, XIII) μέμψαιτο δ'ἄν τις . . . . . Σοφοκλέους δὲ τὴν ἀνωμαλίαν. And in the *De Sublimitate*, XXXIII, 5 we read ὁ δὲ Πίνδαρος καὶ ὁ Σοφοκλῆς ὁτὲ μὲν οἷον πάντα ἐπιφλέγουσι τῇ φορᾷ, σβέννυνται δ'ἀλόγως πολλάκις καὶ πίπτουσιν ἀτυχέστατα.

suggestion is one which cannot be definitely proved or disproved. The fact that some actors are known to have excelled in playing certain parts in his tragedies[1] may be regarded as evidence in support of that theory. In the time of Aristotle it was not unusual for good poets to write for special actors.[2]

DELINEATION OF CHARACTER

Greek tragedy as developed by Sophocles has as its distinguishing feature the delineation of character. This has long been recognized,[3] and is apparent even to the most casual reader of his plays. The poet's method is to select some outstanding personage in old Greek story—an Oedipus, an Ajax, or an Electra—and then through the action of the drama to portray his conduct under various trying circumstances. The skill with which these trials are introduced and woven into a consistent plot constitutes the chief excellence of his tragedy.

According to a tradition handed down in the *Life*, Sophocles learned tragedy under Aeschylus,[4] and it would, in fact, be strange if he were not influenced by the older dramatist early in his career;[5] but the extant tragedies, all of which date from the poet's maturity when he had already developed a characteristic style of his own, show comparatively little trace of that influence. The tragedy of Aeschylus is dominated by the idea of an inexorable fate. Fate, too, has a part in the tragedy of Sophocles; but it is fate brought to its consummation through the character of the individual. The oracle had declared that Oedi-

[1] E.g., Cleidemides (Aristoph. *Frogs*, 791 and scholia). Two generations later Polus won fame by his acting the part of Oedipus in the *Oedipus Tyrannus* and *Oedipus at Colonus* (Stobaeus, *Flor.* XXXIII, 28).

[2] *Poet.*, p. 1451b 37 ὑπὸ δὲ τῶν ἀγαθῶν διὰ τοὺς ὑποκριτάς. But cf. Bywater, *Aristotle on the Art of Poetry*, p. 196.

[3] *Vita*, 20 ἠθοποιεῖ τε καὶ ποικίλλει καὶ τοῖς ἐπινοήμασιν τεχνικῶς χρῆται.

[4] *Vita*, 4 παρ' Αἰσχύλῳ δὲ τὴν τραγῳδίαν ἔμαθε.

[5] See p. 275. In the essay *Quomodo quis suos in virtute sentiat profectus*, ch. 7 which has come down under the name of Plutarch (*Mor.* p. 79 b) Sophocles is quoted as telling how he abandoned the bombastic style of Aeschylus and developed a style of his own.

pus was destined to kill his father and marry his mother; but the fate which he sought so hard to avoid was brought about largely through his own unyielding disposition, through his determination to have his own way. In general the trying situations in which his principal characters find themselves as his various plots develop are due in each case to some defect in the characters themselves. This is in accord with Aristotle's declaration, that the tragic hero should be neither a very good nor a very bad man, but one of distinction who meets with disaster through some failing of his own.[1]

But the characters of Sophocles are always live characters. They are not merely the conventional figures of the tragic stage, but are human beings with all the feelings and passions of real men. This is apparent at once when one reads the extant tragedies and it is, perhaps, for that reason that the gods are so rarely represented in his drama. Take, for example, Ajax in the play of that name. The burly hero of the Trojan war, universally recognized as second only to Achilles in valor, has been wronged, grievously wronged. The reward which was his just due has been given to another man inferior in every way except in wit. Stung by a bitter sense of the injustice done him he broods over his wrong until he becomes temporarily insane. To be sure the dramatist here introduces the supernatural in the character of Athena and thus in a way makes Ajax the victim of a higher power when he slays the sheep and so injures the army. When, however, he recovers his reason he is overcome with remorse and there is nothing left for him but suicide. Here, then, the dramatist has shown us a great soul tried too deeply for human endurance.

Something of the same sort may be said of Oedipus. His character is drawn true to nature. The self-confident man who, through his own ability, has raised himself to the supreme power in the state finds himself checked and thwarted in his plan to

[1] *Poet.*, p. 1453a 9 f. . . . . *δι' ἁμαρτίαν τινὰ τῶν ἐν μεγάλῃ δόξῃ ὄντων καὶ εὐτυχίᾳ, οἷον Οἰδίπους καὶ Θυέστης κ.τ.λ.*

relieve his people. His irascibility and his determination to carry out his purpose are what would be expected of such a man. So, too, in his refusal to be diverted from tracing out his lineage. Here we have a truly human Oedipus, and the same is true of the Oedipus of the later play.

Philoctetes is another character moved by purely human impulses. Like Ajax he has been wronged, though his enemies had some justification for their action. They wished to be rid of a comrade who was suffering from an offensive affliction. Philoctetes has the stubbornness of Oedipus and a hatred even more intense than that of Ajax, not to be appeased by ordinary means. With Ajax the end could be nothing but death by his own hand; with Philoctetes, through the intervention of a superhuman agency, it becomes a transition to a happier life. These are the most important male characters in the seven extant tragedies.

When we come to the female characters the situation is much the same as with the male. They stand out as individuals and, like the men, are consistently represented. This will be found to be true whether the dramatist is setting before us the character of Jocasta or Antigone or Ismene or Electra or any other; and it is in accord with the rule laid down by Aristotle.[1] We find women with strong characters like Clytaemnestra and Electra; and weak and timid women like Ismene and Chrysothemis. But the quality which Sophocles seems to have admired most in women and upon which he lays most stress in the extant plays is devotion. Thus he portrays the wifely devotion of Deianeira and, we must add, of Jocasta; the devotion of Tecmessa both to Ajax and to her little boy; the devotion of Antigone to her father and to her brother Polynices; and the devotion of Electra to Orestes. This will be made clearer in our discussion of the separate plays. It should, however, be added here that what has been said of the dramatist's delineation of character applies equally well to the less important figures in his tragedy. They, too, are real personages.

[1] *Poet.*, p. 1454a 26.

The question is sometimes asked how Sophocles attempts to justify the suffering of Oedipus, or Philoctetes, or Heracles; or the death of Antigone, or Deianeira. The answer is plain. He does not attempt to justify them. He is not a theologian who must seek a logical explanation for all good and evil in the world. Evil comes to the good man and the bad alike in real life, and it is the task of the dramatist to interest his audience in this, not to offer explanations of it.

But Sophocles excelled not only in his ability to depict character clearly and naturally. He had a keen sense for dramatic situations. He had a vivid imagination and he knew how to clothe his thoughts in lofty and at the same time fitting language. Perhaps the anecdote told about him by Aristotle,[1] that he said that he represented men as they should be, and Euripides as they were, may be true.

IRONY

One feature of the tragedy of Sophocles which is especially famous is his so-called "irony." This was discussed at length by Thirlwell[2] many years ago, and has been treated by various other Greek scholars since his time. It was by no means confined to Sophocles. The other tragic poets used it to a limited extent, but Sophocles employed it so frequently and so skilfully that it became a recognized characteristic of his drama. Examples of it occur in all the extant tragedies and in some cases, as in the *Oedipus Tyrannus*, it dominates the play.

Irony is found in the dialogue where the words of the speaker mean one thing to the person addressed and quite a different thing to the audience in the theatre, for the audience is always in the secret. In such cases it may be intentional on the part of the speaker, where he wishes to be misunderstood by the person whom he is addressing. Examples of this are the hidden allusions of Ajax to his intended suicide.[3] Or, again, the speaker

[1] *Poet.*, p. 1460b 33.
[2] *Philological Museum*, II, pp. 483–537; also *Philologus*, VI, pp. 81 ff. and 254 ff.
[3] *Ajax*, 657 ff.; 691 f.

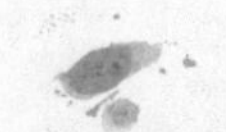

may be wholly unconscious of the irony of his words. Thus in the *Oedipus Tyrannus* when Oedipus pronounces his curse on the slayer of Laius he does not realize that he is laying that curse on himself; and when he says that the man who slew Laius might wish to attack him[1] he has no suspicion of the real situation.

Examples of intentional irony are especially frequent. One of the most striking is to be found in the *Electra*[2] in the scene where Clytaemnestra and Electra hear from the old slave the fictitious account of the death of Orestes. Another is the scene in the *Philoctetes* in which Neoptolemus meets the afflicted hero.[3] The whole passage is full of irony, as are numerous words and phrases.

Irony is not necessarily restricted by Sophocles to the words of the dialogue. He makes use of it in the action as well. Oedipus stayed away from Corinth for fear of the oracle which declared that he must slay his father and marry his mother, but by his very act in coming to Thebes he brings about the fulfilment of the oracle which he sought so hard to avoid. A more ironical situation would be hard to conceive. So, too, when he persists in his purpose to find out his lineage he brings disaster and ruin on himself and his family. Still another striking example of irony in the action comes at the conclusion of the *Electra* when Aegisthus, expecting to see the dead Orestes, removes the covering from the body and finds the slain Clytaemnestra.[4]

But it is needless to discuss at greater length this interesting characteristic of the dramatic art of Sophocles. It is most effectively used in the *Oedipus Tyrannus*, although Jebb[5] sees it in its most subtle and artistic form in the *Antigone* and the *Philoctetes*. All the tragedies have noteworthy examples of it, especially the *Ajax*, the *Trachiniae*, and the *Oedipus at Colonus*.

[1] Lines 224 ff. and 139 f.
[2] Especially 764 ff.
[3] Lines 219 ff.
[4] Line 1475.
[5] *Essays and Addresses*, p. 31.

THE SUPERNATURAL

In the composition of his dramas Sophocles availed himself of all the devices usual with the tragic poets of his time. His primary interest was, to be sure, in the development of character; but he did not hesitate to use the marvelous or the supernatural where it might be employed to advantage. Examples of this may be found in the extant tragedies. The most noteworthy is in the scene in the *Oedipus at Colonus* in which Oedipus goes to his death. The ominous thunder, the blind man suddenly moving away as if he had the power of sight, the messenger's report of the supernatural voice calling Oedipus, and finally the latter's mysterious disappearance reveal the skill of the poet in his use of the marvelous.

The supernatural is also to be found in the appearance of gods in certain of the plays. Athena in the *Ajax* and Heracles in the *Philoctetes* are examples of divinities represented on the stage. In the *Trachiniae*, however, Heracles is a hero, not a god. In general the gods did not have an important part in the tragedy of Sophocles so far as their actual appearance in the theatre is concerned. The lost *Triptolemus* seems to have been an exception in that respect, but that was an early play.

HORROR. DRAMATIC SILENCE

Closely allied to the supernatural and the marvelous is his use of horror. Sophocles did not hesitate to shock his audience on occasion if the tragic effect which he wished to produce could be brought about more vividly by that means. A notable example is when Oedipus with his bloody eyes is brought before the spectators. The horror which his presence on the stage produced in those who saw him could be no greater than that inspired in the minds of his readers by the words which the poet uses to describe the scene.[1] Other examples of horror in the extant plays are Philoctetes with his loathsome sore; and the tortured and dying Heracles in the *Trachiniae.* In both of these cases the poet's language is as frightful as their appearance must have been. Still another example is his description of the dying Haemon staining the pale cheek of Antigone with his blood. The modern reader may be unduly disturbed by such scenes, but it should be remembered that Aristotle[2] declared that suffering (*πάθος*) was an essential part of tragedy.

Here should be mentioned another device of the dramatist which was, however, by no means confined to Sophocles, that is, the silence of a character in some tense situation. Such silence is often more dramatic and more effective than any words the character might utter. The writer of the essay *On the Sublime*[3] notes this in the *Odyssey* in the passage where Odysseus meets the shade of Ajax in the Lower World.[4] Striking examples in the extant plays are the silent departure of Eurydice in the *Antigone* (l. 1244) when she hears of the death of her son Haemon; and the silent exit of Deianeira in the *Trachiniae* (l. 813) when she learns of the ruin which her gift has brought upon Heracles.

HUMOR

Humor from its very nature is not to be expected in tragedy, and yet the extant plays are not without some touches of it. For example, the guard in the *Antigone* (ll. 223 ff.), when he comes in to tell of the dust thrown on the dead body of Polynices, can hardly be called a tragic character; and this may be said also of the messenger in the *Trachiniae* (ll. 180 ff.) when, in expectation of a reward, he hastens in to announce the approach

[1] Aristotle, *Poet.*, p. 1453b 3 ff. declares that the tragic poet should produce just this effect. *δεῖ γὰρ καὶ ἄνευ τοῦ ὁρᾶν οὕτω συνεστάναι τὸν μῦθον ὥστε τὸν ἀκούοντα τὰ πράγματα γινόμενα καὶ φρίττειν καὶ ἐλεεῖν ἐκ τῶν συμβαινόντων· ἅπερ ἂν πάθοι τις ἀκούων τὸν τοῦ Οἰδίπου μῦθον.*

[2] *Poet.*, p. 1452b 10 ff.

[3] IX, ll. 21 f. *ἡ τοῦ Αἴαντος ἐν Νεκυίᾳ σιωπὴ μέγα καὶ παντὸς ὑψηλότερον λόγου.*

[4] XI, 543 ff.

of Heracles. The Shepherd from Corinth in the *Oedipus Tyrannus* (ll. 924 ff.) is represented as something of a wag. To these examples there should be added the cowardly conduct of Odysseus in the *Ajax* (ll. 74 ff.) when Athena proposes to call the madman from his tent. In all these cases there are traces of what may be called humor. The purpose of the dramatist in introducing them was evidently to divert his audience for a moment before the tragic scenes which were to follow.

But Sophocles was by no means lacking in a sense of humor, as the fragments of his *Ichneutae* show. In fact he could write a rollicking farce for a satyr play and apparently enjoy writing it, but that phase of his genius will be treated later in our discussion of his satyr dramas.

STAGE DEVICES

In presenting his plays Sophocles, as might be expected, employed the mechanical devices usual in the Greek theatre. Thus we find him using the *eccyclema* to show the dead body of Clytaemnestra in the *Electra* (l. 1465), and that of Eurydice in the *Antigone* (l. 1293); also Ajax among the slain sheep; and the *deus ex machina* for the supernatural appearance of Heracles in the *Philoctetes* (l. 1408). Furthermore he did not hesitate to bring animals on the stage. In the *Oedipus at Colonus*, for example, Ismene enters riding on a pony (l. 324). In the same play he uses thunder effectively, as we have already seen. He is skilful in his introduction of silent characters such as the two little girls Antigone and Ismene in the *Oedipus Tyrannus*, and the little son of Tecmessa in the *Ajax*. But these are matters which do not call for any lengthy discussion.

STYLE

The style of Sophocles is characterized by dignity, beauty, clarity, and smoothness together with vigor. His verse has the appearance of having been written almost without effort, but a careful examination of it reveals the fact that in reality its apparent simplicity and its grace are due to skilful composition on the part of the poet. He was a master of the "art of concealing art." He always knew what he wanted to say, and he had ready at hand the right words with which to say it. He frequently attained distinction in his verse by the use of rare words, or of words with unusual meanings.[1] Examples are numerous, but three taken at random are sufficient to illustrate the point. In the *Oedipus Tyrannus* l. 1111 we find the verb σταθμᾶσθαι which normally means to "measure" used in the sense of to "conjecture"; and in l. 1124 the expression ἔργον μεριμνῶν ποῖον meaning "attending to what work"—a rare meaning for μεριμνάω. Again in the *Oedipus at Colonus* l. 663 πέλαγος which regularly means "sea" is used in the sense of "distance." It is unnecessary to multiply examples, but an examination of the different passages shows that the poet is justified when he indulges in this practice. Sometimes he coined new words. There are, for example, in the *Oedipus at Colonus* some thirty ἅπαξ λεγόμενα, or words not found elsewhere in Greek literature.[2] His usage is, in fact, in accord with Aristotle's rule as to the proper diction for the tragic poet,[3] that he should occasionally employ a strange word or metaphor in order to keep his diction from becoming commonplace, but he should not overdo the practice.[4] Occasionally a construction which is difficult to parallel occurs in the plays, and then the question arises as to whether or not our text is sound.

If we examine his verse further we do not find in it the loud-sounding, sonorous compounds of which Aeschylus is so fond. This does not mean that Sophocles avoided compounds; for a

[1] About one-third of the fragments of the lost plays (368 by actual count) consist of one word quoted either because it is rare, or used in an unusual sense; or because of some peculiarity of form. A. Juris, *De Sophoclis vocibus singularibus*, has collected the words not found elsewhere in Greek, or found only rarely.

[2] See C. Schambach, *Sophocles qua ratione vocabulorum significationes mutet atque variet*, p. 6.

[3] *Poet.*, p. 1458a 18 ff.

[4] Twice Sophocles uses the very rare first person dual in -μεθον namely λελείμμεθον in *Electra*, 950 and ὁρμώμεθον in *Philoctetes*, 1079. There is but one other example of this form in all Greek literature, περιδώμεθον in *Iliad*, XXIII, 485.

common device of his is to use verbs compounded with an adverb or a preposition, usually to give more force to the simple verb.[1] But the delicacy and beauty of form which are the most striking characteristics of his verse he attained by his skill in the choice of words and their combination. His vocabulary in the extant plays does not vary greatly.[2] This is what might be expected, for they all date from his maturity; and Sophocles had the great good fortune to retain to the end the same characteristics which brought him fame earlier in his career. He had no period of decline.

Occasionally we can see something of his methods of composition. Thus at the beginning of the *Oedipus Tyrannus* he sees that it will be necessary for him to use a verb meaning "to sit" several times. If he repeated the same word it would detract from the loftiness of the whole passage and that would be fatal. He avoids the difficulty by using different words. In line 2 he uses *θοάζετε*, a rare word in this sense; in line 15 *προσήμεθα*; in line 20 *θακεῖ*; and in line 32 *ἑζόμεσθα*. We thus find four different words used to express the same idea.

A favorite device by which he gives dignity to his style is the use of the verb "to be" with a participle where the simple verb might have been expected. Examples of this are very numerous. Thus in the *Oedipus Tyrannus* line 580 we find *ᾖ θέλουσα* instead of *θέλῃ*; in line 747 *βλέπων ᾖ* instead of *βλέπῃ*; in line 970 *θανὼν εἴη* instead of *θάνοι*; in line 1045 *ἔστι ζῶν* instead of *ζῇ*; in line 1146 *σιωπήσας ἔσῃ* instead of *σιωπήσεις*, etc., etc. Further consideration of the poet's diction is not called for here. It would take us too far afield. An elaborate study of his language including grammar and syntax was published by Campbell[3] in his edition of the plays, and to that the reader may be referred.

[1] See P. Kriebitzsch, *Quaestiones de usu verborum cum praepositionibus compositorum apud Sophoclem*.

[2] Various critics have found the language of the *Antigone* less easy and more severe than that of the later plays, and have pointed to this as an indication of an earlier as compared with a more mature style. T. B. L. Webster, *op. cit.*, pp. 143 ff. presents in detail the evidence for such a development.

[3] Vol. I, pp. 1–107.

A peculiarity in the composition of his iambic trimeter verse should, however, be mentioned, namely the ending of a line with an elided syllable. This device was called by the ancient grammarians the σχῆμα Σοφόκλειον. In the extant plays six examples of it are found in the *Oedipus Tyrannus*, one, perhaps two, in the *Oedipus at Colonus*, one in the *Electra* and one in the *Antigone*.[1] In all these cases the following line begins with a vowel.

If anyone has any doubt as to the beauty of the iambic trimeter verse of Sophocles he will find an excellent test ready at hand. Let him read aloud the opening lines of the *Oedipus Tyrannus*, or of the *Antigone*, or of the *Electra*, and he will be convinced.

THE CHORUS

In the seven tragedies which have come down to us the members of the chorus always have an important part. This seems to have been in keeping with the poet's usual custom; for Aristotle in the *Poetics*, while laying down the law that in the drama the chorus should have the place of an actor, says that such was the practice of Sophocles as contrasted with that of Euripides.[2] His choruses are always interested in the fortunes of the chief personage, and thus in a way they do have the part of another speaking character. In one place in the *Ajax* (l. 814) they actually leave the stage as an actor might and return after a time (l. 866). In the *Oedipus Tyrannus* we find the chorus consisting of elderly citizens of Thebes who are deeply concerned for the welfare of their city and their king. In the *Antigone* again they are elderly Thebans. In the *Oedipus at Colonus* they are citizens of Colonus. In the *Ajax* they are sailors from Salamis, comrades of Ajax; and in the *Philoctetes* sailors from Scyros, followers of

[1] *Oed. Tyr.*, ll. 29, 785, 791 and 1224 δ'; l. 332 ταῦτ'; l. 1184 τ'. *Oed. Col.* l. 17 δ'; and perhaps l. 1164 μολόντ'. *El.* l. 1017 δ'. *Ant.* l. 1031 δ'. See J. H. Wright, *Harv. Stud. in Class. Philol.* XII, 1901, pp. 151 ff.

[2] *Poet.*, p. 1456a 25 ff. καὶ τὸν χορὸν δὲ ἕνα δεῖ ὑπολαβεῖν τῶν ὑποκριτῶν, καὶ μόριον εἶναι τοῦ ὅλου καὶ συναγωνίζεσθαι μὴ ὥσπερ Εὐριπίδῃ ἀλλ' ὥσπερ Σοφοκλεῖ.

Neoptolemus. In the *Electra* they are women from Mycenae, and in the *Trachiniae* women of Trachis. In all these cases it is natural that the chorus should have the part assigned to it in the development of the plot; and yet in the last-mentioned play alone does the chorus give its name to the tragedy. This, however, was by no means an isolated case in the drama of Sophocles, for an examination of the titles of the lost plays shows no fewer than twenty-five of them which seem to have taken their titles from the chorus.

When one comes to examine the regular choral songs, or stasima, for their content he finds that in them the members of the chorus frequently comment on the scene which has just preceded. Thus in the *Ajax* ll. 597–645 the subject of their song is the madness of Ajax manifested in what has gone before; again in ll. 693–718 they express their joy at the attitude of the hero in the scene which has just ended; and in ll. 1185–1222 they comment with sadness on his death. Sometimes they express their hope that something good is about to come to pass. For example, in the *Trachiniae* ll. 633–662 they pray that Heracles, influenced by the anointed garment which Deianeira is sending him, may return to her; and in the *Oedipus Tyrannus* ll. 1086–1109 they declare their conviction that Oedipus will be proved to be a Theban citizen. Then again they meditate upon some topic suggested to them by something they have just heard. Thus in the *Antigone* ll. 332–383 they moralize on Man and his doings, and conclude that obedience to the laws of the land is necessary for the prosperity of a city; and in the *Oedipus at Colonus* ll. 1211–1248 the folly of wishing for a long life and the ills attendant upon old age form the subject of their song. Only rarely does a choral ode have little to do with the action. A notable example is found in the famous lines in praise of Attica (*Oedipus at Colonus* ll. 668–719). Though suggested by the promise of Theseus to protect Oedipus, they really have little connection either with what has preceded or with what is to follow. The relative importance of the choral odes in the development of the plot will be set forth more fully in our discussion of the separate plays.

The amount of space given to the chorus varies with the play. Thus in the *Ajax* and the *Antigone* they have about one-fourth of the total number of lines; while in the *Electra* they have only about one-seventh. These are the two extremes. With the other plays the proportion is about one in five in the *Oedipus Tyrannus* and the *Oedipus at Colonus*, and one in six in the *Trachiniae* and the *Philoctetes*.

There is also considerable variation in the number of iambic trimeter lines spoken by the leader of the chorus; for whereas there are eighty-two such lines in the *Ajax*, there are but fifteen in the *Philoctetes*. So, too, there is great difference in the use of anapaestic verse. There are seventy-five anapaestic lines given to the chorus in the *Antigone* and forty-six in the *Ajax*, while there are but three in the *Electra* and four in the *Trachiniae* and the *Philoctetes*.[1]

The parodos, or entrance song of the chorus, is treated differently in the different plays. In but one of them, the *Ajax*, is it written in anapaests. In the *Oedipus Tyrannus* and in the *Trachiniae*, lyric, that is logaoedic, verse is used; while in the *Antigone* there is a combination of lyric and anapaestic verse. In the remaining tragedies the parodos is in the form of a lyric dialogue. It is hardly safe to generalize from so small a number of plays, but it would appear that Sophocles preferred to bring in his chorus with some form of lyric verse rather than with the simpler anapaests.

[1] These variations will be clear from the following table.

	Total number of lines	*Number of lines of chorus*	*Iambic trimeters of chorus*	*Lyrics of chorus*	*Lyric dialogue of chorus*	*Anapaests of chorus*	*Trochaic tetrameters of chorus*
Ajax	1420	362	82	175	59	46	—
Antig.	1353	362	50	208	29	75	—
Oed. Tyr.	1530	323	57	223	26	7	7
Trach.	1278	220	49	164	3	4	—
Electra	1510	227	41	94	89	3	—
Philoc.	1471	224	15	130	75	4	—
Oed. Col.	1779	375	64	162	144	5	—

The fondness of Sophocles for writing lyric verse was recognized in antiquity,[1] and his skill in this type of composition may be seen to advantage today in the choral odes of his extant dramas. In them we find that same facility which appeared in the composition of his iambic trimeter lines. He is equally felicitous in his handling of the metre and in expressing the thought. In general his metres are simpler than those of Aeschylus, but are well adapted to the ideas which he wished to express. His odes often have great beauty, due in part to the fact that lyric verse from its very nature affords the writer a greater opportunity to give play to his imagination, and this opportunity the genius of Sophocles did not neglect.[2] His ode in praise of Attica is one of the most admired pieces of Greek poetry that have survived. The little ode in which the chorus express their conviction that Oedipus will be proved to be a Theban (*Oed. Tyr.* ll. 1086 ff.); the ode in the *Antigone* about Man (ll. 332 ff.); and that in the *Philoctetes* addressed to Sleep (ll. 827 ff.) are other lyrics which have excited the admiration of lovers of Greek verse.

Quite apart from the beauty of the odes as a whole there are single phrases full of poetic feeling which may be found here and there in all the tragedies. For example when the poet speaks of Love sleeping on the soft cheek of a maiden (*Ant.* 783); or a sunbeam as the eye of golden Day (*Ant.* 102); or Time as a gentle god (*El.* 179); or the oracle of Apollo as the child of golden Hope (*Oed. Tyr.* 158). Or again when he calls the mourning Electra a plaintive nightingale (*El.* 1078); or when he declares that the blood-stained man must "ply his foot in flight more swiftly than the horses of the storm winds" (*Oed. Tyr.* 465); or speaks of Insolence reaching the highest summit and crashing down to precipitous ruin (*Oed. Tyr.* 875). It is needless to

[1] Suidas, s.v. Σοφοκλῆς, speaks of his elegiac verse and his paeans.

[2] This seems to have been true also of the music which accompanied his odes. The writer of the *Life* (23) states on the authority of Aristoxenus that he was the first of the Athenian poets to use the Phrygian scale for his lyrics.

multiply examples when they may be found in almost every choral ode. They furnish further evidence, if that is needed, that Sophocles was equally great as a lyric and a dramatic poet.

Whether the audience in the theatre could appreciate the beauty of the choral odes which they heard has long been debated. It should, however, be remembered that Sophocles was writing not merely for the spectators, but for readers as well; and the latter were certainly not insensible to the beauty of the lines they had before them. It is easy to see that his lyrics were a labor of love for the poet,[1] and the fame which they brought him, especially in later times, certainly repaid him for all the care that he lavished upon them.

[1] Suidas, s. v. Σοφοκλῆς, says that he wrote a prose work on the chorus (ἔγραψεν. . . . λόγον καταλογάδην περὶ τοῦ χοροῦ.)

Chapter III

THE SATYR DRAMAS

No adequate knowledge of the satyr drama of Sophocles[1] was available to modern scholars previous to the publication in 1912 of a papyrus containing considerable portions of the *Ichneutae*, or *Trackers*.[2] Before that time the great dramatist had regularly been thought of as supreme among the tragic poets of Greece, and little if any attention was paid to the scanty fragments of the satyr dramas which he was known to have written. This is not surprising when one remembers the meagerness of those fragments and, furthermore, that there is no statement in ancient literature that his satyr plays enjoyed any particular fame. In fact, in contrast with what we are told about the satyr dramas of Aeschylus the natural inference would be that they did not. Thus the general opinion of scholars before the publication of the papyrus seems to have been that such satyr plays as Sophocles wrote were composed in order to conform to a convention of the Attic stage with no special excellence of their own. That he could have entered into this form of composition with spirit and with evident enjoyment could not have been anticipated.

In its origin the satyr drama goes very far back in the history of the Greek people. According to Suidas,[3] Arion from Methymna in Lesbos, who lived at the court of Periander of Corinth, first set up a chorus and sang the dithyramb; that he gave the name to the song sung by the chorus, and introduced satyrs

[1] See Bates, *Class. Stud. Edw. Capps*, pp. 14 ff.

[2] See p. 211.

[3] S. v. Ἀρίων . . . λέγεται . . . πρῶτος χορὸν στῆσαι καὶ διθύραμβον ᾆσαι καὶ ὀνομάσαι τὸ ᾀδόμενον ὑπὸ τοῦ χοροῦ καὶ σατύρους εἰσενεγκεῖν ἔμμετρα λέγοντας.

speaking in verse. This would take us back to the latter part of the seventh century B.C. but we cannot imagine satyrs appearing then for the first time. Mumming has always been a favorite amusement among primitive peoples, especially in connection with religious rites, and we cannot be far wrong if we imagine that men dressed themselves in goat skins with horses' tails and took part in religious dances and songs at a very early period.[1]

It has been generally recognized that from some such form of the dithyramb as that presented by Arion tragedy was derived; that men dressed in goat skins played the part of satyrs, the traditional companions of Dionysus, in whose honor the performance was being held; and that tragedy got its name from the song of these *τράγοι* or goat men.[2] But the satyrs soon dropped out as an essential element in the performance, and tragedy was left to develop along its own lines without them. This was the case also with comedy. We cannot, however, imagine the satyr choruses as being altogether discontinued. They were too deeply rooted in the affections of the people ever to have been completely abandoned. It is, indeed, probable that they were kept up in an impromptu way during the time that tragedy and comedy were attaining definite form until, like them, the satyr drama was evolved as a distinct dramatic type.

The first man to write satyr dramas, according to Suidas,[3] was Pratinas, an older contemporary of Aeschylus. This statement probably means that he was the first to give them literary form. He specialized in this type of composition, as is clear from the statement that of the fifty plays which he is said to have written thirty-two were satyr dramas. They enjoyed a

[1] An animal disguise in a ritual scene seems to be represented on a fresco from the earlier palace at Tiryns. See Rodenwaldt, *Tiryns* II, pl. II, fig. 7. With this might be compared certain Minoan-Mycenaean gems having upon them figures which are usually interpreted as demons. Perhaps these demons may be regarded as the ancestors of the satyrs of Dionysus and their human impersonators.

[2] For other ancient theories for the origin of the word "tragedy" see *Etym. Mag.* s. v. *τραγῳδία*.

[3] S. v. *Πρατίνας. . . . . πρῶτος ἔγραψε σατύρους.*

great reputation in antiquity. Pausanias,[1] writing in the second century A.D., says that after those of Aeschylus the satyr plays of Pratinas and of his son Aristias were the most famous.

Like tragedy, the satyr drama no doubt underwent a development which cannot now be traced. In modern times previous to the publication of the *Ichneutae* papyrus it was known from the *Cyclops* of Euripides,[2] the only example of this type of composition to come down in the regular channels of literary tradition. From that play we learn that the satyr drama was short. The *Cyclops* has 709 lines, or about half the length of the average tragedy; but in form it is more like tragedy than comedy. The episodes and the lyric parts are short and there are no formal stasima; and, furthermore, the lyric metres are simple, implying that the dances were simple as would be expected. Then, too, in the iambic trimeter lines of the dialogue anapaests are occasionally permitted elsewhere than in the first place, but they are nowhere used with the same freedom as in comedy. There is also a certain amount of coarseness which would have been entirely out of place in tragedy.

During the great period of the Attic stage we find a satyr play regularly forming the fourth member of the tetralogy with which the tragic poets competed against one another. Who first adopted this arrangement there is no means of knowing. Perhaps it was Aeschylus, to whom the Athenians were indebted for so many innovations in their theatre. He used the satyr drama in that way, whereas Pratinas evidently did not, as the number of his plays shows. But the custom was beginning to give way as early as 438 B.C., when Euripides concluded a tetralogy with the *Alcestis*. It is known, however, that satyr dramas continued to be performed down into late Greek times.[3]

When we come to consider the works of the three great tragic poets we find that eight titles of Aeschylus are definitely known

[1] II, 13, 6.
[2] See Bates, *Euripides*, pp. 80 ff.
[3] See e.g. *C. I. G.* 1584, 24 and 1585.

to have been those of satyr plays.[1] They are the *Cercyon*, the *Circe*, the *Kerykes*, the *Leon*, the *Lycurgus*, the *Prometheus* (i.e. Πυρκαεύς),[2] the *Proteus*, and the *Sphinx*; and about as many more may with some reason be added to this list.

In the case of Euripides, the anonymous writer of the *Life* states that in his day there were still preserved under the name of the poet eight satyr dramas of which one was spurious.[3] Seven titles are known. They are the *Autolycus*, the *Busiris*, the *Cyclops*, the *Eurystheus*, the *Sciron*, the *Syleus*, and the *Theristae*.

For Sophocles we have a longer list. Seventeen of his plays may be identified as satyr dramas either because they are expressly designated as such by some ancient writer, or because the extant fragments make it clear that they could not have been tragedies. These are the *Amphiaraus*, the *Amycus*, the *Cedalion*, the *Dionysiscus*, the *Heracleïscus*, the *Heracles at Taenarum*, the *Hybris*, the *Ichneutae*, the *Inachus*, the *Kophoi*, the *Krisis*, the *Lovers of Achilles*, the *Marriage of Helen*, the *Momus*, the *Pandora*, the *Salmoneus*, and the *Telephus*. Besides these there are eight other titles which may with varying degrees of probability be regarded as belonging to satyr dramas. With the exception of the *Ichneutae* the fragments of all these plays are so short that at first sight they might seem to afford little evidence for reconstructing their plots. Since the publication of the papyrus, however, many of them have taken on new significance, for knowing how Sophocles handled his material we are now in a position to recover something of the plots of most of them. They will all be

[1] Sidgwick, *Aeschyli Tragoediae* (Oxford text), *Fragmenta, passim.*

[2] It might be pointed out that on a red-figured crater in the Ashmolean Museum at Oxford, dating from about 425 B.C., Prometheus is represented with three satyrs whose names, Komos, Sikinnis, and Simos, are written beside them. He is holding the reed in which he has brought down the fire from heaven, and the satyrs hold reeds, too. See *Am. Jour. Arch.* XLIII, 1939, pp. 618 ff. The drawing may be a reminiscence of this play, though there is a possibility that it may have been inspired by the *Kophoi* of Sophocles.

[3] See Bates, *Euripides*, pp. 15 f. The spurious play seems to have been the *Sisyphus*, which was probably the work of Critias.

considered under their separate titles. We learn from the *Ichneutae* that Sophocles did not hesitate to alter a traditional story in order to bring about a dramatic situation; and, furthermore, that in his satyr dramas Dionysus might have little or nothing to do with the plot. An ancient tale might thus easily be converted into a rollicking farce which might come as a welcome relief to an audience which had just been listening to three tragedies.

When one looks over what is left of these satyr plays he cannot help being surprised that the great tragic poet who produced such masterpieces as the *Oedipus Tyrannus*, the *Antigone*, and the *Electra* could stoop to such compositions. But Sophocles had a sense of humor and could indulge in fun where it was appropriate, as in these satyr dramas. A study of their fragments reveals the dramatist in a very different light; and the finding of a large part of one of them, which had been copied at the end of the second century A.D. with marginal notes on the text, astonishing as it may seem, proves that, like the tragedies, they were studied by scholars and like them were read and enjoyed down into late Greek times.

CHAPTER IV

THE EXTANT TRAGEDIES

THE seven tragedies of Sophocles which have come down to modern times represent an edition of seven selected plays. Who made the selection, and at what period he made it is unknown. Presumably some one in late Greek times picked out the tragedies which for one reason or another he thought interesting and published them, including with his text also a selection of the scholia of the ancient commentators. This may have been in the fifth century A.D. or later.[1] Some of the plays would obviously be included in any edition of the poet's works. They were great masterpieces; but why the *Philoctetes* and the *Trachiniae* were chosen in preference to other plays now lost is not so plain.

In Byzantine times there was in circulation, and apparently much used in the schools, an edition of three plays, the *Ajax*, the *Electra*, and the *Oedipus Tyrannus*; to which the *Antigone* was occasionally added. Many such manuscripts still exist. Pearson in his Oxford text edition of Sophocles quotes fourteen which contain the three plays mentioned, and six more which have the *Antigone* in addition. Other combinations are found in other manuscripts dating from the fourteenth and fifteenth centuries.[2] For the text of the seven tragedies there are two outstanding manuscripts. One is Laurentianus XXXII, 9 in Florence dating from the eleventh, or last part of the tenth,

[1] Mazon, *Sophocle*, I, p. xiii thinks it may have been considerably later because of two apparent references to the *Dionysiaca* of Nonnus in the scholia on *Antigone* 1147 and *Ajax* 695.

[2] Campbell, *Sophocles*, I, pp. xvii ff. records 106 manuscripts which contain at least some part of Sophocles. This list does not include papyri.

century;[1] and the other is Parisinus 2712 in the Bibliothèque Nationale in Paris dating from the thirteenth century.[2] The former is much the more important of the two. The order in which the plays come in these manuscripts differs slightly. In the Laurentian the *Ajax* comes first followed by the *Electra*, the *Oedipus Tyrannus*, the *Antigone*, the *Trachiniae*, the *Philoctetes*, and the *Oedipus at Colonus*. In the Paris manuscript the *Oedipus at Colonus* comes fifth in order, following the *Antigone* and preceding the *Trachiniae* and the *Philoctetes*. Why the plays should have any particular order is not clear. At first sight it might be imagined that the Laurentian manuscript preserved a tradition of the date at which they had originally been brought out, for the *Ajax* is recognized as an early play and the *Philoctetes* as late; and, furthermore, tradition says that the *Oedipus at Colonus* was brought out in the archonship of Micon, that is in the year 402 B.C., by the poet's grandson, in the fourth year after his death.[3] The only other play for which a definite date is preserved is the *Antigone*, brought out in 441 B.C. Both dates have, however, been questioned.[4]

The problem of the dating of the tragedies of Sophocles has been much discussed. Perhaps the most complete study of the whole subject has been made by H. Siess,[5] who has examined all the plays carefully for internal evidence as to their dates. He tests them for elision, crasis, synezesis, aphaeresis; for the frequency of γε in the dialogue as compared with its use by Aes-

[1] This contains besides the seven plays of Sophocles the seven extant tragedies of Aeschylus, but with lines 349–1067 and 1160–1673 of the *Agamemnon* and the beginning of the *Choephoroe* missing; and has also the *Argonautica* of Apollonius Rhodius.

[2] In addition to the seven tragedies of Sophocles it contains the *Hecuba*, the *Orestes*, the *Phoenissae*, the *Andromache*, the *Medea*, and the *Hippolytus* of Euripides; and six comedies of Aristophanes, the *Plutus*, the *Clouds*, the *Frogs*, the *Knights*, the *Birds*, the *Acharnians*, together with lines 1–157, 169–234 and 250–282 of the *Ecclesiazusae*.

[3] See p. 59.

[4] See p. 73.

[5] *Wiener Studien*, XXXVI, 1914, pp. 244–294; XXXVII, 1915, pp. 27–62.

chylus in the *Agamemnon* and Euripides in the *Orestes*; and finally tests them for the resolutions in the iambic trimeter lines. As a result of this investigation he concludes that the *Ajax*, the *Trachiniae*, and the *Antigone* stand together in an earlier group, and the *Oedipus Tyrannus*, the *Oedipus at Colonus*, and the *Philoctetes* in another later group; and that the *Electra* came between the two. He imagines the order of the plays to have been *Antigone*, *Ajax*, *Trachiniae*, *Electra*, *Oedipus Tyrannus*, *Oedipus at Colonus*, and *Philoctetes*. These conclusions have not, however, met with general acceptance; and it may be questioned whether the phenomena which he has examined furnish satisfactory criteria for determining the dates. Such indications for this as we have either from the plays themselves or from other sources will be considered later when the separate tragedies are discussed.

I

The Oedipus Tyrannus

THREE of the extant tragedies are concerned with the story of Oedipus. They do not, however, form a trilogy in the ancient sense, like the *Oresteia* of Aeschylus, for the evidence seems to be conclusive that they were brought out at widely different times. Thus, as already noted, there are good reasons for assigning an early date to the *Antigone*, and a late one to the *Oedipus at Colonus*. The date of the *Oedipus Tyrannus* is unknown. R. J. Walker in his edition of the *Ichneutae*[1] has revived the idea of a trilogy, arguing for 411 B.C. as a date for all three tragedies; but his arguments are not convincing. In fact, as the case now stands, we must regard the three plays as composed at different periods in the poet's career.

The story of Oedipus was an ancient one. It was told at length in two old epic poems, the *Oedipodeia* and the *Thebais*, of

[1] *Ichneutae*, pp. 595 ff.

which scanty fragments alone survive, and very briefly in the *Odyssey*;[1] and two of the incidents in it—Oedipus meeting his father and Oedipus attacking the Sphinx—seem to be represented on gold seals found in a rock tomb near Thisbe in Boeotia (Fig. 1) dating from about 1500 B.C.[2] Sophocles is known to have followed the poems of the Epic Cycle closely in his plots,[3] though how closely he did so in the case of the Oedipus legend we cannot say. Aeschylus had already made it familiar to an Athenian audience.[4]

FIGURE 1.
OEDIPUS (?) ATTACKING SPHINX
From a Gold Seal from Thisbe, Boeotia. Date ca. 1500 B.C.

The first of the three tragedies from the point of view of the story is the *Oedipus Tyrannus*, universally regarded as the greatest masterpiece of the ancient stage. Its reputation in antiquity may be quickly ascertained by turning the pages of Aristotle's *Poetics*.[5] It is clear that this great authority on the origin and development of tragedy regarded it as a sort of model

[1] XI, 271 ff.

[2] Sir Arthur Evans, *Jour. of Hel. Studies*, XLV, 1925, pp. 27 ff., figs. 31 and 33.

[3] See p. 14.

[4] Besides the extant *Seven against Thebes* Aeschylus wrote a *Laius*, an *Oedipus*, and a *Sphinx*, the four plays presumably forming a tetralogy.

[5] The references are: *Poet.*, p. 1432a 24 ff.; (cp. p. 1432a 33); p. 1453b 7; p. 1453b 31; p. 1454b 8; p. 1455a 18; p. 1460a 30 and p. 1462b 2.

for tragic poets in the treatment of plot. Modern critics have admired not only the dramatic skill of the poet in it, but also his beautiful verse.

No statement of any kind has come down to us in regard to its date, and although this has been much discussed no conclusion satisfactory to everyone has yet been reached. Dates assigned on stylistic or metrical grounds are very uncertain. Jebb[1] thinks that "internal evidence warrants belief that it was composed after the *Antigone* and before the *Oedipus Coloneus*," and suggests roughly 439–412 B.C. as the limits within which it was produced. Almost all scholars would assent to that. It is possible that it may be referred to in the *Acharnians* of Aristophanes.[2] In that case it would be earlier than 425, when that comedy was presented. There is nothing in the tragedy itself which would conflict with such a date; and the scholars who have thought that in the opening scene there was an allusion to the great plague in Athens at the beginning of the Peloponnesian War would seem to have good reason for their inference.

The question has been raised as to whether the word *τύραννος* formed part of the original title of the play. It seems likely to have been added afterwards to distinguish it from the *Oedipus at Colonus*.[3]

The scene of the *Oedipus Tyrannus* is laid at Thebes in front of the palace of King Oedipus. Before the action begins, a band of suppliants enters led by an aged priest. It consists of men of different ages, youths and boys who wear white bands about their hair and carry in their hands olive branches twined with wool. They take seats upon the steps of the altars of the gods on which they lay their suppliant branches. The central doors

[1] *Oedipus Tyrannus*, pp. xxix f.

[2] Lines 1174 ff. of the *Acharnians* are clearly a travesty of some tragic scene, which may be *Oedipus Tyrannus* 1182 ff. See Bates, *Am. Jour. of Philol.* LIV, 1933, pp. 166 ff.

[3] See Hypothesis II, *ὁ Τύραννος Οἰδίπους ἐπὶ διακρίσει θατέρου ἐπιγέγραπται.* Also Hypothesis III, *ὁ Τύραννος Οἰδίπους πρὸς ἀντιδιαστολὴν τοῦ ἐν Κολωνῷ ἐπιγέγραπται.*

of the palace are thrown open and Oedipus comes forth and inquires the reason for their presence. The venerable priest of Zeus replies, reminding him of the terrible pestilence which is laying waste the land. Crops have withered away and women and cattle alike have failed to bring to birth living offspring. Overwhelmed by their distress they have come to him as the one person most likely to help them in their trouble. By his conquest of the Sphinx in former times he had shown that he had ability beyond that of other men, and now he is besought to use all his powers to relieve his people. Oedipus replies that he, too, is terribly distressed and that he has already sent the queen's brother, Creon, to the oracle at Delphi to inquire how he might free the state from its calamity. It is time for him to have returned. He is, in fact, seen to be approaching, and a moment later enters. Oedipus at once asks what tidings he brings and Creon replies "Good"; but seems reluctant to tell what his message is. He feels that his words are for the king's ears alone. Oedipus, however, bids him speak out before them all, and he then explains that the oracle has directed them to banish or put to death the man who slew Laius, their former king, for it is this unavenged murder that is the cause of their misfortunes. Oedipus asks for further information and is told that Laius, while on a mission to the oracle at Delphi, had been murdered by robbers and that one man alone of his party had escaped. The boldness of such an attack makes Oedipus think that it must have been inspired by a political intrigue in Thebes; but he is told that the Sphinx then devastating the land made a thorough investigation impossible. Oedipus declares that he will probe the matter to the bottom, for the men who caused the death of Laius might well plot against his own life. He orders the people to be summoned, and dismisses the suppliants with the assurance that he will do everything for their relief. He then retires into the palace.

The character of Oedipus in this scene is noteworthy. He is the great king fully conscious of his power and of his obligations as a monarch, and he speaks with dignity and confidence. The audience remembering the story would be greatly interested in some of his statements made in complete innocence, as when he says (l. 105) that he had never seen Laius, and that (l. 142) in avenging Laius he was helping himself.

The criticism has sometimes been made that the one weakness in the plot of the play lies in the fact that Oedipus does not know more about the death of Laius. Aristotle condemns improbabilities in general, but would seem to think Sophocles justified here because the death of Laius lies outside the immediate action of the play.[1] In view of all that happened to Oedipus after he came to Thebes the poet might well feel that his young hero, busy with his own affairs, would be content to accept the statement as to the death of the former king without further inquiry. The improbability may thus be defended.

When the suppliants have withdrawn, the chorus consisting of Theban elders enter. They represent the Theban people summoned by the king. They sing a song full of apprehension (ll. 151–215). They call upon Zeus and upon Apollo, Artemis, and Bacchus for aid against the terrible god of the pestilence, Ares. It may be rendered thus:

(*Strophe α'*) Oh! sweetly speaking voice of Zeus,
With what intent hast thou come here
To glorious Thebes from Pytho rich
In gold?
My tortured mind is filled with fear;
With awe I tremble, Delian god,
Thou healer, greeted with loud cries,
In dread of what thou wilt bring forth
Anew, or at recurring times;
Thou child of golden Hope speak out,
Immortal voice.

[1] See *Poet.*, p. 1460a 27 ff. *τούς τε λόγους μὴ συνίστασθαι ἐκ μερῶν ἀλόγων, ἀλλὰ μάλιστα μὲν μηδὲν ἔχειν ἄλογον, εἰ δὲ μή, ἔξω τοῦ μυθεύματος, ὥσπερ Οἰδίπους τὸ μὴ εἰδέναι πῶς ὁ Λάιος ἀπέθανεν, κ.τ.λ.*

(*Antistrophe α′*) Immortal daughter of great Zeus,
Athena, first I call on thee,
And Artemis, protector of
This land,
Thy sister, on her famous throne
Encircled in our market-place;
On Phoebus, the far-darter, too,
I call. Oh! ye defenders three,
Appear; if ever in the past
Ye drove away the flame of woe
Come also now.

(*Strophe β′*) Oh! woe for my countless ills;
Sick are my people, one and all,
No shaft of thought is there to help;
No crops spring forth from our famous land,
And childless the women arise from their pangs.
And like a well-winged bird ye would see
One follow another with greater speed
Than resistless fire to the distant shore
Of the evening god.

(*Antistrophe β′*) Deaths countless our city holds!
Pitiless in the plain there lie
Her unpitied offspring causing death,
And there at the altar's edge bewail
Both wives and gray-haired mothers, too,
On all sides begging relief from their woes.
A paean rings out and a wailing cry.
For which, Oh! golden daughter of Zeus,
Send us fair-faced help.

(*Strophe γ′*) Ares the fierce who without his bronze shield
Meets and consumes me amid shouts and cries
Send on his course with a favorable breeze
Back from my native land;
Either to Amphitrite's vast deep

Or to the midst of the billows of Thrace,
  Land with no friendly port.
For if the night lets anything pass
That thing day completes when it comes.
Thou who directest the lightning flash,
Father Zeus, with thy thunderbolt
  Slay him, I pray.

(*Antistrophe* γ') Oh! thou Lycean god, fain would I wish
That from thy gold-twisted bowstring there fly
Missiles invincible for my defense
  Marshaled against my foes;
Also those fiery, bright-shining flames,
Torches of Artemis with which she darts
  Over the Lycian hills.
Gold-snooded Bacchus I call upon, too,
Ruddy-faced, bearing the name of this land,
Comrade of Maenads and hailed with "Euoi!"
Holding bright torches to ward off that god
  Scorned among gods.

Oedipus reënters from the palace as the members of the chorus are concluding their prayer. He tells them that they may hope for a favorable answer if they will listen to him though he is a stranger enrolled as a citizen since the death of the former king. He then makes the following proclamation (ll. 223–275):

To all Cadmeans these things I proclaim.
Whoever of ye knows by what man's hand
King Laius, son of Labdacus, was slain
I bid that man tell everything to me.
And if he is afraid, let him speak out
Himself against himself and so remove
The charge, and he shall suffer nothing bad,
But all unharmed depart from out this land.
Or if he knows one from another land
To be the slayer let him not keep still;
For I will give him a reward and thanks.

But on the other hand if ye keep still,
And one of ye in terror for a friend
Or for himself rejects this word of mine,
Then he must hear what thing I shall do next.
For I proclaim that no one in this land
In which I hold the sovereignty and throne,
Shall take that man into his house or speak
To him, whoe'er he be, or join with him
In prayers or sacrifices to the gods;
Or share the holy water, but that all
Shall thrust him from their homes, for it is he
Who is to blame for the pollution here,
As now the Pythian oracle has shown.
This is the way that I assist the god
And aid the man who died. And now I lay
This curse upon the doer whether he
Be one, or joined with others who remain
Unknown, that he in evil plight shall wear
His evil and ill-fated life away.
And should he be an inmate of my home
With my full knowledge, then I pray that I
May suffer what I just called down on him.
Now all these things I lay on ye to do
For me and for the god and for this land
Which lies thus ruined, barren, and accursed.
For even if this were not by the gods
Commanded, it was not a seemly thing
To leave the crime unpurged when he who died
Was noble and a king, but track it out.
Now since I chance to have the office which
He had before, and have his bed and wife—
And we should both have had a common pledge
Of children, too, had not misfortune come
Upon his family—because of this,
Since fate has leaped upon him I will fight
For him as if he were my very sire,
And will resort to every plan and seek
To take the perpetrator of this crime

Upon the son of Labdacus who was
The son of Polydorus who in turn
Was son of Cadmus of a former age,
The offspring of Agenor long ago.
And for those people who do not do this
I pray the gods may not send from their land
A harvest, or yet children from their wives,
But that they perish by this present fate,
And even worse than this. But for the rest
Of ye Cadmeans, who these words approve,
May Justice be with ye as your ally,
And all the gods forever happily.

The chorus hasten to assure the king that they know nothing of the murderer, and they suggest that he send for the old blind prophet Tiresias that he may give them his assistance. Oedipus replies that he has already done so. Then they remind him of the story that Laius was slain by wayfarers, and express their conviction that the guilty man will flee from the land as soon as he hears the king's proclamation. A few moments later the blind seer enters guided by a small boy. Oedipus addresses him with words of respect and veneration and asks for his help, but the old man is surly and seems reluctant to speak. He asks to be sent home. Oedipus cannot understand his motive and urges him still further, but without success. This persistent refusal of the prophet to coöperate with him, or give him any help, angers the king and he speaks sharply to him. The action now moves rapidly, for the idea suddenly comes to the king that the reason why Tiresias is unwilling to speak is because he was involved in the plot to kill Laius, and he boldly accuses him. Tiresias in his turn becomes angry and declares that it is Oedipus himself who is to blame for the pestilence. The impossibility of such a thing is so apparent that Oedipus at once suspects a political intrigue with the object of dethroning him and making Creon king, and he is not slow to say so. Both men are now thoroughly enraged, and Oedipus even goes so far as to taunt the seer with his blindness.

After this heated dialogue Oedipus in a longer speech shows how deeply he is hurt that Creon, his friend from the beginning, should have proved a traitor in the hope of gaining the throne, for he is convinced that that is what has been planned. As for the prophet, he has nothing but scorn for him.

The chorus, who have been listening, now rather timidly suggest that both men have spoken in anger, but that what is really needed is to obey the oracle of Apollo. Tiresias, however, is not to be deterred from defending himself. He reminds the king that he is not his slave, but Apollo's, and gives terrible hints as to what is in store for Oedipus. He speaks as follows (ll. 407–428):

> I, too, must have the right to make reply
> At equal length although thou art the king.
> Of this I am the master; for I live
> Not thy slave, but Apollo's so that I
> Shall not be written down as Creon's man.
> But since thou tauntest me with being blind
> I say that thou hast sight and dost not see
> In what an evil plight thou art, or where
> Thou dwellest or with whom. Come, dost thou know
> From whom thou hadst thy birth? Thou dost not see
> That to thine own beneath the earth thou art
> An enemy, and to those still alive.
> And swiftly shall the double-lashing curse
> Of mother and of father drive thee forth
> Outside this land though seeing now aright
> But then in darkness. Then what haven shall
> Be free from cries of thine? Cithaeron, too,
> Shall speedily reëcho with them when
> Thou hast perceived that marriage in the house,
> To which with favoring breezes thou didst sail,
> Was no safe harbor. And thou seest not
> The multitude of other evils which
> Shall make thee and thy children equals all.
> On Creon, therefore, and upon my words

Heap thy reproaches; for no mortal man
Shall meet with utter ruin worse than thou.

Oedipus is still further enraged by this speech and he bids the seer begone from the palace. The old man starts to go; but lets fall the puzzling words that the parents of Oedipus thought him wise even if Oedipus does not. The king is startled and tries to question him; but Tiresias is angry and utters terrible but obscure words, though the audience understands that he is foretelling the fate of Oedipus. He says (ll. 446–462):

I go, first telling that for which I came,
With no fear of thy face; for there's no way
By which thou wilt destroy me. But I say
To thee that that man whom thou long hast sought
With threats, proclaiming search into the death
Of Laius, he, I say, is near at hand,
A stranger by report, but he shall prove
To be a native Theban, and that lot
Will not delight him; for instead of rich
A beggar, and instead of having sight
A blind man he will go with groping stick
Unto a foreign land; and will be shown
To be his children's brother and their sire,
And of the woman of whom he was born
Both son and husband; of his father, too,
The slayer and the sharer of his bed.
Do thou go in and ponder well these things;
And if thou findest that my words are false,
Say I know naught of the prophetic art.

At the conclusion of this speech his boy attendant leads the old man away, and Oedipus reënters the palace. The chorus then come forward for their formal song and dance. They are very much disturbed at what they have just heard. They wonder who the slayer of Laius can be, and imagine him like a solitary bull moving through woods and caves seeking to escape the punishment which is always hovering over him. They cannot understand the accusation that Tiresias has made. They have never heard of a quarrel between the families of Laius and Polydorus which might have led to the death of their former king. They conclude by expressing their confidence in Oedipus, who, by actual test when he slew the Sphinx, proved himself the city's benefactor.

As the ode comes to an end Creon enters in haste. He has heard of the serious accusation that the king has made against him and he comes to defend himself. Oedipus enters from the palace and at once begins to upbraid him. He has no doubt in his own mind that his brother-in-law has been plotting with the prophet to seize the throne, and he tells him so in no doubtful language. Creon defends himself at length and wins the approbation of the chorus, but Oedipus will listen to no argument. He is determined that Creon shall pay for his treason with his life. The queen has heard the high words passed between the two men and now comes from the palace to put an end to the dispute. Her first words are a rebuke to them for quarreling when the city is in such distress. Creon declares his innocence and Jocasta and the chorus both urge Oedipus to believe him. He yields at length though reluctantly and much against his will. The chorus urge the queen to take Oedipus into the palace, but she wishes first to know the cause of the quarrel. Oedipus explains that it arose from the charge made against him by the prophet; and Jocasta to quiet him tells him of an old oracle which had declared that Laius should die at the hands of his son; but the baby within three days of its birth was cast out on a barren mountain and so died, while Laius was slain by robbers where three roads meet. Here she says is proof of the futility of oracles. The mention of the place where Laius was slain stirs the recollection of Oedipus and he asks for further information. He is told that the murder occurred shortly before he came to Thebes. There were five in the party, and Laius, a man of middle age with hair just turning gray, rode in a chariot. One man alone had survived to tell the story. Oedipus remembers a fight he had had at a similar place with just such a company. He asks that the man who had brought the news be sent for at once. He is very apprehensive, and when the queen asks the reason why he tells the following story (ll. 774–833):

> My father was Corinthian Polybus,
> My mother Dorian Merope, and I
> Was held to be the greatest person there
> Among the citizens until this chance
> Befell me—something worthy of surprise,
> But not of serious thought. For at a feast
> A man filled overfull with wine called out
> That I was not my father's real son.
> Distressed at this I scarce restrained myself
> That day; but on the next I went and asked
> My mother and my father and they both
> Were angry at the man who had let fall
> The word. Now I was pleased at what they said,
> But yet the thing annoyed me for it spread
> Afar. And I without the knowledge of
> My mother and my father then set out
> For Delphi; but Apollo told me naught
> Of that for which I came; but other things
> Distressing, frightful, terrible he told—
> That I must wed my mother and show forth
> A race that no man could endure to see,
> And be my father's slayer. When I heard
> These things I fled, and thenceforth knew the land
> Of Corinth only by the stars that I
> Might never see those evil oracles
> Fulfilled. And as I went along I came
> To that place where thou say'st this king was slain.
> And, lady, I will tell thee all the truth.
> When I was near that place where three ways meet
> A herald met me and a man upon
> A carriage drawn by colts, as thou hast said.
> And there the leader and the aged man

Himself both tried to drive me from the road
By force, and I in anger struck the man,
The leader, who was thrusting me aside.
And when the aged man saw this he watched
As I was going by and from the car
Came down with double goad upon my head.
He more than paid the penalty for this,
For smitten by my staff he quickly fell
Upon his back, and rolled out of the car.
And then I slew them all. Now if some tie
Exists between the stranger in the car
And Laius, what more wretched man is there
Than I, whom neither stranger may receive
Nor citizen within his house, nor yet
Address him, but must thrust him from their homes.
And it was no one else than I who laid
These curses on myself. And with my hands,
The hands by which he perished, I defile
The dead man's bed. Am I an evil man?
Am I not utterly unclean? Since I
Must flee, and fleeing cannot see my friends
Or set my foot in my own land or else
Must wed my mother and slay Polybus,
My father, who begat and brought me up.
Would not a man be right who judged these things
To come upon me from a cruel god?
Ye holy and revered gods, may I
Not see that day, but may I vanish first
From human kind before I come to see
The stain of this misfortune brought to pass.

The chorus are filled with anxiety, but they urge Oedipus to have hope until he can hear from the eyewitness. He agrees; for if the man stands by his earlier story that robbers were to blame, that will prove that he, Oedipus, is guiltless. Jocasta declares that the man cannot change his tale, and to reassure the king reminds him of the oracle she had mentioned before, that Laius should die by the hands of his son when in reality the boy had died as a baby long before. This, she thinks, is a convincing proof of the futility of prophecy. The two then enter the palace to await the arrival of the man.

The chorus now come forward for their second formal dance and song. They pray that they may ever observe a pious holiness in all they do and say in accordance with laws ordained on high. Insolence creates the tyrant and brings him to his doom. They pray that an evil fate may come upon the haughty man who has no reverence for the gods. The oracles about Laius must come to pass, or confidence in the gods will fade away.

Jocasta now comes from the palace with offerings for Apollo, for she wishes to quiet Oedipus. She explains that she is going to the temple of Lycean Apollo because it happens to be nearest.

At this moment an old shepherd arrives from Corinth and inquires for the king. He is referred to Jocasta whom he greets politely like a well-trained old servant. He has brought the news that King Polybus is dead and that it is reported that the people will make Oedipus their king. Jocasta at once sees in this the falsity of the oracle that Oedipus should kill his father, and she quickly sends her maid to summon the king. Oedipus enters and hears the sad, yet welcome tidings. Polybus is dead and he has had nothing to do with his death. His faith in oracles is shaken and he is almost ready to have as little regard for them as Jocasta; and yet he fears the part which relates to his mother. All this time the old shepherd has been standing by and listening to the conversation between the king and queen, and now he asks of what woman Oedipus is afraid. The king says of his mother, Merope; and then he tells him of the terrible oracle which had declared that he should kill his father and marry his mother, and that that is the reason why he had stayed away from Corinth. The old man had made the journey to Thebes in the hope of receiving a reward for his news, and now he thinks he sees a chance to relieve the king of his anxiety. He tells him that Polybus was not his father; and, when Oedipus in astonishment questions him, declares that he himself had given him when he was a baby to the childless queen Merope.

He had received the child from a shepherd of Laius, but knows nothing further about him. Oedipus now sees an opportunity to find out about his origin, and on asking who the shepherd was is told that he is probably the very man for whom they have been looking as the eyewitness of the death of Laius.

All this time Jocasta has been listening with horror and she tries to divert Oedipus from his inquiry. And here comes one of the most tragic scenes in the whole play. Jocasta now knows the dreadful truth, that Oedipus is really her son, and her one desire is to shield him, to keep him from knowing. Oedipus wholly misunderstands her. He thinks that she, the proud queen, is afraid her husband will be proved to be of humble birth, and he scorns the thought. When Jocasta finds that her efforts are unavailing, with a wild cry she rushes into the palace and hangs herself. Oedipus remains fixed in his purpose to learn who he really is, and he waits for the coming of the shepherd.

The chorus sing a short and joyful song. They are sure that Oedipus will be proved a Theban and they wonder if it was not some local nymph who bore him to Pan or Apollo or some other god.

The shepherd is seen approaching, and Oedipus asks the Corinthian if this is the man he meant. When he is told that it is he roughly bids the man answer his questions. The Theban shepherd does not recognize the Corinthian until the latter reminds him how long ago, for three years in succession, they had pastured their sheep near each other on Mount Cithaeron for periods of six months. The next question is startling, for the Corinthian asks if he remembers giving him a baby to bring up, and then points to Oedipus as that child. The old Theban curses him and threatens to strike him, but Oedipus interferes and takes up the questioning. Bit by bit by means of threats he at length forces the man to tell that the baby was said to be the child of Laius; that it was given to him by the queen to abandon on the mountain because of the oracle which foretold that the child would kill its parents. Overcome with horror at his dreadful discovery Oedipus rushes into the palace.

The chorus sing of the insignificance of man. Oedipus had accomplished great feats and won great renown and now he has encountered utter ruin. It was he who saved them in their direst need, and now he has brought upon them great sadness.

A messenger enters in haste from the palace. He is filled with horror at the sights he has beheld and he tells what has happened within the house; but first of all he announces the queen's death by her own hand. When she had rushed into the palace in her mad frenzy she threw herself upon her bed calling upon Laius and bewailing her terrible fate. Then Oedipus with a dreadful cry dashed in, begging for a sword as he moved back and forth and calling for Jocasta. Suddenly the closed doors of her bedroom caught his eye and he hurled himself against them and burst in. There she was seen hanging by the neck, dead. He quickly took down the body and tearing the brooches from her garments struck his eyes with them that they might never behold in the future the sights they should never have seen. And now he is calling upon them to open the doors that he may cast himself from the land. But his strength is not sufficient.

The horror of this narrative grips the imagination. It affects the reader as it must have affected the listener in the theatre even more profoundly than if he had beheld the dreadful deeds actually taking place. Aristotle felt this, as we have already seen.[1] Indeed no passage in all the plays of Sophocles illustrates more clearly the dramatist's power to stir the feelings of his hearers.

The doors of the palace open and reveal the blinded king with his face stained with blood. The chorus are horrified at the sight. A lyric dialogue follows between Oedipus and the chorus in which the former bewails his terrible fate ordained for him by Apollo, while the chorus, though full of sympathy, can but join him in the wish that his life had not been saved when he was exposed as a baby on the mountain. Even now it would be better for him to be dead than to live blind.

[1] See p. 22.

But Oedipus defends his self-inflicted blindness in a speech which is noble and yet at the same time full of anguish. He expresses the wish that he might have been able to deprive himself of the sense of hearing as well as sight. Then, overcome by the thought of all the horrible things which he has done, he begs the chorus to kill him or cast him into the sea where he may never more be seen.

Creon now enters as king and, shocked at the spectacle before him, immediately orders the removal of Oedipus to the palace. Oedipus feels deeply the injustice with which he had treated Creon, but begs him to send him to Mount Cithaeron that he may end his wretched existence there. He is convinced that no illness will bring about his end, but that he is reserved for some terrible fate. Two other requests he makes, that Jocasta have the proper rights of burial and that he be permitted to touch with his hands his two little daughters. Creon declares that he must hear from the oracle of Apollo before he decides what to do with him; but the little girls are brought in and a pathetic farewell scene with their father follows. Oedipus finds it very hard to part from them, but they are separated by Creon's command and the blind king is led out, while the chorus moralize on the vicissitudes of human fortunes and recall the old adage that one should call no man happy until he is dead.

When one has finished reading the play he cannot help feeling that the common judgment of antiquity in regard to its excellence was justified. And yet, if we may believe a statement attributed to Dicaearchus, when it was presented Sophocles was defeated by the tragic poet Philocles,[1] whom Suidas calls a nephew of Aeschylus. Philocles is known to have been a voluminous writer of tragedies,[2] but we do not hear that any of them obtained particular distinction. It should, however, be remembered that Sophocles presented two other tragedies and a satyr

[1] Hypothesis II, 3 f. . . . . καίπερ ἡττηθέντα ὑπὸ Φιλοκλέους, ὥς φησι Δικαίαρχος.

[2] Suidas, s. v. Φιλοκλῆς, says, that he wrote one hundred tragedies among which he mentions an *Oedipus*.

drama at the same time with the *Oedipus*. What these other plays were we do not know; but it may well be that the group as a whole made a less favorable impression on the minds of the judges than the tetralogy of Philocles.

It has already been pointed out that the tragedies of Sophocles are distinctly studies of character. That such is the case with the *Oedipus Tyrannus* one sees very clearly in reading the play. In fact, for his purpose, the dramatist could not have found a better subject than the Theban king. Governed by a destiny which he is helpless to control, through no intentional wrong-doing on his part, he experiences all the vicissitudes of fortune from extremely good to extremely bad. In the early part of the play he is a mighty monarch, absolutely self-confident, master of himself and of his people, and devoted to his wife. At the end he is a wretched blind man suffering tortures in mind and body wrought by himself. He thus conforms to Aristotle's ideal tragic hero.[1] The skill with which the dramatist brings about the transition could not be surpassed, and it is here that he shows himself the great master of plot. The introduction of the two little daughters of Oedipus at the end of the play adds a pathetic touch, and hints at a tender side to the king's character not brought out in the earlier part of the drama.

The character of Jocasta, too, is finely set forth. She lacks the dignity of Oedipus, but knows her power and does not hesitate to chide her husband and her brother. She is scornful of the gods and their oracles, for she has had what seems to be a clear example of their uselessness; but at the same time she is not without a certain nobility of character. This is shown in her attempt to shield Oedipus when she realizes the true situation, and to prevent him from knowing; and again in her suicide. The version of the story which makes her survive would have been impossible for the Jocasta of Sophocles.[2]

[1] See p. 17.

[2] This version is followed in the *Phoenissae* of Euripides. See Bates, *Euripides*, pp. 176 ff.

Compared with the clarity with which the characters of Oedipus and Jocasta are drawn, that of Creon seems rather colorless. He has done loyally all that has been asked of him and he is naturally deeply hurt when he is unjustly accused. We can hardly imagine the Creon of the early part of the play plotting to seize the throne; though at the end, when he has become king, he does assume a certain dignity and authority.

The character of Tiresias is clearly set forth. He is not merely a prophet in whom the people have implicit confidence, but he is confident of his own powers and of his position. At the same time he is irascible and unable to control his temper. With these characteristics he is made to play an important part in the development of the plot.

Two other characters are worthy of attention—the two shepherds. And here one could not have a better example of the skill with which Sophocles depicts his minor characters. They are both men of humble station, both herders of sheep, but they have distinct individuality. The man from Corinth, as we have seen, has made the journey to Thebes in the hope of receiving a reward for his tidings. He is the type of the well-trained, polite old servant, and his well-intentioned but meddlesome revelations lead to ruin. His good nature is in contrast with the surliness of the Theban shepherd. The latter, to be sure, has good reason to be apprehensive. He knows that the king is the man who slew Laius; and when he is reminded of the child of long ago he feels that he must make every effort to hide the secret which he is finally forced to divulge. There is good reason for the difference between the two men.

The chorus are represented as a band of dignified old men, loyal to the king, yet having absolute confidence in the gods. Their sympathy for Oedipus and their sorrow for his misfortunes are very real. They have a well-defined part in the advancement of the plot.

The story of Oedipus was so well adapted to tragedy that it is not surprising that each of the three great tragic poets of Greece made use of it, as did various minor dramatists.[1] No doubt there were many variations in detail in their different plays. There is good reason to believe that in the old epic version of the story Jocasta was not represented as the mother of the children of Oedipus;[2] and his blinding by the servants of Laius seems to have been included in the plot of the *Oedipus* of Euripides.[3] What all these variations were, however, it is needless to inquire.

With the revival of classic themes by the dramatists of the seventeenth and eighteenth centuries it is not surprising that the story of Oedipus was again represented on the stage. Thus Corneille in 1657 and Voltaire in 1718 in France, and Dryden in 1679 in England produced tragedies with Oedipus as the hero. In modern times, however, French and English translations from the Greek have been more popular, and these have had long and successful seasons in the United States, England, and France. In Athens the *Oedipus Tyrannus* has often been played both in ancient Greek and in modern Greek translation. And the opera *Oedipe* by the Rumanian Georges Enesco, brought out in 1934, and W. B. Yeats's version for the modern stage, published in 1928, are further evidence for the vitality of this ancient story.[4]

II

The Oedipus at Colonus

THE *Oedipus at Colonus* is a play very different in character from the *Oedipus Tyrannus*, and yet in a way it is quite as remarkable as the earlier and more famous tragedy. Its plot has to do with

[1] For example, Achaeus, Carcinus, Diogenes, Meletus, Nicomachus, Philocles, Theodectes, Xenocles, and, in the third century B.C., Lycophron in two plays.

[2] So Pausanias, IX, 5, 10. *παῖδας δὲ ἐξ αὐτῆς* (*'Ιοκάστης*) *οὐ δοκῶ οἱ γενέσθαι μάρτυρι 'Ομήρῳ* (*Odys.* XII, 271 ff.) *χρώμενος . . . . . ἐξ Εὐρυγανείας δὲ τῆς 'Υπέρφαντος ἐγεγόνεσαν. δηλοῖ δὲ καὶ ὁ τὰ ἔπη ποιήσας ἃ Οἰδιπόδια ὀνομάζουσι.*

[3] See e.g. Bates, *Euripides*, pp. 265 f.

[4] In the Gennadion at Athens there is a prose translation of lines 1–560 and 863–881 of the *Oedipus Tyrannus* written in an interleaved copy of the edition of Foulis (Glasgow, 1777). It has been attributed to the poet Shelley.

the last hours of Oedipus. According to tradition it was the work of the poet's extreme old age[1] and it is full of feeling for his native deme of Colonus Hippius. There the scene was laid in the sanctuary of the Furies.[2] A story has been handed down by several ancient authors to the effect that his son Iophon brought the aged Sophocles into court charging that he was incapable of managing his affairs, and that the poet in his defense merely repeated lines from the first stasimon of the *Oedipus at Colonus* (ll. 668 ff.) which he was then composing, and was acquitted.[3] According to the unknown writer of the second Hypothesis to the play it was brought out after the poet's death by his grandson, Sophocles the younger, in the archonship of Micon, that is, in the year 402 B.C.[4] This date has been questioned and it has been argued that it was not presented then for the first time. There seems, however, to be no good reason to doubt the traditional date which is given with so much explicitness.[5]

For a setting we have the grove of the Furies at Colonus and the country in its immediate vicinity. The time is supposed to be twenty years or more after the events which had brought the *Oedipus Tyrannus* to a conclusion. The play begins in dramatic fashion in the midst of the action. The aged Oedipus, blind and in beggar's rags, enters on the arm of his daughter Antigone. They have been able to keep themselves alive all these years through the charity of others, and now, after long

[1] The writer of Hypothesis I, 13 ff. says, *τὸ δὲ δρᾶμα τῶν θαυμαστῶν· ὃ καὶ ἤδη γεγηρακὼς ὁ Σοφοκλῆς ἐποίησε, χαριζόμενος οὐ μόνον τῇ πατρίδι, ἀλλὰ καὶ τῷ ἑαυτοῦ δήμῳ· ἦν γὰρ Κολωνῆθεν.*

[2] See Hypothesis I, 20 ff. *ἡ σκηνὴ τοῦ δράματος ὑπόκειται ἐν τῇ Ἀττικῇ ἐν τῷ ἱππίῳ Κολωνῷ, πρὸς τῷ ναῷ τῶν σεμνῶν.*

[3] The story is told with some variations by the author of the *Life* (13), perhaps on the authority of Satyrus; Plutarch, *An seni sit res pub. ger.* III, 3; Cicero, *De senectute*, VII, 22; Lucian, *Macrobii*, 24; Apuleius, *Apol.* p. 298; Valerius Maximus, VIII, 7, 12.

[4] Lines 1 ff. *τὸν ἐπὶ Κολωνῷ Οἰδίπουν ἐπὶ τετελευτηκότι τῷ πάππῳ Σοφοκλῆς ὁ υἱδοῦς ἐδίδαξεν, υἱὸς ὢν Ἀρίστωνος, ἐπὶ ἄρχοντος Μίκωνος, ὅς ἐστι τέταρτος ἀπὸ Καλλίου, ἐφ' οὗ φασιν οἱ πλείους τὸν Σοφοκλέα τελευτῆσαι.*

[5] Campbell, *Sophocles* I, ed. 2, pp. 277 ff. suggested that the play was brought out in 411 B.C., a date for which some other writers have argued.

wandering, they have reached a grove where they sit down to rest their weary limbs. A man approaches, and as soon as he sees them warns them off, for they are sitting in the grove of the Furies at Colonus which no one is permitted to enter. When Oedipus hears to what place he has come he knows that his end is near, for Apollo in his oracle had foretold that he would end his days in a sanctuary of the Furies, a blessing to those who received him and a curse to those who had sent him forth. The man is touched by the noble dignity of the blind beggar and he hastens away to tell his fellow citizens of the presence of the stranger in the forbidden place. Oedipus is apprehensive, and after the man has gone withdraws further into the grove.

A band of aged citizens of Colonus (that is, the chorus) soon enters looking for the blind man. Oedipus after some delay comes forward and shows himself. The chorus are shocked at his dreadful appearance and order him to leave the grove at once. He consents to do so and at length moves from the spot when the old men promise that nobody shall take him away. Painfully, resting on the arm of Antigone, he passes beyond the forbidden ground and with her help is seated on a rock at the edge of the grove. The chorus ask him who he is. He tries to put them off and, when he can do so no longer, tells them that he is Oedipus. They are horror-stricken and tell him that he must leave the country. They think that they have been imposed upon, and will not stand by their promise. Antigone makes a pathetic appeal for herself and for her father and although the old men acknowledge that they feel pity they are fearful. This whole scene must have been very effective in the theatre. There is, to be sure, little action in it, but the situation becomes tense and the sympathies of the spectators are fully aroused for the unfortunate man and his daughter.

Oedipus now addresses the chorus (ll. 258 ff.):

What profits reputation or fair fame
That slips away in vain, when people say
That Athens is most reverent towards the gods,
That she alone can save an injured man,

Alone protect the stranger? Tell me where
I find this service, ye who raised me up
From my seat here and now will drive me forth
Not fearing me, nor yet the deeds I've done,
But just my name; since if I must recall
The stories of my mother and my sire
For which ye dread me—that I know full well—
My deeds were those of one who suffered, not
Of one who acted first. How, then, am I
By nature evil, wicked, just because
When I was injured I struck back again?
If I had acted with full knowledge I
Should not thus be accounted a bad man.
And now unknowing I went where I went,
But they knew what they did who sought my death.
For which I beg ye, strangers, by the gods
To save me since ye made me leave my place.
And do not in your honor of the gods
Make gods of no account; but rather think
They see the pious man, and also see
The wicked, and no sinful mortal can
Find an escape. With their assistance, then,
Do not incline towards impious deeds and hide
The glorious fame of Athens, but protect
And guard me, just as when with solemn pledge
I was received a suppliant. And I pray
When ye look on my poor disfigured face
Cast not dishonor on me, for I come
A holy, pious man who brings to all
These citizens a guerdon, and when he
Who is your ruler comes ye shall hear all
And understand. Before that time do not
Show yourselves base.

The chorus are won over by this speech and agree to await the arrival of the king, who has already been summoned by messenger. Oedipus has grave doubts about his coming, but is assured that his name will surely bring him.

Antigone now sees approaching a woman on horseback and,

although she can hardly believe her eyes, she at length identifies her as her sister Ismene. Ismene enters accompanied by an attendant. She has been living at Thebes and has now, with considerable difficulty, sought out her father and sister to tell them of the developments which have taken place there. Oedipus inquires for his two sons who have so neglected him, and contrasts their unfilial conduct with that of his daughters. It makes him think of the land of Egypt.[1] Ismene explains that at first they had left the throne to Creon, but afterwards had decided to seize the royal power. Eteocles, the younger son, had made himself king and driven out his elder brother Polynices.[2] The latter is now at Argos, where he is planning the invasion and conquest of his native land.

But Ismene has other news, namely that the oracle at Delphi had declared that the welfare of Thebes depended upon the presence there of Oedipus, living or dead;[3] that Creon is now coming to take possession of him in order to place him near the city where he can have control over his person, without permitting him to dwell in Theban land. On learning that his sons knew of this oracle Oedipus declares that he will never help them, for they had preferred the throne to him. He tells the chorus that if they are willing to protect him he himself will prove to be a benefactor to their state. The old men agree to help him, but advise him to make an offering to the Furies whose holy precinct he has entered. Oedipus is willing and is instructed in the ritual to be followed, but because of his blindness Ismene undertakes to enter the grove and perform the rite for him. Antigone is to remain behind to protect him. The

[1] In comparing the conduct of the children of Oedipus with the habits of men and women in Egypt (ll. 337 ff.) Sophocles clearly has in mind a passage in the history of his friend Herodotus (II, 35). For other references to the work of Herodotus by the poet see p. 11.

[2] Sophocles makes Polynices the elder brother, apparently for dramatic effect, thus giving greater justification to his claim to the throne. Other authorities make Eteocles the elder, e.g., Euripides, *Phoenissae*, 71.

[3] C. R. Post, *Harv. Stud. in Class. Philol.* XXIII, 1912, p. 85, suggests that this oracle is the invention of Sophocles.

chorus question Oedipus about himself and drag from the unhappy man the admission that the reports they had heard about him are true.

While this scene is taking place Theseus is on his way from Athens to Colonus, and he now enters and addresses Oedipus, whom he recognizes at once. He assures him of his sympathy and help even before he hears what request he has to make. Oedipus explains that an attempt will be made by the Thebans to get possession of him from fear of an oracle which foretold their defeat if Oedipus alive or dead remained in Attic territory. Theseus, however, can see no reason why the friendship between Thebes and Athens should be broken. Oedipus replies in a noble speech as follows (ll. 607 ff.):

Oh! dearest son of Aegeus, gods alone
Escape old age and death; all other things
All-conquering time confuses. Strength of soil
And strength of body fade, faith perishes
Distrust springs up and confidence does not
Remain the same for friends, nor yet between
One city and another. Either now
Or at a later time their joys become
First bitter and then pleasant once again.
And if fair weather now prevails at Thebes
In its regard for thee, advancing time
Will bring to birth both many nights and days
In which those pledges now harmonious
Shall by the spear be scattered, all because
Of a slight word. Then my dead body shall
Though cold and sleeping, hid beneath the ground,
Drink their warm blood, if Zeus still Zeus remains
And Phoebus his true prophet. But to speak
Of things forbidden is not well. Let me
Leave off where I began, but guard thy pledge
And never shalt thou say thou didst receive
Me, Oedipus, a useless dweller here
Within this land, unless the gods prove false.

Theseus assures Oedipus that he will be permitted to remain, and even invites him to go with him to Athens. But Oedipus knows that he must stay where he is and, though apprehensive, is reassured by Theseus. The latter now returns to Athens and the chorus come forward and sing the first stasimon (ll. 668–719). This is one of the finest odes in Sophocles. It is full of feeling for his native Colonus and for Attica. It is the ode already mentioned which Sophocles was said to have recited before his judges. Whether there is any truth in that story or not there is no means of knowing, but it was popular in antiquity, as the many references to it prove. The ode runs something as follows:

(*Strophe α'*) Stranger, into this land thou hast come,
Into earth's fairest abode,
To white Colonus famed for its steeds,
Where 'mid coverts of greenery
Many and many a time
Nightingales warble their clear-voiced song,
Hiding in ivy dark as wine
In the thick foliage laden with fruit,
Sacred, dear to the god, unharmed
Either by sun or by winds of the storm.
Here Dionysus, the reveler god,
Always comes with his train of nymphs.

(*Antistrophe α'*) Thriving under the heavenly dew
With its fair clusters of flowers
Narcissus always day after day
Blossoms, just as in ancient times
It crowned the goddesses twain.
Here, too, is crocus with golden sheen;
Here never fail the sleepless springs
Of the Cephissus which with its pure flood
Wanders over the swelling plain
Giving a speedy return from the soil.
Here come the Muses in choruses and
Aphrodite with golden rein.

(*Strophe β′*) I have not heard that in Asian land
Or in old Pelops' great Dorian isle
Such a tree lives as thrives mightily here,
Ever unconquered, renewing itself,
Terror to enemies' spearmen, the gray
Olive which nurtures our sons.
Youth shall not harm it with ravaging hand,
Nor one advanced in his years, for Zeus,
Lord of the sacred olives, keeps watch
As does Athena with gray-blue eyes.

(*Antistrophe β′*) One other tale I have also to tell,
Glorious tale of a gift from a god,
Mightiest boast of our own mother land,
Famed for its horses, its colts, and the sea.
Thou, son of Cronos, Poseidon our lord,
Gavest her reason to boast.
Here thou didst first show the bit for the horse;
Here does the well-fitted oar in our hands
Leap forward briskly, following close
After the Nereids' hundred feet.

At the conclusion of this song Antigone sees Creon approaching with a band of followers. Oedipus is apprehensive although the chorus promise their protection. Creon enters and makes a specious plea to Oedipus to return with him to Thebes; but Oedipus knows that he has no intention of taking him there, tells him so plainly and refuses to go. Creon threatens, and then orders his guards to seize Antigone, who, in spite of the chorus, is carried away. Ismene had already been captured. Creon is about to leave when the chorus lay hold of him. He throws them off and tries to drag Oedipus away. The chorus shout for aid as Theseus enters with his bodyguard and demands the cause of the uproar. Oedipus quickly explains that his daughters have been carried off by the followers of Creon. Theseus orders them to be pursued and declares that Creon shall be held until the two girls are safely returned. Creon pretends that his action was justified by the crimes of Oedipus and that he knew that Athens would never endure the presence of such a man. To this Oedipus replies in a speech full of deep feeling. He reminds them all that the dreadful deeds of which he had been guilty had been committed with entire innocence on his part, and declares his belief that his father Laius, if he could come back to life again, would not deny it. As to Creon—he has shown what sort of man he is by recalling his sister's shame. He concludes his speech by appealing to the Furies for help. Theseus now forces Creon, in spite of his obscure threats, to accompany him and help in the rescue of Antigone and Ismene. Oedipus is instructed to remain where he is until they return.

This lively scene, full of action, is in marked contrast with the greater part of the play where the plot is developed quietly and with little action.

The chorus now sing the second stasimon. They express the wish that they might be present at the combat which they foresee is about to take place between Theseus and the followers of Creon. They predict a victory for the former and pray to Zeus, Athena, and Apollo to bring it to pass.

A few moments later Antigone and Ismene are seen approaching with Theseus, and a touching meeting between the blind father and his daughters takes place. Oedipus expresses his gratitude to Theseus, who accepts it and then recalls that as he was about to set out he had found a relative of Oedipus as a suppliant at the altar of Poseidon, and that the man wished to speak to him. When the king mentions Argos, Oedipus knows that it is his son Polynices, and he declares that he will not see him; but he does at length consent to do so when persuaded by Antigone.

The scene thus comes to an end and the chorus sing the third stasimon. With the experiences of Oedipus before them they moralize on the folly of wishing for a long life with all its tribulations. They declare rather gloomily (ll. 1224 ff.) that

Not to be born is the best thing of all;
But when one has come into this world
Leaving it speedily is the next best.

Polynices is recognized by Antigone as he approaches alone. He professes to be deeply distressed at the wretched plight of his father and sister, clad as they are in foul and unseemly garments. Oedipus remains silent; and Polynices, encouraged by Antigone, sets forth the reasons why he has come. He has been banished from Thebes by his younger brother, Eteocles, who had gained the support of the city. From Thebes he had gone to Argos, married the daughter of Adrastus and organized an expedition. He is now about to march against his native city and, having learned of the oracle which declared that victory would fall to those with whom Oedipus sided, seeks his aid. He promises to bring back his father to Thebes if he will assist him.

Oedipus replies in a long speech declaring that he would not have spoken at all if it had not been for Theseus. But the treatment which he had received from Polynices in the past still rankles in his breast and he speaks very bitterly. He reminds him that it was he, when he was on the throne, who drove him out and so became the cause of the very miseries which he now pretends to deplore. He curses his unfilial son, and prays that he and his brother Eteocles may both perish, each by the other's hand. Polynices is crushed by his father's words; but although Antigone begs him to turn back his army and not persist in his invasion of his native land, her words are of no avail. He cannot bear the scorn of his younger brother; and even if his father's words do forebode disaster he must go on with his expedition just the same. But he begs his sister, if death is to be his lot, to obtain burial for his body.

When Polynices has departed the chorus comment briefly on the evils which they have seen arise from Oedipus, and on the vicissitudes of fortune. These few lines serve as a transition to the remarkable scene which follows.

A peal of thunder is suddenly heard, and Oedipus knows that

it is a sign from heaven. He asks that Theseus be sent for with all speed. A second peal is heard and the chorus become frightened as the lightning continues to flash and the thunder to resound; but Oedipus knows that his end is near. Theseus arrives in the midst of the storm, and Oedipus tells him that he will show him the place where his life will at length come to an end. This must be regarded as a state secret to be told only to his successor when death approaches, and then to his successor, and so on, and thus it will always remain a protection to Athens against Theban aggression. And now he says he must go, for a divine power urges him on. He arises without assistance, bidding his children follow, but not touch him (ll. 1547–1555):

> Come this way, this way come, for this way leads
> My escort Hermes and that goddess who
> Directs the dead. Oh! light that is no light,
> Which once was mine, but now for the last time
> My body feels thee, for I go to hide
> Myself in Hades. But, my dearest friend,
> Mayst thou, thy land and thy attendants, too,
> Be happy; and when ye have met success
> Remember me though I am dead, and ye
> Forever fortunate.

Then, in what must have been one of the most impressive scenes in all Greek tragedy, the miserable blind man, no longer timid, but as if guided by a higher power and with full confidence in himself, moves off the stage.[1]

The chorus sing the fourth stasimon. It is a short prayer to the deities of the Lower World that the passing of Oedipus to the abode of the dead may be free from pain.

A messenger now enters to announce the death of the stranger. When questioned by the chorus he explains that Oedipus advanced forward until he came to the Brazen Threshold—a well-known place. Then he sat down, loosened his wretched gar-

[1] Shorey, *Martin Class. Lectures*, p. 74, quotes De Quincey as declaring this scene to be one of the most sublime in literature.

ments and asked his daughters to bring him water that he might bathe and offer a libation. When he had completed his bath and put on the dress of the dead, thunder from the god of the Lower World was heard. He then bade the two girls farewell as they clung to him weeping; and all were terrified as a voice was heard summoning Oedipus and bidding him delay no longer. The messenger's narrative continues thus (ll. 1629–1666):

When he perceived the god was calling him
He begged King Theseus to draw near and said,
"Dear friend, thy solemn pledge give to my girls.
And ye, my daughters, also give him yours.
And promise that thou never willingly
Wilt fail them, but accomplish happily
Whatever thou dost purpose for their good."
And, like the noble man he is, the king
Took oath that he would do this for his guest.
Then Oedipus straightway with groping hands
Felt for his children, saying "Daughers mine,
Ye must be bold of heart and leave this place,
And not think ye should see what ye should not,
Nor hear us speaking. Go, then, with all speed
And let the king alone remain and learn
What things are done." So much we heard him say.
And grieving, with eyes full of tears we left
Together with the maidens; but we soon
Turned and beheld the man no longer there,
But Theseus with his hand before his face
To shade his eyes, as if some dreadful sight,
One unendurable, had met his gaze.
And then we saw him bow down to the earth,
And hail Olympus in the selfsame prayer.
But by what fate the stranger met his end
No mortal man save Theseus could reveal.
No fiery thunderbolt destroyed the man
Nor whirlwind from the sea in that short time;
But either from the gods a messenger,
Or else a parting of earth's floor below,

Removed him, free from pain; for without groan
And with no suffering from disease he went—
An ending marvelous among mankind.
Now if I seem to utter foolish words
I would not ask those to believe who think
I am devoid of reason.

When the messenger has finished his speech Antigone and Ismene enter, and a lament in lyric verse follows. This assumes the form of a dialogue between the chorus on one side and Antigone and Ismene on the other. The purport of it is that Oedipus has died as he wished and where he wished, that is, in a foreign land; but his daughters cannot help grieving for him, or from being apprehensive for their own future.

Theseus now returns and urges them to refrain from weeping and, when Antigone begs to look upon her father's burial place, tells her that a strict injunction from Oedipus himself requires that the place should be kept secret. He will, however, send them to Thebes, where Antigone hopes to prevent bloodshed between her two brothers. The chorus feel that what has happened was destined, and with these words the play ends.

The *Oedipus at Colonus*, like most of the other extant tragedies of Sophocles, affords a marvelous opportunity for a great actor. The dramatist undertakes to show us Oedipus as he conceives him after long years of pain and sorrow. At the conclusion of the *Oedipus Tyrannus* we find Oedipus, the powerful king, utterly crushed by the dreadful crimes which he had unwittingly committed. In the *Oedipus at Colonus* we see the same man after long suffering attaining a certain degree of tranquility and peace. He is now convinced that, black as his deeds may seem, they were done with entire innocence on his part, and that no man can justly hold him guilty. This is his settled conviction when he reaches the place where it had been foretold he must end his life.[1]

[1] In *Harv. Stud. in Class. Philol.* XXXIII, p. 11, C. R. Post argues that where Sophocles wrote two plays on the same subject the second play dealt with the

The appearance of Oedipus, unkempt and dressed in filthy rags, in outward aspect a very wretched beggar, is in striking contrast to the nobility of his mind. In fact at times he reminds us of the Oedipus whom we find at the beginning of the *Oedipus Tyrannus*, and we almost forget his personal appearance as we read the lines. Perhaps we might wish a different attitude towards his son, Polynices, but the injury received from him is too great, and has hurt him too deeply, to be lightly forgiven. And here we see his anger blazing up as fiercely as we saw it in the earlier tragedy. The noble spirit and the hot temper of the younger Oedipus are still with him in his old age. The element of the supernatural introduced in the account of his death is in keeping with the events of his life. Oedipus could not be made to meet his end like any ordinary mortal.

The remaining characters call for little comment. Theseus is what an Athenian audience would like to have an Attic king—a ruler having the esteem of his people, and a protector of the weak against the strong. Creon is no longer the Creon of the *Oedipus Tyrannus*, but more like the Creon of the *Antigone*. He is tricky, unscrupulous and very ready to use force to attain his ends. Polynices, the recreant son, is represented as a rather weak man who knows that he has done his father great wrong; but nevertheless has the effrontery to ask for his forgiveness and even assistance. Antigone and Ismene are both devoted to their father, but the devotion of Antigone is the greater for she has voluntarily shared in her father's wretched life as a beggar. The marked difference in character between the two daughters which is so strongly emphasized in the *Antigone* is not found here. The messenger tells his story of the end of Oedipus directly and simply. His speech is an excellent example of the messenger's part as employed by Sophocles.

---

purification of the main character for the sin for which he was punished in the first play. He thinks this principle applies not only to the *Oedipus at Colonus*, but to several of the lost plays such as the *Philoctetes at Troy*, the *Teucer*, the second *Athamas*, etc.

The *Oedipus at Colonus* is the longest of all the extant Greek tragedies, containing as it does 1,779 lines. Furthermore, a fourth actor seems to have been employed in its presentation This might be avoided by having the part of Theseus divided between two actors, and the part of Ismene presented in the same way. Such an arrangement would be very surprising, if not impossible.

The *Oedipus at Colonus* was not read in the schools of Byzantium as was the *Oedipus Tyrannus*, and in consequence the extant manuscripts of it are not particularly numerous. Pearson in the Oxford edition of *Sophocles* notes twelve manuscripts, of which nine date from the fourteenth or fifteenth century.[1] On the other hand, an anecdote told by Plutarch in his *Life of Demetrius*[2] is good evidence for its fame in antiquity. He says that Demetrius, whose aged father Antigonus had been killed in battle some years before, invaded Caria to seize that territory, which was ruled by Lysimachus. His invasion was unsuccessful and he led his army away into Phrygia, hoping eventually to reach Armenia. At this time some wag in the army fastened to the general's tent a parody of the opening lines of the *Oedipus at Colonus* changing the name Antigone to Antigonus, so that they read:

> τέκνον τυφλοῦ γέροντος Ἀντιγόνου, τίνας
> χώρους ἀφίγμεθα;

The story would have little or no point if the play were not well known and the parody readily recognized.

No other dramatist than Sophocles is known to have written a tragedy with the last hours of Oedipus for its subject. This may be due to the fact that they failed to see the dramatic possibilities of the story; but it should not be forgotten that

[1] The three earlier manuscripts which contain it are L (Laurentianus xxxii, 9) of the eleventh century; A (Parisinus 2712) of the twelfth century; and Ven. (Marcianus 468) of the thirteenth century.

[2] *Demetrius*, XLVI, 4.

Colonus was the birthplace of Sophocles and that a local tradition made Oedipus meet his end there.[1]

III

The Antigone

The *Antigone* is the last of the three great tragedies of Sophocles dealing with the Oedipus legend—last, that is, from the point of view of the story, for in actual composition it was certainly earlier than the *Oedipus at Colonus* and probably also earlier than the *Oedipus Tyrannus*. It has already been pointed out[2] that we have good evidence for its date in the statement in the Hypothesis to the play attributed to Aristophanes of Byzantium, that there was a tradition that Sophocles was made general in the Samian War because of the fame which he acquired from the performance of his *Antigone*.[3] The date of that war is known to be 440 B.C.[4] and the play was, therefore, presumably brought out the year before, that is, in 441; and certainly not more than two years before.[5] It was said to have been his thirty-second play.[6]

[1] The scholiast on l. 1593 says πιθανῶς δὲ Σοφοκλῆς πρὸς χάριν τῆς Ἀττικῆς φησιν ἐνταῦθα (that is, the place where Theseus and Peirithous made their compact) τὴν εἰς Ἅιδου κατάβασιν Οἰδίποδος γενέσθαι. According to Pausanias (I, 28, 7) the tomb of Oedipus was located at Athens between the Areopagus and the Acropolis. Other writers placed it at Colonus, or in Boeotia. Homer (*Iliad*, XXIII, 679 ff.) speaks of Mecisteus going to Thebes for the funeral of Oedipus, thus implying his burial there. A scholium on *Oedipus at Colonus* 91, perhaps going back to Didymus says that he was eventually buried in a sanctuary of Demeter at Eteonus in Boeotia. For a discussion of these sites see Frazer *Pausanias*, II, pp. 366 ff.

[2] See p. 9.

[3] φασὶ δὲ τὸν Σοφοκλέα ἠξιῶσθαι τῆς ἐν Σάμῳ στρατηγίας εὐδοκιμήσαντα ἐν τῇ διδασκαλίᾳ τῆς Ἀντιγόνης.

[4] Thucydides, I, 115, 2. ἕκτῳ δὲ ἔτει (i.e., the sixth year after 445 by Greek reckoning) Σαμίοις καὶ Μιλησίοις πόλεμος ἐγένετο περὶ Πριήνης.

[5] R. J. Walker's argument for 411 must be rejected. See p. 38.

[6] Hypothesis, 14 f. λέλεκται δὲ τὸ δρᾶμα τοῦτο τριακοστὸν δεύτερον. This passage has been much discussed and the interpretation given above questioned.

The fame of the *Antigone* has always been great, from the time of its first performance.[1] In the century after the poet's death, when it was customary at Athens to revive the tragedies of the three great masters, it was played repeatedly.[2] It is possible even that it may have been brought out a second time during the poet's life; for if there is anything at all in the story that he died of joy when he was proclaimed victorious with his *Antigone*,[3] it would seem to be that the play was put on the stage again many years after its first appearance. At the same time the word *ἀνάγνωσιν* may imply some competition in which plays were read; but if that is the case nothing more is known about it. We have no other evidence for the presentation of a tragedy by Sophocles at Athens a second time during the fifth century B.C. The plays of Aeschylus were, however, by special decree reënacted after their author's death.[4] In modern times

---

Similar numbers are found in notices of other plays. Thus the *Alcestis* of Euripides is said to have been his seventeenth play (*τὸ δρᾶμα ἐποιήθη ιζ'*); the *Birds* of Aristophanes his thirty-fifth (*ἔστι δὲ λε'*); the *Dionysalexander* of Cratinus his eighth (Διονυσ[αλέξανδρος] ῆ Κρατ[είνου].*Ox. Pap.* IV, p. 71); and the *Imbrians* of Menander his seventy-[first, third, sixth, or ninth] (*ταύτην [ἔγρα]ψεν ἐπὶ* Νεικοκλέο[υς . . .]*την καὶ ἑβδομηκοστ[ήν]*. *Ox. Pap.* X, No. 1235, ll. 105 ff.). R. C. Flickinger (*Class. Philol.* V, 1910, pp. 1 ff.) argued that the numbers were those the plays had in the Alexandrian Library. R. J. Walker denies that this is possible and argues (*Ichneutae*, pp. 598 ff.) that in the case of the *Antigone* the number thirty-two means that that play belonged to the thirty-second tetralogy of Sophocles, though Sophocles is said to have written but 123 plays. Whether the statement of the Hypothesis is correct or not the Greek is clear, that the *Antigone* was said to have been the thirty-second play of Sophocles.

[1] In the museum at Lahore there is a fragment of a vase of local manufacture found near Peshawar, similar to the Megarian ware produced in the third and second centuries B.C., on which is represented an older man who has seized a young girl, while a younger man apparently supplicates him. This has been supposed to represent Creon, Antigone, and Haemon, and has been taken as evidence that Sophocles was known in Northern India. See *Jour. of Royal Asiatic Soc.*, 1909, pp. 1060 f. and pl. III, a; also Tarn, *op. cit.*, p. 382.

[2] Demosthenes, *de Fals. Leg.* 246, Ἀντιγόνην δὲ Σοφοκλέους πολλάκις μὲν Θεόδωρος, πολλάκις δὲ Ἀριστόδημος ὑποκέκριται.

[3] *Life*, 14, οἱ δὲ ὅτι μετὰ τὴν τοῦ δράματος ἀνάγνωσιν, ὅτε νικῶν ἐκηρύχθη, χαρᾷ νικηθεὶς ἐξέλιπεν.

[4] *Life of Aeschylus*, 11, Ἀθηναῖοι δὲ τοσοῦτον ἠγάπησαν Αἰσχύλον ὡς ψηφίσασθαι μετὰ θάνατον αὐτοῦ τὸν βουλόμενον διδάσκειν τὰ Αἰσχύλου χορὸν λαμβάνειν.

the *Antigone* has been one of the most read and most admired of Greek tragedies.[1]

The scene of the play is laid at Thebes in front of the royal palace. A great battle has just been fought and the invading Argive army defeated and put to flight. In the battle the two sons of Oedipus, Eteocles the king and Polynices the leader of the invading host, have met in single combat and each perished by the other's hand. Antigone and Ismene, the two daughters of Oedipus, enter from the palace in conversation. Antigone asks her sister if she has heard of the proclamation made by their uncle Creon, who has become king and commander of the Theban army since the death of Eteocles. Ismene has not, and Antigone explains that she has brought her outside the house to tell her. Creon has honored Eteocles with appropriate funeral rites, but the body of their other brother, Polynices, he has proclaimed shall be left unwept and unburied, a prey to the carrion birds. Anyone who violates this decree shall be stoned to death. She asks Ismene if she will help her to bury the body, but Ismene is afraid. She recalls the misfortunes of her family, reminds Antigone that they are weak women and Creon a powerful man, and says she will ask pardon of the dead, but will obey the king's decree. Her decision does not deter Antigone, who declares that she will defy the decree and bury her brother. She is willing to die if she accomplishes this. Ismene tries to dissuade her though she dare not help her, and finally bids her go, foolish as she thinks her, but true to her dead brother. She returns into the house, while Antigone goes to perform her solemn task.

The chorus, consisting of Theban elders, now enter and sing a joyous song, a song of thanksgiving for the Theban victory over the invading Argives. The death of the two royal brothers is but lightly touched upon; the victory of their fellow townsmen

[1] Demosthenes apparently had this play in mind at the time of his death, if the story told by Plutarch (*Demosthenes*, XXIX, 4) is true. When he felt the poison which he had taken working he said to the leader of the Macedonians, "Οὐκ ἂν φθάνοις ἤδη τὸν ἐκ τῆς τραγῳδίας ὑποκρινόμενος Κρέοντα καὶ τὸ σῶμα τοῦτο ῥίπτων ἄταφον,"—a manifest allusion to Creon's treatment of the body of Polynices.

is the dominant thought in their minds. The structure of this ode is peculiar, anapaestic lines following the logaoedic in each strophe and antistrophe.

The king is seen approaching from the palace. He had previously ordered the elders to meet him, and when he has come forward he addresses them in a dignified speech. He tells how the royal power has come to him, and says that although new to his position and untried he means to observe certain principles, namely not to keep quiet when disaster to the state impends and not to regard any public enemy as a friend. With these preliminary remarks he tells of his proclamation that Eteocles, who had died fighting for the city be buried with all suitable honors, but that the body of Polynices be cast out to be mangled by birds and dogs. In this speech of forty-two lines Sophocles gives us a glimpse of Creon's character, which is brought out in greater detail as the play develops. He seems to distrust himself. His first concern is to impress upon the old men who form the chorus that he is legally king and that he regards the interests of the state above all else. Having accomplished that he tells of his proclamation about the two brothers. The chorus readily acknowledge his authority and assent to his commands. He is giving them further instructions when a rustic guard is seen reluctantly entering. There is something almost ludicrous in the way in which the man comes forward and tells his story. He has been sent by his companions to tell the king bad news, and he is afraid to tell it. He therefore begins by explaining the misgivings he has had on his way to the palace, and then declares that he did not do the deed nor see anyone do it, before he makes known what has actually happened. Then, after beating about the bush, he at length blurts out his story that somebody has thrown dust upon the body of Polynices, thus effecting the necessary rites of burial. But there is no mark of pick or trace of cartwheels to give a clue to the perpetrator of the deed. The chorus suggest that some god may be responsible, and by their words arouse the anger of the king. He is sure that disloyal subjects are to blame and he threatens the chorus if they fail to find out the guilty persons. The guard tries to say a word, but is quickly silenced, and Creon with a parting threat enters the palace.

The chorus now come forward for their first stasimon. The short ode which they sing is an interesting one. They moralize on man and his wondrous ways. There is no accounting for him. Many things he accomplishes, but sometimes he does what he should not and meets disaster. Their thoughts have evidently been suggested by what has just transpired. The ode may be rendered thus (ll. 332–383):

(*Strophe α'*) Many and wondrous things there are
And none more wonderful than Man.
Over the hoary sea he goes,
The stormy south-wind drives him on,
With billows surging round about.
Earth, supreme among the gods,
Imperishable and intact,
He wears away from year to year
With courses of his mule-drawn plough.

(*Antistrophe α'*) Families of the thoughtless birds,
The different kinds of savage beasts,
Denizens of the briny deep,
With meshy folds of nets he takes,
This subtle, clever creature, Man.
By devices he subdues
The mountain-roving animals;
He tames and yokes the rough-maned horse
And the unwearied mountain bull.

(*Strophe β'*) Speech hath he taught himself,
Thought swift as the wind,
The will to live in law-abiding towns,
And the keen darts of frost and rain to flee.
He's unprepared for naught that is to come,

Save only Death, from which he cannot flee.
From grievous ills he hath devised escape.

(*Antistrophe β′*) Skilful beyond belief,
Wise craft doth he have
Which brings him now to evil, now to good.
When he observes his country's laws he thrives
With justice from the gods; but when he sins
Hath nothing good; no city. May that man
Not share my hearth nor think the same with me.

FIGURE 2.
ANTIGONE BEFORE CREON
From a Lucanian Amphora in the British Museum

At this moment Antigone is led in by the guards, and the chorus are shocked and distressed at the sight (Fig. 2). The man who had brought the message is with them and speaks up, declaring that she was caught in the act of performing the burial. He asks for Creon who is just entering from the palace. The guard briefly explains the situation and turns Antigone over to him. He has done what he was ordered to do and found the guilty person. But Creon is in no mind to let him go so lightly. He wants details and they are given. With the other guards he had swept the dust from the corpse and otherwise put it as far as possible in the same condition as when it was first exposed. Then they had hidden behind a hill and watched. At length they saw Antigone approach. When she saw the body she uttered a cry of wailing like a distressed bird and proceeded to repeat the rites she had previously performed. The guards rushed down and seized her and accused her of the former violation of the king's decree, and, when she did not deny it, brought her to the palace. Creon asks her if she denies the deed. She does not, and what is more declares that she knew the decree, but had followed divine laws, superior to those of any mortal man. Her speech may be rendered thus (ll. 450–470):

> It was not Zeus who gave me these commands,
> No Justice dwelling with the gods below
> Ordained such laws to be among mankind.
> I did not think thy edicts had such force
> That one who was a mortal could o'erride
> The laws of gods, unwritten and secure.
> They are not of today or yesterday,
> But live eternal, and no man knows whence
> They first appeared. For violating these
> I did not mean to pay the penalty
> Before the gods, because I feared man's will.
> I knew I was to die. Why not? And that,
> Though thou didst not proclaim it publicly.
> And if I die before my time I say
> It is a gain. For does not one like me,
> Who dwells amid great sorrows, gain by death?
> For me to meet this fate is no great pain.
> But if I left unburied that dead man
> Of my own mother born I should be grieved;
> At what I've done, I am not. Therefore if
> My deed seems foolish now, I am, perhaps,
> Condemned for folly by a foolish judge.

Here the character of Antigone stands out. She has never thought of the possibility of disregarding divine law and leaving the body of her brother unburied. Creon, too, shows his true nature. His authority has been flouted. To yield to Antigone and condone her offense would be to relinquish his royal prerogative. She must be punished, and he condemns her to death.

Ismene, who now enters, is bitterly assailed by Creon, who wishes to find out if she had shared in her sister's deed. She answers that she did take part and is willing to bear her share of the blame; but Antigone will not permit this. Ismene, she explains, was not willing to help her and she must not be involved in her punishment. Antigone is rather severe in her attitude towards Ismene, who has nothing of her strength of character but is, nevertheless, devoted to her. Now that Antigone is in trouble she thinks that there is nothing for her to do except to die with her. There is something noble about Ismene even if she is weak.

The chorus now moralize. Happy are they whose life is free from evil. A family whose house is shaken by the gods experiences misfortune from generation to generation. Such has been the fate of the house of Labdacus. The power of Zeus is invincible and naught can disturb it. Man in his folly may hope to escape the inevitable, but he soon burns his foot in the fire. It is a wise saying that evil seems good to him whom the god leads to ruin. He escapes but for the briefest moment.

Haemon, the son of Creon, enters and with his very first words seeks to placate his father, readily acknowledging his parental authority. Creon accepts this as his natural due, and proceeds to justify his conduct towards Antigone. This speech again illustrates well the pettiness of the king. Antigone's act of disobedience is in his opinion a blow to his prestige as ruler of the land, and that is something that he cannot tolerate. The chorus agree with the sentiments which he expresses. Haemon begins by pointing out that people when talking among themselves say that Antigone did right, and he urges his father to give heed to this popular feeling and yield. His speech (ll. 683–723) deserves quoting:

Good understanding, Father, from the gods
Comes to a man, the best of all good things.
I could not say—nay, may I not know how—
That thou dost not correctly say these things;
And yet another man might be right, too.
I am by birth the one to watch what's said
About thee, or what's done, or what is blamed.
Thy eye excites fear in the common man
Of telling things thou would'st not like to hear.
But I can hear in secret things like these,
The sad laments the town makes for this maid,
How "She, of all her sex, most undeserved
Dies wretchedly for a most noble deed.
Her own dear brother slain in deadly strife
She did not leave unburied nor permit
To be destroyed by savage dogs or birds.
Some golden honor surely she deserves."
Such things does rumor darkly spread abroad.
But, Father, when thou farest happily
I have no dearer joy. For what delight
Have children greater than when glorious fame
Comes to their father; or what father's joy
Is greater than when children win success?
And now hold not to one idea alone
That what thou sayest and naught else is right.
For they who think that they alone are wise,
And have a tongue and mind like no one else,
Have been found lacking when brought to the test.
But if a man is wise it's no disgrace
For him to learn much and be not too set.
Thou seest beside the furious winter streams,
The trees which yield preserve their branches safe
While those resisting perish root and branch.
And so, if on a ship one holds the sheet
Close hauled and does not slack he soon upsets
And navigates with benches upside down.
But change thy purpose and give up thy wrath.
If I, a younger man, have any sense

> I say it's best by far for every man
> To have by nature wisdom in full store.
> But when the balance does not so incline,
> It's well to learn from those who say what's right.

Creon takes offense at the suggestion. He does not propose to be influenced by one of Haemon's age. A wordy dialogue follows. Haemon keeps his temper, but Creon becomes enraged and orders Antigone to be sent for that she may die in the presence of the man to whom she is betrothed. Haemon is in despair. He vows that this shall never be and, declaring that his father shall never see him more, leaves the stage.

In this scene the poet has brought out in striking fashion what he conceives to be the difference in character between the father and the son. On the one hand we have the petty, small-minded Creon, resentful and fearful that his authority will not be fully respected; and on the other the gentle Haemon filled with anxiety for the fate of his affianced bride and, at the same time, deeply conscious of his duty to his parent. He tries to persuade him by every legitimate means, and restrains himself even when goaded by Creon's bitter jibes. The farthest that he goes is when he says (l. 755):

> If thou wast not my sire I'd call thee fool;

and again (l. 765) as he leaves the stage:

> Rave on with those who wish to rave with thee.

Haemon, it may perhaps be said, is lacking in spirit; but he is so completely dominated by his overbearing father that he feels utterly helpless.

The chorus are disturbed by the last words of Haemon's speech, in which they find a certain foreboding of evil; but Creon regards them merely as a boyish threat. He sends for Antigone and Ismene, but makes it plain to the chorus that he will not injure Ismene if she really has had no part in the burial of

Polynices. Antigone is, however, to be immured alive in a rocky grotto with such small amounts of food as will free him from moral stain, and there she is to meet her end. The chorus sing a short, but beautiful ode (ll. 781–799) on the power of love:

(*Strophe*) Love, invincible in fight,
Love, who lightly scatters wealth,
Thou art present all the night
On the maiden's dainty cheek.
Thou dost go beyond the sea,
Thou art in the savage home.
No immortal can escape
From thy power, nor mortal man.
Mad is he whom thou dost hold.

(*Antistrophe*) Thou dost draw aside the minds
Of the honest to their hurt;
Thou this present kindred strife
Hast stirred up between these men.
Plain desire from fair bride's eyes
Clearly wins its victory
Firmly fixed on principles
Of great laws, for still supreme
Goddess Aphrodite sports.

Antigone is brought in, and a short lyric dialogue ensues in which she sings in logaoedic verse while the chorus reply in anapaests. She laments her coming death. No marriage song will accompany her. She likens herself to Niobe turned to stone on Mount Sipylus with the tears streaming down her cheeks. She calls Thebes to witness her unhappy fate. The chorus remind her of her father's misfortune, and she bitterly recalls that she is sprung from an accursed union and now unwept, without friends, unwedded, she is going to her doom.

This weakening on the part of Antigone is true to nature. Her duty has been accomplished and a reaction from her lofty purpose was bound to come. Creon orders her removed and entombed; but with her terrible fate before her she recovers her poise and goes away to her death bravely and with dignity. In her last speech she tells how her love for her brother led her to defy Creon. The passage (ll. 891–928) runs thus:

> Oh! tomb, my bridal chamber under ground,
> Forever guarding me, to which I go
> To friends departed, whom Persephone
> In numbers has received among the dead.
> I last, and far most wretched, pass below
> Before I've reached my proper span of life.
> However, when I've gone I have this hope,
> That I shall come there welcomed by my sire,
> And by thee, too, my mother and by thee,
> Dear brother; for when ye had passed away
> With my own hands I took and laid ye out
> And poured libations at your burial mounds.
> And, Polynices, now because thy corpse
> I buried I have punishment like this.
> And yet I rightly honored thee as they
> Will think who know. But if the case had been
> That I had children, or that the dead man
> My husband was, then I should not have dared
> To run this risk against the people's will.
> By virtue of what law do I say this?
> Why, if my husband died, another man
> I might have married; or another child
> Might then have had if this one I had lost.
> But when my mother and my father, too,
> Lie dead in Hades there could not be born
> Another brother. Therefore by this law
> I honored thee, dear brother, though I seemed
> To Creon to do wrong and dare bold deeds.[1]

[1] The commentators have doubted the genuineness of this passage, and point to Herodotus III, 119 as its source. Here, when Intaphernes and all his relatives have been arrested for plotting against Darius, the king grants the wife of Intaphernes the life of one of the condemned and she chooses her brother, using the same arguments as Antigone. But the passage was in Aristotle's text of Sophocles

And now by force of hands he takes and leads
Me off, unwedded; when I've had no part
In bridal song, or marriage; had no part
In rearing children; but ill-fated I,
Abandoned by my friends, while still alive
Go to the burial chambers of the dead.
What statute of the gods have I transgressed?
Why should I wretched still look to the gods—
Or what ally address—since I have gained
A name, though pious, for impiety?
If these things please the gods then I shall know
When I have suffered, that I have done wrong.
But if those in authority are wrong
May they not suffer worse things than they do
To me unjustly.

The guards lead Antigone away, while Creon upbraids them for their slowness. As she leaves the stage she addresses a few despairing words to Thebes and the gods of her race.

The chorus now sing of others of royal birth who have suffered by imprisonment—Danaë by her father Acrisius; Lycurgus by command of Dionysus; and Cleopatra, daughter of Boreas, by her husband, Pheneus. Cleopatra's sons were blinded as well as imprisoned. Fate was cruel to all of these.

A new character is introduced in the next scene in the person of the old, blind seer Tiresias, who is led in by a small boy. Creon is surprised and inquires the purpose of his unexpected visit. Tiresias bids him follow his advice as he had done on previous occasions, and then proceeds to tell the reason that had brought him into the king's presence. When he went to his usual seat for augury he found the birds uttering discordant

---

(*Rhet.* p. 1417a 32 ff.); and even if Herodotus was the source from which it was drawn that would not prove it spurious, but rather would be an argument for its genuineness. Sophocles is known to have used Herodotus elsewhere, as has already been pointed out (p. 11). The argument apparently did not seem to the Greeks to be far-fetched, and introduced into Antigone's speech becomes another reason for justifying her conduct.

cries and tearing at one another with their talons. He then turned to burnt sacrifice and the fire would not burn. This failure of his auguries he attributes to Creon, for the altars of the gods and the city's hearths have been polluted by the flesh of the unfortunate Polynices, carried there by the carrion birds. The gods do not, therefore, accept their sacrifices. He urges the king to rectify his mistake and to permit the burial of the dead man. Creon is annoyed. He thinks that Tiresias has been bribed by his enemies to invent this tale, and refuses to permit the burial. A brief altercation ensues in which the aged seer loses his temper and foretells the death of Creon's son in retaliation for the punishment of Antigone and his treatment of the dead. Creon is frightened as the old man departs and asks the advice of the chorus. They urge him to release Antigone at once and to bury Polynices. Creon yields and gives orders to see that both things are done.

The chorus now sing a dance song. It is an appeal to Dionysus to help his native Thebes in the present crisis.

A messenger enters and moralizes on the uncertainties of human fortune as exemplified in the case of Creon. The chorus question him and learn that Haemon has died by his own hand. Eurydice, the queen, is seen approaching. She has heard lamentations and she wants to know the meaning of them. The messenger in a long speech tells the whole story. He had followed the king to the spot where the body of Polynices lay and had seen it properly interred. A cry of mourning was then heard at the place where Antigone had been immured. Hastening there they found the stones of the entrance torn away and in the back part of the tomb Antigone hanging by the neck and Haemon embracing her dead body and lamenting. Creon called to him to come out. The boy in a mad frenzy rushed at his father with his sword drawn, and then thrust it into his own side and died clasping the body of Antigone. Eurydice listens intently and then without uttering a word reënters the palace. Both the messenger and the chorus are worried at her conduct, and the former follows her. In the meantime Creon enters with his escort bearing the body of Haemon. He is deeply depressed and bitterly laments his own conduct. A messenger comes from the palace and tells him that the queen is dead. The *eccyclema* is now brought into play and an inner room shown with the body of Eurydice lying near an altar where she had stabbed herself. Creon, lamenting and crushed by his misfortunes, is led away. The leader of the chorus, as they leave the stage, points out that wise thoughts lead to happiness; that one must be pious in his doings towards the gods; that proud words meet with severe punishment and so bring wisdom to old age.

Such is the *Antigone*. As one thinks it over he realizes at once that the plot is in itself very simple with no startling developments. A high-minded young girl defies the constituted authority of her land, performs an act that is forbidden, and, as a result, pays the penalty with her life. That is all. The facts that she had compelling reasons for her deed, that her punishment was too severe for the offense committed, and that in consequence it reacted to the grievous injury of her enemies, are merely details added to the central theme. It was the dramatic instinct of Sophocles that saw in what was a comparatively simple incident the elements for a great tragedy. The skill with which he utilized and developed them is sufficiently attested by the success of the play.

But the story itself has nothing modern about it. It belongs rather to the life of ancient Greece. The modern reader cannot feel, as the ancient Athenian did, the importance of the rite of burial to the peace of the dead man; nor can he quite understand how a handful of dust thrown on the corpse sufficed to quiet the unhappy shade. He may be shocked and offended that any dead body should be thrown out and exposed to mutilation by dogs and birds of prey; but that is as far as his sympathy can go. One might suppose, therefore, that the *Antigone* would not make any especial appeal to a modern audience. Such, however, has not been the case. The play has been, and still is, one of the most popular of all the old Greek tragedies. The reason is that it is one of the most pathetic. It does not call for any profound knowledge of ancient customs to sympathize with a young girl who meets a terrible death because of her devotion to a dead brother. It would be strange otherwise. The poet, indeed, touches a chord which stirs the emotions of all mankind. That is enough for the modern reader, and that explains the continued popularity of the play. Because of this human appeal the *Antigone* belongs to all time, not to the fifth century B.C. alone, and for that reason it will probably continue to be as much admired in the future as it has been in the past.

To the reader who knows ancient Greek well and can read the text freely the *Antigone* makes still another appeal in the beauty of its verse. This, to be sure, is characteristic of the best work of Sophocles, as we have already seen. His skill in the composition of iambic trimeter lines has never been surpassed.

When one stops to consider the *dramatis personae* he finds that the principal character is, as it should be, Antigone. She dominates the play from the beginning, although a counting of the lines shows that she is not on the stage as much of the time as Creon. She is before the audience while 435 lines are spoken, while Creon is present during 789. The play, according to the generally accepted text, contains 1,353 lines. And yet one cannot imagine the play named for Creon.

There is nothing in the character of Antigone as the dramatist presents her which calls for profound psychological analysis. It is, indeed, very simple. She is a sincere young girl inspired by a lofty purpose which she conceives to be a solemn duty. The idea that this duty is something which she might, perhaps, avoid does not for a moment occur to her; nor that she must avoid it to save her life. It is with her, as Aristotle says,[1] a case of the

[1] Aristotle, *Rhet.* p. 1375a 31 καὶ ὅτι τὸ μὲν ἐπιεικὲς ἀεὶ μένει καὶ οὐδέποτε μεταβάλλει, οὐδ' ὁ κοινὸς (i.e. νόμος), κατὰ φύσιν γάρ ἐστιν, οἱ δὲ γεγραμμένοι πολλάκις· ὅθεν εἴρηται τὰ ἐν τῇ Σοφοκλέους Ἀντιγόνῃ· ἀπολογεῖται γὰρ ὅτι ἔθαψε παρὰ τὸν τοῦ Κρέοντος νόμον, οὐ παρὰ τὸν ἄγραφον,

οὐ γάρ τι νῦν γε κἀχθές, ἀλλ' ἀεί ποτε.
ταῦτ' οὖν ἐγὼ οὐκ ἔμελλον ἀνδρὸς οὐδενός.

universal law superior to the written law. The penalty is a detail to which at the moment she gives no serious thought. With this firmly fixed in her mind it is not surprising that she cannot understand the attitude of her sister Ismene. But Sophocles has no intention of representing her as if she were a religious enthusiast bent on martyrdom, so that we should not be surprised at the reaction which comes to her after the deed is done (ll. 891 ff.). Many commentators have not understood this, especially ll. 905 ff. where she says that she would not have done it for a husband or a son. But she has never had either. The whole passage has been declared spurious by some critics, as we have seen, and by others called an example of Sophoclean bathos. Erroneously, I think. The poet wants to show that Antigone is, in reality, not so very different from other people. It is as if she were thinking out loud. She is going over and over in her own mind all that has occurred. Life is as dear to her as to anyone, and she is convinced now that she never could have done what she did for any other than Polynices. This moment of weakness is surely natural, and the fact that the poet felt it to be so is evidence of his dramatic instinct. It does not detract from our interest in or our pity for her. She is a pathetic figure to the end, the most pathetic of all the characters of Sophocles, except Oedipus after his downfall.

It has been suggested that Antigone's regard for her brother is really an instance of the age-old principle of loyalty to family or clan; that it was not so much love for Polynices as regard for him as a Labdacid and pride in her Labdacid ancestry that influenced her.[1] Whether Sophocles may have felt this and to what extent it is impossible to say.

In direct contrast with Antigone is the character of Ismene. She is represented as a timid young girl with none of the resoluteness of purpose which her sister has, nor her high moral sense of duty. She is terrified by the king's edict and dares not aid her sister. Her feelings are well expressed in ll. 61 f.:

[1] See Robert, *Oidipus*, I, pp. 334 ff.

> But this we must remember that we are
> Born women and not fit to fight with men.[1]

And again, l. 67

> Those in authority I shall obey.[2]

Antigone cannot understand this attitude of mind and scorns it.

> I love not one who loves me just with words,[3]

she says (l. 543). But when Antigone's guilt has been established and she has been condemned, Ismene, though innocent, is ready to share in her punishment. Ismene may be of common clay, yet the poet does not wish us to imagine her as lacking in courage or in sisterly affection. The difference in character in the two daughters of Oedipus is, however, sharply drawn.

The part of Creon calls for little comment. He is the villain in the play and is represented consistently. He is a man of small mind conscious of his weakness, but very jealous of his prerogatives. He is king and he is determined to seem a great man to all his people. His edict must be law regardless of all consequences. Such a character is not hard to understand. In his punishment of his enemies, of all in fact who oppose him, he is too severe, and this severity results in his own ruin. Creon is punished as it was right that he should be, and in the end utterly crushed. It will be noticed that the Creon of the *Antigone* is quite a different person from the Creon of the *Oedipus Tyrannus*.

Haemon is a gentle youth whose love for Antigone is sincere. He wants to help her; but at the same time is overawed by the importance of his father's official position and by dread of him. When, near the end of the play, he rushes at Creon sword in hand and then turns the weapon against himself, it is the despair of a

[1] ἀλλ' ἐννοεῖν χρὴ τοῦτο μὲν γυναῖχ' ὅτι
ἔφυμεν, ὡς πρὸς ἄνδρας οὐ μαχουμένα.

[2] τοῖς ἐν τέλει βεβῶσι πείσομαι.

[3] λόγοις δ' ἐγὼ φιλοῦσαν οὐ στέργω φίλην.

timid soul. Aristotle cites this as an example of a person about to do a dreadful deed knowingly and then refraining, a rather rare motive in tragedy which he condemns as untragic.[1] Unusual, too, is the love motive. The character of Haemon is, however, as clearly drawn as is that of Antigone or Creon.

Of the remaining personages in the play, Tiresias is represented as in the *Oedipus Tyrannus*. He is the same blind seer whose powers are unquestioned by the Thebans and yet, with all his prophetic art, very irascible; and just as in the *Oedipus Tyrannus* he utters dreadful prophecies which turn out true. Tiresias is consistently represented in both plays.

Eurydice, the wife of Creon, has a short but striking part. She speaks but nine lines, listens intently to the report of the messenger and then departs without a word. This silent exit of the queen must have been very effective in the theatre. No speech which she could have uttered could have produced the same effect as this tragic silence. One could not find a better example of the dramatic skill of Sophocles. The device is one that he used elsewhere.[2]

The guard is particularly well handled by the dramatist. He is a man of the lower class, upon whom has been laid an unpleasant and dangerous duty which he cannot avoid. He must tell the king that his edict has been defied and the culprit not detected. He is worried and tries to conceal his anxiety by treating the matter lightly. He thinks he can best save his own skin by playing the buffoon. All this is natural. Alongside of him we must place the shepherd of Laius in the *Oedipus Tyrannus*. Sophocles was particularly happy in depicting such characters.

There is little to say about the messengers other than that they tell the stories which they have to tell clearly, but without the vividness characteristic of messengers' speeches in Euripides. Lines 1192–1243 give us a good example of such a speech in Sophocles.

[1] *Poet.*, p. 1453b 37 ff.

[2] See p. 22.

The criticism may, perhaps, be made that the *Antigone* does not afford a great tragic actor a good opportunity to show his skill. This is true. There is no part in the play which can be compared with that of Oedipus in the *Oedipus Tyrannus*. The *Antigone* was not written with such an end in view. It depended for its success upon the way in which the incidents of the plot were presented. The play is good proof that a tragedy may be great without providing a rôle for a great actor. At the same time it is evident that the *Antigone* might be effectively presented even with actors of moderate ability, and no doubt that often happened.

In its metrical structure the *Antigone* is the severest of the extant tragedies of Sophocles. Jebb, for example, points out (*Antigone*, p. xlviii) that there are but forty resolutions of any foot in the trimeters, including the proper names, whereas in the other plays the resolutions are more numerous. So, too, the lyric portions of the play are much longer than in the other dramas. This has often been regarded, and naturally so, as evidence of an early date.

It should not be forgotten that the *Antigone* of Sophocles in spite of its fame was not the only tragedy of that name on the ancient stage. Euripides, too, wrote an *Antigone*, now lost, which enjoyed some popularity.[1] This play apparently had a happy ending. The Roman poet Attius also wrote an *Antigone* of which six fragments remain,[2] but it is impossible to tell from them whether he followed Sophocles or not. In modern times the most famous work inspired by the *Antigone* is Mendelssohn's music, originally composed for Donner's translation of the play.

[1] See Bates, *Euripides*, pp. 219 ff.

[2] Ribbeck, *Scaen. Rom. Poes. Frag.* I, pp. 153 ff.

IV

The Ajax

THE *Ajax* of Sophocles has to do with the tragic story of the madness and death of one of the great heroes of the Trojan War. It is, therefore, in this respect very different in plot from the *Antigone*; but, surprising as it may seem, there are certain resemblances between the two plays. Thus in both the chief character dies by suicide; and in both the burial of a dead body is forbidden by those in authority and their edict defied and disregarded. Furthermore there is resemblance between individual characters. Thus the Menelaus of the *Ajax* (ll. 1071 ff.) resembles the Creon of the *Antigone*, as was pointed out by Jebb;[1] and certain similarities in the metrical composition of both tragedies have been noted.[2]

The play was known in antiquity as the *Whip-bearing Ajax* (Αἴας Μαστιγοφόρος)[3] from the fact that Ajax enters at line 91 carrying a heavy whip with which he has been lashing a great ram; and the special title was given it to distinguish it from another play by Sophocles, the *Locrian Ajax*, now lost. The Alexandrian scholar Dicaearchus is said to have called it the *Death of Ajax* (Αἴαντος Θάνατος).[4] In the *didascaliae*, or official record, it was called simply Αἴας,[5] and this is no doubt what Sophocles called it.

The scene is laid in the Greek camp at Troy before the tent of Ajax. To the right may be seen the other tents of the camp, and to the left the open country of the Troad. The play opens with action. Odysseus is seen cautiously examining footsteps near the tent. The goddess Athena appears and addresses him.

[1] *Ajax*, p. 163, note on l. 1071.

[2] E.g., the use of anapaests in the parodos.

[3] Hypothesis, l. 8, ἐν οἷς ἐστί τις καὶ κριὸς ἔξοχος, ὃν ᾤετο εἶναι 'Οδυσσέα, ὃν δήσας ἐμαστίγωσεν, ὅθεν καὶ τῇ ἐπιγραφῇ πρόσκειται Μαστιγοφόρος, ἢ πρὸς ἀντιδιαστολὴν τοῦ Λόκρου.

[4] *Ibid.* l. 11 Δικαίαρχος δὲ Αἴαντος Θάνατον ἐπιγράφει.

[5] *Ibid.* l. 12, ἐν δὲ ταῖς διδασκαλίαις ψιλῶς Αἴας ἀναγέγραπται.

She is supposed to be invisible to him,[1] though in plain view of the spectators. Her divine power makes this possible, for when Ajax enters at line 91 she makes him unable to see Odysseus[2] though he apparently sees her. Athena speaks and tells him that Ajax is in the tent, but asks why he has been trying to find out. He explains that the cattle belonging to the army have been slain during the night and that he is trying to find out if Ajax is responsible for the deed, as is suspected. Athena tells him that he is; that he had planned to kill all his enemies in the camp and was on the point of carrying out his intention when she caused him to become violently insane and in that condition to attack the cattle. Some of these he had killed and others he had driven to his tent where he was torturing them, still under the delusion that they were his enemies. She proposes to call him out, but Odysseus in terror begs her not to do so. She promises that Ajax will not see him and summons the madman from his tent. A dialogue ensues between the goddess and the insane hero in which Ajax is led to say that he has slain Agamemnon and Menelaus, and means to flog Odysseus to death. He then reënters the tent. Odysseus is deeply moved by the pitiful condition of his adversary, and Athena takes the opportunity to read him a lesson which he scarcely needs, always to have due respect for the gods. The passage runs as follows (ll. 118–133):

ATHENA

Odysseus, dost thou see what mighty strength
The gods possess? What man could there be found
With greater foresight, or more fit than he
To do the things demanded by the times?

ODYSSEUS

I know of no one, and I pity him,
The wretched man, although he is my foe;

[1] See l. 15 *κἂν ἄποπτος ᾖς ὅμως.*
[2] See ll. 83–88.

For he is bound fast to an evil doom
And I think less of his fate than of mine.
I see that we who live are nothing else
Than phantoms, or just unsubstantial shades.

ATHENA

Beholding this do thou thyself refrain
From speaking haughtily against the gods,
Assuming swelling pride, if with thy hands
Or with excess of wealth thou hast prevailed
Above another man; since just a day
Lays low and raises up all man's affairs.
The gods love prudent men, the bad they hate.

The chorus consisting of sailors from Salamis now enter with a song in anapaestic verse which at line 172, as they take their places in the orchestra, passes into a lyric strophe. They are all followers of Ajax. They have heard rumors that their master has slain the cattle and have come to ask him to show himself and confute his enemies. It is easy, they say, to spread slanders against the great (ll. 157–161):

For envy creeps forth against him who has.
Yet the lowly alone are a poor defense
For a wall; for best will the humble succeed
If joined with the great, and the great in their turn
If aided by those who are weaker than they.

Yet they have a lurking dread that some god may have led him astray.

Tecmessa, captive and wife of Ajax, enters and in a lyric dialogue with the chorus explains that her lord when afflicted with madness slew the cattle. The chorus are much distressed and know that their own lives are in danger as well as their master's. The dialogue is continued in trimeter verse. Tecmessa in a vivid speech tells how in the middle of the night Ajax had gone forth and returned with sheep and cattle. Some of these he slaughtered, others he tortured, shouting in his madness that he had inflicted punishment upon the sons of Atreus and Odysseus. Then, at length, he recovered his reason and asked what it all meant. When told he moaned aloud, though in all previous time he had regarded lamentation as a sign of weakness. And now, she says, he is sitting in the midst of the slaughtered animals, and she asks the chorus to try to help him. This whole passage is a good example of the narrative style of Sophocles. It runs as follows (ll. 284–330):

As partners of this man ye shall know all.
For at the dead of night, when evening lamps
No longer burned, he took his two-edged sword
And started out upon an empty quest.
And I reproved him and I said, "What's this
Thou doest, Ajax? Why without command
Of messengers, nor yet by trumpet called,
Dost thou set forth? Now all the army sleeps."
His answer was both brief and commonplace.
"It's silence, woman, that brings women fame."
I ceased on hearing this, and he rushed forth
Alone. I cannot say what happened next,
But he came driving in bulls closely bound
And shepherd dogs and great horned sheep besides,
As victims. He beheaded some of these
And cut the throats of others. Others still
He cleft in twain, and others in their bonds
He fell upon and tortured as if men.
At length he darted forward through the doors
And shot out words as to some shadowy form
Against the sons of Atreus and against
Odysseus, and he laughed aloud and told
How great a penalty he made them pay.
Then darting back again into the house
At length by slow degrees regained his mind.
And when he saw that ruin filled the house
He smote his head and cried aloud and there,
Among the corpses of the slaughtered sheep,

He fell a wreck amidst the wreck he caused.
And there he sat and with his hands clutched tight
He grasped his hair. So, speechless did he sit
For a long time, and then with dreadful words
He threatened me if I did not explain
The whole calamity that had occurred,
And asked me how the situation stood.
I told him all I knew; and he at once
Bewailed with sad laments such as before
I never heard from him, for he declared
Such wailings were for base and gloomy men.
But he without a sound of shrill distress
Groaned quietly like a low-bellowing bull.
And now in such unhappy state as this
The hero lies, not tasting food or drink,
Right where he fell among the slaughtered herds.
And it is clear he wants to do some harm.
Such is the tenor of his words and grief.
But, friends, for I have come out here for this,
Go in and help him if ye can, for such
As he are influenced by words of friends.

Ajax is heard crying out from within the tent. He calls for his half-brother, Teucer, who is absent on a raid. By means of the *eccyclema*[1] the interior is now shown revealing the hero in the midst of the slain animals. He is now in his right mind and is overwhelmed with shame at the thought of what he has done. He declares that he will live no longer.[2] His shipmates, the chorus, try to console him. The poet indicates his distress of mind by making him speak in lyric verse, chiefly dochmiac, while Tecmessa and the chorus speak in the usual trimeters.

[1] The *eccyclema* is used but twice elsewhere by Sophocles in the extant plays, in the *Antigone* 1294 and the *Electra* 1464.

[2] A famous painting by Timomachus of Byzantium represented the mad Ajax after he had slain the sheep meditating suicide (Philostratus, *Vita Apol.* II, 22). It was purchased for a large sum by Julius Caesar, together with the same painter's Medea, and dedicated in the temple of Venus Genetrix at Rome (Pliny, *Nat. Hist.* VII, 38 and XXXV, 4 and 11).

Following this Ajax soliloquizes. He is speaking partly to himself though really addressing the chorus. He has disgraced himself and his father, and can see nothing ahead but shame if he lives, yet he longs for a chance to redeem his honor. The passage (ll. 430–480) runs thus:

> Alas! Who would have thought my woeful name
> Would fit so well this evil fate of mine.
> For now I cry "Alas!" yes, twice and thrice,
> Such grievous fortunes have I come upon.
> And yet my father from this Trojan land
> Brought home with him great fame when he had won
> The highest prize for valor in the host.
> But I, his son, came to this selfsame land
> Of Troy and having strength no less than his
> Accomplished just as valiant deeds of hand
> And in dishonor by the Argives thus
> Am brought to ruin; yet I know full well
> That if Achilles lived and had to make
> Award to someone of these arms of his
> As prize for valor, no one else than I
> Would then have won them. But now, as it is,
> The sons of Atreus have assigned them to
> A man of wicked mind, and thrust aside
> My prowess. And had not my eyes and mind
> Diverted, turned me from my fixed resolve,
> They never would against another man
> Give such a judgment. But the moment I
> Was stretching forth my hand against those men
> The bright-eyed child of Zeus, invincible
> Divinity, a maddening frenzy cast
> Upon me and made my intent to fail,
> So that with blood of cattle such as these
> I stained my hands, while they escaped and laugh,
> Though that was not my wish. But when some god
> Does harm, the wicked even would escape
> The better man. And now what must I do?
> I, who am clearly hateful to the gods,

Am hated by the army of the Greeks;
And all of Troy detests me and these plains.
Shall I go home across the Aegean Sea
Deserting the Atridae and the ships?
What countenance shall I show Telamon,
My sire, when I present myself to him?
Will he endure to see me thus, without
Those honors of which he himself once held
A glorious crown? Nay, that cannot be borne.
But shall I then go forth against the walls
Of Troy, alone, and doing some fine deed
At length meet death? Why, that would make those sons
Of Atreus happy. I cannot do that.
I must think of some daring deed by which
To show my aged father I am his
And have a valiant nature. For it's base
To wish for long life when there is no change
In evil fortune. For what joy is there
Day after day to be brought near to death
And then escape it? I would not esteem
A mortal man of any worth if he
Is set aglow by vain and empty hopes.
The man well born should either nobly live
Or nobly die. I have no more to say.

Tecmessa makes a pathetic plea to him to live for her sake. She asks him to think of the insults which will be heaped upon her if he dies, and the hard life she will have to live. She begs him to think of his father and mother and his little boy, and finally reminds him that her father and mother are dead and that her only safety lies with him.

This passage is interesting not merely for what it shows us of the character of Tecmessa and the part it has in the development of the plot, but it shows us what Sophocles thought of the position of a woman who had been taken captive in war in the household of her captor. Tecmessa has a certain affection for Ajax even if he is her master, which seems to imply that she had been treated with consideration and that her life in his house had not been unhappy.

Ajax calls for his son, and an attendant leads in the little boy, Eurysaces, who draws back at the sight of his father stained with gore. Ajax speaks (ll. 545–582):

Come, lift him, lift him up, for he will not
Be startled when he sees this new-shed blood
If he is rightly mine and I his sire.
But straightway we must break him to the ways
Of me, his father, savage though they are,
And in his nature he must be like me.
My boy, mayst thou be luckier than thy sire,
But in all else be like him. Then thou wouldst
Prove never to be base. Yet even now
I envy thee in this, because thou hast
No clear perception of these present ills.
For life is sweetest when there is no thought,
Before one comes to know both joy and grief.
When thou hast come to this then thou must show
Among thy father's foes what sort thou art
And from whom sprung; but until then do thou
Upon light breezes feed, and thy young life
Make thrive, a joy unto thy mother here.
No Greek, I know, with grievous injuries
Will do thee wrong, though I am far away.
Such mighty guardian, Teucer, I shall leave
Untiring in thy care, although he now
Is absent in pursuit of enemies.
But, fellow warriors, comrades of the sea,
On ye with him I lay this pleasant task;
Tell him that this is my command that he
Shall take this infant to my home in Greece
And show him to my father Telamon
And to my mother Eriboea, too,
That he may nurture them in their old age,
Until they reach the precincts of the god
Who dwells beneath the earth. And let him see

That those who rule the games shall not set up
My arms as prizes; nor that man who wrought
My ruin. But, my boy, take this my shield
From which thou hast thy name, Eurysaces,
And by its well-stitched handle hold it up
And turn it, for it is unbreakable,
Of ox-hide seven ply. My other arms
Shall be interred within the tomb with me.
(*To Tecmessa*) But with all speed now take the child and close
The house, and do not weep in front of it.
A woman is compassionate, I know.
But quickly close the door. An injury
That needs the knife no skilful surgeon treats
With charms and lamentations.

From the tone of these words Tecmessa fears the worst. Ajax is drawn back into his tent by means of the *eccyclema*, Tecmessa and Eurysaces retire and the stage is free for the chorus for their first formal dance, the first stasimon. In their song they recall their long absence from their native land. They express their distress at the mental condition of their master, and speculate on the sorrow it will cause his father.

Ajax now reënters, holding in his hand the sword which he had once received from Hector in an exchange of gifts. He declares that he will bury it, for the gift of an enemy is bound to bring harm. He says he will be discreet and yield to the sons of Atreus. His speech runs thus (ll. 646–692):

All hidden things the long, unmeasured space
Of time brings forth, and when revealed conceals,
And there is nothing that exists beyond
Man's expectation; but both dreadful oath
And stubborn mind as well are overcome.
For I, who then resisted mightily,
Like tempered steel, was by this woman here
Made soft in my resolve. And at the thought
Of leaving her a widow, and this child
An orphan here amid my foes I'm filled

With pity. But now to the bathing place
And to the meadows by the shore I'll go
That I may purge away these stains of mine
And so avoid the goddess' heavy wrath.
I'll go where I shall find a place untrod
And hide this sword, this hatefulest of blades,
Deep in the earth where it will not be seen.
Let Night and Hades keep it down below.
For I, since in my hand I took this sword,
A gift from Hector, my most bitter foe,
Have not had any honor from the Greeks.
But that old proverb is, I find, too true,
That gifts from foemen are not gifts at all,
Nor useful. Therefore in the future I
Shall know that I must yield unto the gods
And learn the sons of Atreus to respect.
They are the rulers so that I must yield.
Why, things most potent, things that dread inspire,
Give way before those in authority.
The winter storms that fill the ways with snow
Give place to fruitful summer; dreary night
Withdraws and yields to day with her white steeds,
That she may make her light shine forth; the blast
Of stormy winds allows the groaning sea
To rest; and sleep all powerful sets free
Whom it has fettered. It does not hold fast
Forever those whom it has in its grasp.
How, then, shall I not learn to be discreet?
For I have come to understand this fact:
That I must hate my enemy as if
He would in future time become my friend;
And wish to serve and benefit my friend
As one who will not always hold that place.
No haven is there which most men can trust
In friendship. But for matters such as these
It will be well. (*To Tecmessa*) Now, woman, do thou go
Within and pray the gods that I may have
Fulfilled completely what my heart desires.

(*To chorus*) And ye, my comrades, honor these same things
With her; and tell to Teucer when he comes
To care for me and to have friendly thoughts
For ye at the same time; for I shall go
To that place where I must. But do those things
I bid, and ye perhaps will learn that I
Though now unfortunate have found relief.

The sailors are completely deceived by this speech and sing a joyous song. They wish to dance, for they think that the quarrel between Ajax and the Atridae is now unexpectedly over and all will be well.

A messenger enters announcing the return of Teucer. The latter, upon his arrival in camp, had been received with abuse by the Greek soldiers and his life threatened simply because he was a relative of Ajax. The chorus explain that Ajax is not there. The man laments that he had not come before, for Teucer had given strict orders that Ajax should be kept safely within doors until he arrived. Calchas, the prophet, had predicted death for Ajax unless he could pass that day in safety, for he had repeatedly opposed the gods. Tecmessa enters and hears from the lips of the messenger that this going forth of Ajax means his death. She orders everyone to go in search of him, and she herself sets out to try to find him. The chorus, too, join in the search (l. 814). This departure of the chorus from the stage is very unusual in the Greek theatre and, as Jebb has pointed out,[1] it occurs in only three others of the extant tragedies.

The scene now changes to a lonely spot on the seashore. This, too, is very unusual and may be compared with the famous example in the *Eumenides* of Aeschylus where the action shifts from the temple of Apollo at Delphi to the Court of the Areopagus at Athens. What changes took place in the scenery is not altogether clear. It may be taken for granted that the spectators did not have to depend wholly upon their imagination.

[1] *Ajax*, p. 127, note on l. 813. The tragedies are the *Eumenides* of Aeschylus (l. 231), and the *Alcestis* (l. 746) and the *Helen* (l. 385) of Euripides.

Ajax is seen standing at one side. He has fixed Hector's sword firmly in the ground point up and addresses it. He prays that Zeus may send a messenger to Teucer that his brother may take charge of his body before it is cast out to the dogs and birds by some enemy. He calls upon Hermes to send him an easy death and upon the Furies for vengeance against the sons of Atreus. He prays the Sun to announce his death to his aged parents, bids farewell to his country and falls upon the sword. The speech of Ajax may be rendered thus (ll. 815–865):

> The slayer stands where it will be most sharp,
> If one should take the time to think of that,
> The gift of Hector, man detested most
> Of my guest-friends and hateful to behold.
> Here it is fixed in hostile Trojan soil
> New whetted by the iron-biting hone.
> I set it and I trod the earth well round
> That it might prove most friendly to this man,
> The cause of speedy death. I am prepared.
> And, therefore, Zeus assist me first of all
> For it is fair thou shouldst; and I shall beg
> No great reward of thee. Send off, I pray,
> A man to Teucer bearing evil news
> That, when I've fallen on this streaming sword,
> He first may take me in his arms before
> Some hostile eye espies me and I am
> Cast forth to be the prey of dogs and birds.
> So much, Oh! Zeus, I beg of thee; and now
> I call upon that escort of the dead,
> On Hermes, that he give me quiet sleep
> Without convulsions when I quickly fall
> Upon this sword and plunge it in my side.
> Those maidens, too, I call upon for help
> Who live forever and always behold
> Man's sufferings, those beings swift of foot,
> The holy Furies, to observe how I,
> Poor wretch, am made to perish by those lords,
> The sons of Atreus, whom may they destroy

Most evilly since they are evil men,
Slain by themselves as they behold me slain.[1]
Ye swift, avenging Furies come, I pray,
Now sate yourselves and spare this army not
With all its people. And I pray that thou
Who drivest through the lofty vault of Heaven,
Lord Helios, when thou dost see my land
May check thy golden rein and tell my woes
And death to my old father and to my
Unhappy nurse. Poor woman! When she hears
This news she will throughout the town send forth
A mighty wailing. But it is no use
To mourn these things in vain. And now the deed
I must begin and that, too, with some speed.
Oh! Death, Oh! Death, now come and gaze at me.
And yet I shall address thee when we meet
Below. And thee, bright light of shining day,
And Helios, the driver in his car,
I call upon for this last time and not
Hereafter. Oh! thou light, and sacred soil
Of my own land of Salamis, the seat
Of my ancestral home; and Athens, too,
Far famed, and people of a kindred race,
And springs and rivers, and these Trojan plains,
To ye who nurtured me I say farewell.
This final word does Ajax speak to ye.
All else he'll say in Hades to the dead.

At the conclusion of this speech Ajax throws himself upon the sword, probably not, however, in full view of the spectators, for that would not be in accord with the practice of the Greek theatre in the time of Sophocles.[2]

The chorus now return. They are in two groups and have

[1] Line 842 is spurious and, therefore, omitted in the translation. Lines 839–841 have also been questioned but seem to me genuine. There is much difference of opinion. Among modern editors Campbell rejects all four lines; Jebb, 841 and 842; Masqueray, 841 and 842; Radermacher (in the 10th edition of Schneidewin-Nauck) 842; Pearson from *αὐτοσφαγεῖς* in 841 through *ἐκγόνων* in 842.

[2] For a discussion of the manner in which this scene was staged see p. 116.

been searching in vain for Ajax. The scene is dramatic and the situation tense. A commatic passage follows. They call for someone to help them find their master. A cry is suddenly heard. Tecmessa has discovered her husband's body among the bushes. The chorus, now united, rush to her and join in her laments. After her first outcry she speaks in trimeter verse. She spreads a robe over the body, now represented by an effigy, that none may behold it covered with blood. Attendants accompanying Tecmessa bring the corpse forward and lay it down. It remains on the stage until the end of the play,[1] when it is carried out for burial. The chorus moralize on the fate that has overtaken Ajax which they now understand was foreboded by his complaints against the Atridae. The lament continues in the form of a dialogue between Tecmessa and the chorus. She reminds them that the enemies of Ajax in their folly do not know the greatness of their loss. The death of her lord is bitter to her, but it is a relief to himself.

Teucer enters lamenting. He has heard of his brother's death and is informed by the chorus that the report is true. He asks for Eurysaces that he may protect the boy as Ajax wished, and Tecmessa goes to seek him. He approaches the dead body and orders the covering raised. In his distress at the sight he thinks of his own return home and of the harsh reception he is likely to have from his father Telamon, who will think that the death of Ajax was due to cowardice or treachery on his part. He recalls the fact that it was by the belt that Ajax gave him that Hector was fastened to the chariot of Achilles to be dragged to his death;[2] and now Ajax lies slain by the sword he received from Hector in return. Such situations are brought about by the gods.

[1] See, for example, ll. 1002, 1181, 1319, 1326 and 1415.

[2] For the exchange of gifts between Hector and Ajax see *Iliad*, VII, 303 ff. It is noteworthy that Sophocles does not follow the Homeric account (*Iliad*, XXII, 395 ff.) of the death of Hector here. In the *Iliad* the Trojan hero is dead before he is fastened to the chariot. The version of the story followed by Sophocles may have been found in the *Little Iliad*.

Menelaus enters and in an arrogant manner forbids the removal of the dead Ajax. He declares that he has shown himself an enemy to the army, and in consequence his body shall be cast out unburied. The chorus mildly remonstrate and Teucer boldly defies him, declaring that he has no authority over Ajax. Menelaus sneers at him and threatens, and finally withdraws. The chorus are alarmed and urge Teucer to hasten the burial, but he is not afraid.

Tecmessa enters with her little boy. Teucer cuts a lock of hair from his head and the boy with this and with other locks of his own and his mother's in his hands is told to cling to his father's body and to beg it for protection. He must let nobody drag him away. Teucer then leaves to make preparations for the burial.

The chorus sing a short song recalling the hardships they have suffered in the war. Now that their protector is dead they long to return home.

At this moment Teucer hastily reënters, for he has seen Agamemnon approaching and knows that there is trouble ahead. The king loses no time. He soundly berates Teucer, reminds him that he is the son of a mother captured in war, declares that he cannot even understand his foreign speech, and threatens to have him whipped for opposing the authorities. Teucer defends himself with manly and dispassionate words. He calls to mind the valiant deeds of Ajax, points out the ingratitude of Agamemnon, and reminds him of his ancestry and the crimes committed by Aërope and Atreus. As for himself, if his mother was a captive she was a king's daughter. He defies Agamemnon and warns him.

Odysseus now appears. He has heard the loud talk and inquires the cause. Agamemnon briefly explains that Teucer has defied his authority and declared that he would bury the dead Ajax. Odysseus advises Agamemnon to permit the burial, for he would be conforming to the laws of the gods. He himself, he says, was the greatest enemy of Ajax, but now acknowledges his valor and is even ready to take part in his funeral. Agamemnon is forced to yield, though he does so sullenly. Teucer thanks Odysseus. He is, however, afraid that his presence at the grave might give offense to the dead. Odysseus is not offended, but acquiesces and retires. Teucer then gives orders to make ready the grave and prepare for the burial. The body still bleeding is raised from the ground and borne by Teucer and the attendants, and followed by Tecmessa, Eurysaces, and the chorus, it is carried off the stage. As the last of the funeral procession passes out of sight the leader of the chorus turns towards the spectators and moralizes on the uncertainty of the future:

> A mortal can learn many things with his eyes;
> But until he has seen, let him never predict
> How he is to fare in the future.

It is apparent at once from this account of the play that the poet has given us an interesting study of the character of Ajax under very trying conditions. But it is not merely the picture of an unhappy and disappointed warrior. Every man in the theatre who had had any education at all would remember the great hero from Salamis as we find him represented in the *Iliad*, where his bravery and great physical strength are repeatedly emphasized. There we see that he is a large man as well as powerful.[1] He is second only to Achilles among the Greek heroes at Troy.[2] He repeatedly fights with Hector.[3] He

[1] E. g., *Iliad*, III, 226 f. Priam asks Helen,

> τίς τ' ἄρ' ὅδ' ἄλλος Ἀχαιὸς ἀνὴρ ἠΰς τε μέγας τε
> ἔξοχος Ἀργείων κεφαλήν τε καὶ εὐρέας ὤμους;

and the reply is,

> οὗτος δ'Αἴας ἐστὶ πελώριος ἕρκος Ἀχαιῶν.

[2] *Iliad*, XVII, 279 f.

> Αἴας, ὃς πέρι μὲν εἶδος πέρι δ'ἔργα τέτυκτο
> τῶν ἄλλων Δαναῶν μετ'ἀμύμονα Πηλεΐωνα.

Also *Odyssey*, XI, 550 f.

[3] *Iliad*, VII, 182 ff.; XIII, 190 ff.; 809 ff.; XIV, 402 ff.; XV, 415 ff.; XVI, 114 ff.; 358 ff.

kills various antagonists—Simoisius,[1] Amphius,[2] Epicles,[3] Archelochus.[4] It is he who is the mainstay of the Greeks when Hector attacks the ships,[5] and he defends the dead body of Patroclus.[6] Perhaps no one passage in the *Iliad* shows Homer's conception of the character of Ajax better than those lines in the Seventeenth Book[7] in which the hero prays Zeus to remove the mist so that the Greeks may see to fight and then to slay him in the sunlight if such is his wish. This is the man whom Sophocles chose for the chief character in his tragedy; and this would be the picture of him in the minds of most of the spectators when he was brought before them in the midst of his misfortunes. It must be remembered, too, that Ajax had become mad long before the beginning of the play. His constant brooding over his wrongs had deranged his mind to such an extent that he had developed a homicidal mania and determined to murder his opponents. Athena's intervention leading him to mistake the flocks for men merely made his insanity more acute. The tragic situation was thus at the very outset made all the keener both for the spectator and the reader.

The story of the contest for the arms of Achilles in which Ajax was defeated by Odysseus was told both in the lost *Aethiopis*, which continued the tale of Troy from the place where it was left at the end of the *Iliad*, and in the *Little Iliad*, though apparently with some difference in detail. In the late epic poem, the *Posthomerica* of Quintus of Smyrna,[8] which still survives,

[1] *Iliad*, IV, 474 ff.
[2] *Ibid.*, V, 612 ff.
[3] *Ibid.*, XII, 378 ff.
[4] *Ibid.*, XIV, 459 ff.
[5] *Ibid.*, XV, *passim.*
[6] *Ibid.*, XVII, 132 ff.
[7] Lines 645 ff.

> Ζεῦ πάτερ, ἀλλὰ σὺ ῥῦσαι ὑπ' ἠέρος υἷας 'Αχαιῶν
> ποίησον δ' αἴθρην, δὸς δ' ὀφθαλμοῖσιν ἰδέσθαι·
> ἐν δὲ φάει καὶ ὄλεσσον, ἐπεί νύ τοι εὔαδεν οὕτως.

This passage is justly praised for its sublimity by the author of the treatise *De Sublimitate*, IX, 10.

[8] V, 128 ff.

the story appears in the following form. After the funeral games held by Thetis in honor of her son have been completed, she places his splendid armor before the Greeks to be awarded to the man who had rescued his dead body. Ajax and Odysseus both claim it. Ajax asks that a committee consisting of Idomeneus, Nestor, and Agamemnon decide between them. Odysseus is not averse, and declares his willingness to accept the three as judges; but they decline to serve. Then, at the suggestion of Nestor, the award is left to Trojan captives who decide in favor of Odysseus. This version of the story is alluded to in the *Odyssey* (XI, 547)[1] though some editors believe that line to be a later addition. But there were also two other versions. According to a scholium on Aristophanes, *Knights*, (1053, Dindorf), spies were sent from the Greek camp to try to hear the unprejudiced opinion of the Trojans on the merits of the two heroes. They overheard two Trojan girls talking, one of whom declared Ajax superior to Odysseus because he rescued the body of Achilles; the other declared Odysseus the better for having made it possible for him to do so. The spies reported this and the award was made to Odysseus. According to the scholiast this was told in the *Little Iliad*.[2] A third version that the Greeks were the judges is found in Pindar,[3] and that is the story followed by Sophocles. In the *Posthomerica* Ajax is indignant at the effrontery of Odysseus in venturing to compete against him, and very likely this was the case also in the *Aethiopis*. As the second bravest man at Troy by general consent, he had a right to feel that he was entitled to the arms without dispute.

But the motive of Sophocles in writing the *Ajax* was, I think, a broader one than this. It is not so much disappointment at the loss of the prize which has led Ajax to his ruin as the feeling

[1] παῖδες δὲ Τρώων δίκασαν καὶ Πάλλας Ἀθήνη.

[2] See Blaydes, *Aristophanis Equites*, p. 422. The summary of the *Little Iliad* given by Proclus is too brief to confirm or refute this statement.

[3] *Nem.* VIII, 26. Pindar says by a secret vote, κρυφίαισι γὰρ ἐν ψάφοις Ὀδυσσῆ θεράπευσαν.

that he has not been appreciated by his comrades. The poet wants us to understand that the man of ability who has rendered distinguished services has been passed over for the man glib of tongue. The talker has been honored in preference to the doer.[1] Here, then, is the real tragedy; and it does not concern Ajax alone, but is of general application and for all time. The spectator or the reader might well apply the moral to himself, as, in fact, Socrates does.[2] This wider significance of the motive lying back of the play should not be overlooked. It is one of the things which add to its interest today.

The outstanding character in the tragedy is, as it rightly should be, that of Ajax himself. The part is so written that it would give a good actor an excellent opportunity to show his dramatic skill, particularly in the narrative speeches. As the plot develops we see the hero first insane, and then restored to his right mind, but overwhelmed with remorse and shame. We see him exhibiting tenderness in the scene with his little son,[3] and finally possessed by a grim determination to end his life. These variations in mood could be made very effective on the stage.

One might, perhaps, ask why Ajax should be made to suffer as he does. That is part of the original story and for that reason the dramatist cannot be held strictly responsible for it. But he does nevertheless make it clear that just as Jocasta in the *Oedipus Tyrannus* is punished for her sacrilegious attitude towards the gods, so in the *Ajax* it is the hero's scorn of Athena's help that justifies his ruin.

The other characters are all subordinate, though each contributes his part. Teucer, devoted to his half brother, and determined to save his dead body from outrage and disgrace, is second in importance. He is the outstanding figure in the

[1] Cp. Pindar, *Nem.* VIII, 25 μέγιστον δ'αἰόλῳ ψεύδει γέρας ἀντέταται.

[2] *Apology*, p. 41b. The reference is to the story, not necessarily to the *Ajax* of Sophocles.

[3] There seems to be a reminiscence here (ll. 545 ff.) of *Iliad*, VI, 466 ff.

latter part of the play. His loyalty to Ajax even in death is his chief characteristic and would undoubtedly win him the favor of the crowd.

Tecmessa is a captive taken in war, but she has evidently been well treated by her master and has come to love him. The place of honor which she holds in his household is seen in the respect with which she is addressed by the chorus, and in Teucer's attitude towards her. In her treatment of her little boy she shows a mother's natural tenderness. It is clear that the poet wishes us to think of her not as a slave, but as the acknowledged mistress of the household of Ajax.

Of the three great leaders of the Greeks who figure in the play, Odysseus, the enemy of Ajax, appears to best advantage. In the opening scene he is the wily Odysseus of Homer, for he has tracked the slayer of the cattle to his enemy's door; but at the end of the play he shows himself in nobler guise, siding with Teucer against Agamemnon and Menelaus, and so making possible the burial of his former rival.

Menelaus is thoroughly base. It was he who had brought about the defeat of Ajax for the arms (l. 1135), and now that he lies dead he is determined that his body shall be left unburied a prey to dogs and birds. There is nothing noble about him. Agamemnon is not much better, though he does at length reluctantly yield to the arguments of Odysseus and let the burial take place.

The other minor characters call for little comment. It is natural that Athena should appear as the friendly supporter of Odysseus, for as such we find her in the *Odyssey*; but she also shows herself offended at Ajax. His attitude towards the gods had aroused her resentment, so that she is all the more ready to aid Odysseus. [1]

The messenger tells his tale simply, and thus contributes his small part towards the development of the plot. The little boy Eurysaces, on the other hand, does not speak, and yet he is an

[1] Cp. ll. 127 ff. and 767 ff.; also Jebb, *Ajax*, p. xi.

important element in the story. His presence on the stage makes more vivid a tragic situation.

Still more important are the members of the chorus—sailors who are followers of Ajax. They are loyal and devoted to their master, dead as well as living. For them Ajax never ceases to be a great hero. Such conduct would certainly meet the hearty approval of an Athenian audience, for Ajax was a local hero. He was honored with an altar at Athens as late as the time of Pausanias.[1] One of the ten Athenian tribes (Aeantis) was named for him, and his race was supposed still to exist in Athens in the time of Sophocles. Alcibiades, for example, claimed to be descended from him through Eurysaces.[2] Without too much imagination, therefore, Ajax might be claimed by the spectators as one of themselves.

It has often been pointed out that in the *Ajax* we really have two motives, the first coming to a climax with the death of the hero; and the other with the burial of his body. To a certain extent this is true. The spectator, and the reader, too, is so overwhelmed with the tragedy of the suicide which he sees coming and knows cannot be avoided that the contest over the burial of the body plays a minor part in the action. This was felt in antiquity, for a scholium on line 1123 criticizing, as not belonging to tragedy, the dialogue in which Menelaus sneers at Teucer and the latter replies, says that the poet, in wishing to prolong the play beyond the death of Ajax, has made it frigid and spoiled the tragic effect.[3] I cannot altogether agree with this judgment. It was manifestly impossible for the dramatist to end his tragedy with the death of Ajax. That is the climax of the play certainly; but it would not satisfy an Athenian audience to leave the body of the hero—and that, too, a local hero—without more ado. Preparations for the burial are required to complete the picture, to satisfy the dramatic sense.

[1] Pausanias, I, 35, 3.

[2] Plutarch, *Alcibiades*, I, 1.

[3] τὰ τοιαῦτα σοφίσματα οὐκ οἰκεῖα τραγῳδίας· μετὰ γὰρ τὴν ἀναίρεσιν ἐπεκτεῖναι τὸ δρᾶμα θελήσας ἐψυχρεύσατο καὶ ἔλυσε τὸ τραγικὸν πάθος.

The fact that the enemies of Ajax forbade him the usual rights of the dead and that Teucer by his insistance succeeded in obtaining them for him would certainly not be looked upon as a dramatic defect by the great majority of the spectators in the ancient theatre. It would rather be regarded as a natural sequence from what had preceded. It rounds out the story.

The *Ajax* is little read in American colleges at the present time, and it is not surprising that this should be the case. As compared with the *Oedipus Tyrannus*, the *Antigone*, or the *Electra*, the plot seems weak and the action slow. The play is one that would naturally make more of an appeal to an ancient audience than to a modern reader; and yet in the Middle Ages it was one of the most read of the tragedies of Sophocles. In consequence there are many manuscripts of it. The substantial body of scholia[1] that has come down with the text and the finding of papyrus fragments of the play in Egypt testify to the great interest in it in the past.

The date of the *Ajax* is not known, but editors and critics alike agree that it was early. It is usually placed first among the extant tragedies. Jebb[2] thinks it later than the *Antigone* because in the latter play the poet does not admit the division of a line between two speakers, while in the *Ajax* he does (ll. 591–594; 981–983; 985). There can be no doubt that as a general rule a severer style of composition is earlier; but it would not be safe to conclude that because the poet had decided to admit the division of a line between two speakers in one play he could not, a little later, write another play without such division. Evidence of another sort would seem to make the *Ajax* the older of the two. It has already been pointed out that there are important features in which the plot of this play resembles that of the *Antigone*,

[1] Ninety-six pages in the edition of Papageorgios.

[2] *Ajax*, pp. liii f. He is followed by Tycho von Wilamowitz-Moellendorf, *Die Dramatische Technik des Sophokles*, p. 51, n. 1, who believes with Kranz (*De forma stasimi*, p. 52) that these two plays date from about the same time as the *Alcestis*, the *Telephus*, and the *Cressae* of Euripides, that is, 438 B.C.

namely in the suicide of the chief character and in the refusal of the constituted authorities to permit the burial of a dead body. I find it very difficult to imagine how Sophocles could have written those parts of the *Ajax* where these two incidents are elaborated after he had written the *Antigone*. In the latter play the question of the burial of Polynices is the most important incident in the whole plot. It would seem as if the poet after writing the *Ajax* saw the possibilities of developing both incidents so that they should become the chief feature of a new plot and that the *Antigone* was the result. For this reason above all others I should follow the majority of editors and regard the *Ajax* as the earliest of the extant tragedies of Sophocles.[1] If the date of the *Antigone* is shortly before 441 B.C. the *Ajax* would be earlier, though how much earlier cannot be told. Masqueray[2] would, as a guess, set the date at about 450 B.C. The fact that Menelaus, the Spartan, is not represented in a favorable light cannot be regarded as evidence pointing to a later date. The relations between Athens and Sparta were none too friendly long before the outbreak of the Peloponnesian War, so that even granting that Menelaus is represented as he is because he is a Spartan—and that may be questioned—it does not necessarily follow that the date is subsequent to the beginning of the war.

There are two passages in the *Ajax* which call for brief consideration from the point of view of the stage action. At line 346 Tecmessa opens the door of the hut or tent and Ajax is revealed sitting among the slaughtered animals. By means of the *eccyclema* he is then drawn forward into full view of the spectators. This we are told by the scholiast,[3] and it seems to be correct. But Ajax certainly does not remain seated during the entire scene that follows. I imagine that he rises and comes

[1] Of the most recent writers on Sophocles, Pohlenz, *Die Griechische Tragödie* (Leipzig and Berlin, 1930), p. 173, reaches the same conclusion.

[2] *Sophocle*, 1922, Vol. I, p. 9.

[3] On l. 346, *ἐνταῦθα ἐκκύκλημά τι γίνεται ἵνα φανῇ ἐν μέσοις ὁ Αἴας ποιμνίοις . . . . δείκνυται δὲ ξιφήρης, ᾑματωμένος μεταξὺ τῶν ποιμνίων καθήμενος.*

forward to deliver the soliloquy which begins at line 430. The *eccyclema* is not moved, as we see from lines 453 and 546.[1] When Ajax tells the attendant to lift the boy Eurysaces he means lift him off the ground, not place him upon the *eccyclema*, as has sometimes been supposed. At the end of the scene he steps back upon the platform and at line 595 the *eccyclema* is drawn back into the tent.

The second passage is that in which the suicide of Ajax takes place. At line 815 the scene shifts and we are transported from the Greek camp to a lonely spot on the seashore. At line 865 Ajax falls upon his sword. Did the suicide take place in full view of the spectators? If so, it is a direct violation of one of the principles of the Greek drama, that there should be no violent death on the stage. The scholiast on line 815 apparently thinks that it did, and comments on the fact that such scenes were rare "among the ancients" and usually told by a messenger, citing as an example the *Thracian Women* of Aeschylus.[2] He adds that Sophocles may have introduced the change for the sake of novelty. Again a scholium on line 864, commenting on the fame which the actor Timotheus of Zacynthus acquired by his acting in this scene, has been regarded as further evidence in support of this interpretation.[3] Furthermore Hesychius, quoting Polemon (second century A.D.), speaks of a sword with collapsible blade used in acting the part of Ajax.[4] But if Ajax fell on his sword in full view of the audience, at the close of the scene he would have to rise and walk off the stage while the

[1] The scholiast on l. 547 says εἴπερ ἔστιν ἐμὸς οὐκ εὐλαβηθήσεται τὸν φόνον τῶν ποιμνίων.

[2] He says ἔστι δὲ τὰ τοιαῦτα παρὰ τοῖς παλαιοῖς σπάνια· εἰώθασι γὰρ τὰ πεπραγμένα δι'ἀγγέλων ἀπαγγέλλειν· τί οὖν τὸ αἴτιον; φθάνει Αἰσχύλος ἐν Θρῄσσαις τὴν ἀναίρεσιν Αἴαντος δι'ἀγγέλου ἀπαγγείλας· ἴσως οὖν καινοτομεῖν βουλόμενος, κ.τ.λ.

[3] It reads δεῖ δὲ ὑπονοῆσαι ὅτι περιπίπτει τῷ ξίφει καὶ δεῖ καρτερόν τινα εἶναι τὸν ὑποκριτὴν ὡς ἄξαι τοὺς θεατὰς εἰς τὴν τοῦ Αἴαντος φαντασίαν ὁποῖα περὶ τοῦ Ζακυνθίου Τιμοθέου φασὶν ὅτι ἦγε τοὺς θεατὰς καὶ ἐψυχαγώγει τῇ ὑποκρίσει ὡς Σφαγέα αὐτὸν κληθῆναι.

[4] S. v. συσπαστόν· τῶν τραγικῶν τι ἐγχειρίδιον ἐκαλεῖτο ὡς Πολέμων φησί, τὸ συντρέχον, ἐν Αἴαντος ὑποκρίσει. See also Jebb, *Ajax*, note on line 815.

spectators looked on, for there was no curtain to conceal him. This is certainly inartistic, and I do not believe the dramatic instinct of Sophocles would have permitted it. Moreover, when Tecmessa finds the body she is out of sight, for the chorus ask whose cry came from the glen.[1] For these reasons I think that whatever may have been the practice on the later stage—and it should be remembered that the Roman theatre had a curtain—in the fifth century B.C. the usual rule of the Greek theatre prevailed; that Ajax was seen to fix his sword in the ground to one side, where it was not visible to the spectators, and then to cast himself upon it in such a way that he disappeared from view. The anecdote about Timotheus would be equally appropriate if the scene were so staged. The body which is brought in covered up has to be an effigy, for the actor who played the part of Ajax was needed to play the part of Teucer.

The story of Ajax seems to have been a favorite with the ancient dramatic poets. Aeschylus used it for a trilogy, the separate plays being the *Judgment of Arms*, the *Thracian Women*, and the *Women of Salamis*.[2] Sophocles wrote also a *Teucer* and an *Eurysaces*. In the fourth century the younger Carcinus,[3] Theodectes,[4] and the younger Astydamas[5] all wrote tragedies entitled *Ajax*, but our knowledge of them is so scanty that it is impossible to say how closely they resembled the extant play of Sophocles. In Roman times Livius Andronicus wrote an *Ajax Mastigophorus*,[6] the title of which indicates that he probably followed Sophocles. Only two and a half lines of it are preserved. Two lines of an *Ajax* by Ennius[7] are also extant, but give no hint as to their source.

[1] Line 892, *τίνος βοὴ πάραυλος ἐξέβη νάπους.*

[2] The titles in Greek are: Ὅπλων Κρίσις, Θρῇσσαι and Σαλαμίνιαι.

[3] Cf. Pauly-Wissowa, *Real-Encyclopädie*, s. v. Karkinos.

[4] Aristotle, *Rhet.* p. 1399b 28.

[5] Suidas, s. v. Ἀστυδάμας ὁ νέος.

[6] Ribbeck, *op. cit.* II, p. 2.

[7] *Ibid.*, *op. cit.*, p. 17.

V

The Electra

IN WRITING the *Electra* Sophocles turned for his plot to the history of the house of Atreus, which furnished the tragic poets with numerous subjects for their dramas. Aeschylus, in fact, wrote four tragedies on this theme, Sophocles at least ten,[1] and Euripides nine, not to mention the plays of the minor poets. Each of the three great dramatists wrote a tragedy about Electra, all of which have survived. Aeschylus, to be sure, entitled his the *Choephoroe* and made it the second play in the trilogy of the *Oresteia*; but Euripides gave Electra's name to his tragedy. The *Electra* of Sophocles has been generally regarded as the most powerful of the three, and one of the masterpieces of the Attic stage. The death of Clytaemnestra at the hands of her son Orestes is the most important incident in all of these plays; but the part that Electra has in the murder is treated differently by the three dramatists.

The date of the *Electra* is unknown. It has been generally assumed to have been earlier than that of the *Electra* of Euripides, which seems to have been brought out about 413 B.C.,[2] and such was the conclusion reached by Siess[3] from internal evidence. M. A. Elisei, on the other hand, who has published an elaborate study of the two *Electras*,[4] concluded that the *Electra* of Euripides was the earlier of the two—an opinion also held by A. S. Owen.[5]

[1] They are the *Aletes*, the *Atreus or Mycenaean Women*, the *Chryses*, the *Erigone*, the *Hermione*, the *Iphigenia*, the *Oenomaus*, and the three tragedies entitled *Thyestes*. To this list should be added the *Aegisthus* and the *Clytaemnestra* if Sophocles really wrote tragedies with those titles, and perhaps the *Demand for Helen*.

[2] See Bates, *Euripides*, pp. 88 f.

[3] See p. 38.

[4] *Rendiconti Accad. dei Lincei*, 6th Series, VII, 1931, pp. 93–169.

[5] *Greek Life and Poetry*, Oxford, 1936, pp. 145 ff. Other noteworthy discussions are those of Wilamowitz-Moellendorf, *Hermes*, XVIII, 1883, pp. 214 ff. and Steiger, *Philologus*, LVI, 1897, pp. 561 ff. The words Ἠλέκτραν κατ' ἐκείνην

The scene of the tragedy is laid at Mycenae in front of the royal palace. To the right and the left the spectator has glimpses of the neighboring country. The play opens in the midst of the action. Orestes and Pylades enter in earnest conversation with an old slave who is pointing out the important sights which lie before them—the Argive plain, the market-place of Lycean Apollo, the famous temple of Hera,[1] and finally the royal palace. The slave is the very man who rescued the young Orestes at the time of his father's murder and has been living with him in Phocis. The time is early morning. Orestes, who feels sure that the old man will not be recognized because of the lapse of time, instructs him to enter the palace and announce that he has come from Phocis with news that Orestes was thrown from his chariot at the Pythian games and killed. In this way he will learn the situation in the palace; for Apollo had foretold that he would obtain vengeance by craft and not by force of arms. In the mean time he and Pylades will go to the tomb of Agamemnon and make suitable offerings and then return with the bronze urn, supposedly containing the ashes of Orestes, which they had hidden in the bushes. They hastily leave the scene as the voice of Electra is heard lamenting within the house.

Electra now enters and bewails her slaughtered father. She calls upon the Powers of Darkness and the Furies to avenge him, and begs them to send her brother to help her. The chorus of Mycenaean women approach, and there ensues a lyric dialogue which is afterwards continued in iambic trimeter verse. They point out to Electra the futility of her insatiate grief. They have no sympathy for the murderers and know that Zeus is not unmindful of their crimes. Electra appreciates their friendly feelings, but her unhappy surroundings are such as constantly to remind her of the tragedy. There is Aegisthus sitting on her father's throne and living with her wicked mother,

---

in the parabasis to the *Clouds* of Aristophanes (ll. 534 f.) clearly refer to some tragedy, which may have been the *Choephoroe*.

[1] In reality the Argive Heraeum was not visible from Mycenae.

who celebrates every month with choruses and sacrifices the day on which Agamemnon died. The members of the chorus are alarmed at Electra's unrestrained expressions, but she assures them that Aegisthus is away and that she can speak without danger. She tells them that her brother Orestes has promised to come to her relief, and she cannot understand why he has delayed so long. The chorus express their confidence in him.

This dialogue is interrupted by the appearance of Electra's sister Chrysothemis, who tells her that she feels just as Electra does, but she realizes that the prudent course is to accept things as they are. Electra rebukes her for her cowardice. The chorus try to reconcile the two sisters, and Chrysothemis explains that she has the welfare of Electra at heart, for she has heard that Aegisthus will confine her in an underground chamber when he returns to the palace if she does not cease from her lamentations. Electra, however, is not in the least frightened. She questions her sister about the meaning of the offerings which she is carrying and in reply is told that she has been sent by her mother to pour libations at Agamemnon's grave. Clytaemnestra has had a disconcerting dream. Agamemnon had appeared to her and planted his sceptre at the hearth, and from this a shoot had sprung forth and shaded the whole land of Mycenae. Electra urges Chrysothemis to throw the offerings away and in place of them to lay on the tomb a lock of her hair and one of Electra's, and also Electra's girdle, and to pray Agamemnon for help against his enemies. The chorus urge Chrysothemis to comply and she agrees to do so, but with some apprehension.

The chorus now sing the first stasimon. Clytaemnestra's dream, they are convinced, is an omen foretelling punishment for her and for Aegisthus; and they moralize on the misfortunes of the house since the charioteer Myrtilus was cast into the sea.

Clytaemnestra enters, accompanied by an attendant carrying offerings of fruit, and is surprised to find Electra outside the palace. If Aegisthus were there this would not have been possible. She takes her to task for her constant reproaches, and declares Agamemnon's death was justified because of his sacrifice of Iphigenia. Electra replies that even if that were true it did not justify her murder of her husband; but it is not true. Love for Aegisthus was her real motive; and as for Iphigenia, her sacrifice was required by Artemis in fulfilment of an ancient vow. Electra is not afraid of her mother who has treated her so badly and she boldly declares that, if she could, she would have her pay the penalty she deserves. Clytaemnestra is angered by her words, tells her she should be ashamed and threatens her with punishment when Aegisthus returns. She then orders her attendants to place the offerings upon the altar of Apollo and she herself prays to the god to fulfill her dream if it is for her good, but, if it is not, to cause it to result in injury to her enemies. She prays that she may live unharmed and continue to rule in the house of Agamemnon.

The whole purpose of the dramatist up to this point is evidently to impress upon his audience the bitter hostility which exists between mother and daughter. The hatred of Electra for her mother is too deeply seated for reconciliation; while Clytaemnestra's hatred of her daughter is due to fear. At this place comes the turning point in the play. From here on the action is concerned with the plot for slaying the murderers of Agamemnon, and its successful accomplishment.

The old slave who had accompanied Orestes now enters and inquires politely, like a well-trained servant, if this is the house of Aegisthus and if the lady is his wife. His bearing and his questions are like those of the messenger from Corinth in the *Oedipus Tyrannus*. When assured that he is right he says that he has come from Phocis and brings the news that Orestes is dead. Electra is overwhelmed with grief, but Clytaemnestra in glad surprise asks for particulars. The old man then begins his narrative (ll. 680–763):

> I'll tell you all, for I was sent for this.
> For he went to that famous spot in Greece
> For competition in the Delphian games.

And when he heard the herald in loud tones
Announce the foot-race, first of the events,
He entered shining and admired by all.
And in the race his deeds were not unlike
His nature, for he won the splendid prize
Of victory; and where there's much to tell
I say but little, for no man I know
Is such in prowess and achievements too.
And know this one thing, that in those events
The stewards of the games announced, he won—
The double race and contests which make up
The pentathlon—and was thought happy when
He was proclaimed an Argive and by name
Orestes, son of Agamemnon who
Once gathered that famed armament of Greece.
So much for this. But when a god wills harm
No strong man even can make his escape.
For on another day, at sunrise, when
The contest of the chariot race took place,
He entered it with many charioteers.
One was Achaean, one from Sparta, two
Were Libyans skilled in knowledge of yoked cars,
And fifth among them came Orestes, who
Was driving his Thessalian mares. The sixth
Came from Aetolia with his light brown colts.
The seventh was Magnesian; and the eighth
An Aenian with white horses; and the ninth
From Athens founded by the gods. The tenth
Was from Boeotia making the full list.
Now when the men appointed for that task
Had cast the lots and stationed every car
They waited for the brazen trumpet's call
And started. Then each driver shook his reins
And shouted to his horses; and the track
Was filled with noise of thundering chariots,
And dust flew upward. And together they
All intermingled did not spare their goads;
They sought each one to pass the others' cars

And snorting horses. For about their backs
And rolling wheels the foam fell on them and
The horses' breath assailed them. At each turn
Orestes with his wheel just grazed the post
In keeping close beneath it, letting out
The trace-horse on the right while he held back
The inner horse. So far the chariots all
Remained uninjured. Then with violence
The Aenian's hard-mouthed colts went rushing on,
And, swerving as they finished the sixth lap
And started on the seventh, struck head on
The car from Barca. Then from that mishap
Car after car was shattered and fell back
And all the plain of Crisa was filled full
Of broken chariots. Seeing this the man
From Athens, skilful in the chariot race,
Drew over to one side and checked his team
Thus leaving in the midst the surging mass.
Orestes at this time was driving last
And holding in his horses, for his trust
Was in the finish. But when he beheld
Just one opponent still left in the race
He uttered a sharp cry to his swift steeds
And started in pursuit. Then the two teams
Drove side by side, now one and then again
The other leading by a head. Now he,
Ill-fated that he was, had finished all
The other laps in safety, both himself
Secure and with his chariot still unharmed;
But loosing his left rein as his horse turned
Quite unawares he struck the turning-post
And broke his axle-box in two. Then he
Was hurled out of his chariot and became
Entangled in his well-cut reins. His steeds,
As he fell to the ground, broke loose and fled
Into the middle of the course. Now when
The people saw him thrown out of the car
They cried aloud in grief for this young man

Because, when he had done such noble deeds,
He met a fate so dreadful, sometimes dashed
Against the ground, then feet up towards the sky
Until at length some chariot-drivers stopped
The horses in their course and freed the man
All stained with blood, so that none of his friends
Could recognize his wretched body. Then
They straightway burned him on a pyre. And now
Appointed Phocian men are bringing here
The wretched ashes of that splendid form
Concealed within a little urn of bronze,
That he may find a grave in his own land.
Such is the tale, a grievous one to tell.
To us, however, who looked on it was
The saddest sight that I have ever seen.

This vivid narrative produces a different effect upon the different characters in the play. No one has any suspicion that it is not true. The chorus are shocked and distressed that the house of Agamemnon should have come to such an end. Clytaemnestra is clearly delighted, although at first she pretends to be distressed. When the old slave suggests that his errand seems to have been useless she acknowledges that the death of Orestes has relieved her of fear both from him and from Electra, who has been the more troublesome of the two. Electra is overcome with grief and has no spirit to answer her mother's taunts. Clytaemnestra invites the messenger into the house, and Electra is left alone with the chorus. She speaks partly to herself and partly to the chorus (ll. 804–822):

Did that most wretched woman seem to you
Like one distressed and pained, to weep and mourn
Her son thus dead? Why, rather, with a laugh
She left. Oh, woe is me! My brother dear,
Orestes, by thy death thou hast destroyed
My life, for thou hast gone and hast removed
The only hopes remaining in my mind

That thou wouldst live and some day come and wouldst
Avenge thy father and unhappy me.
And now where shall I go? For all alone
I am bereft of father and of thee.
I must again become the slave of those
Whom I hate most, the slayers of my sire.
Think ye that this is well? Nay, not again
Shall I become an inmate of their house,
But out here by the gate I shall lie down
And waste my life away bereft of friends.
If I have angered anyone within
Let that one slay me. It is joy to die,
A sorrow if I live, for no desire
Have I for life.

Electra cannot restrain her tears, and a lyric dialogue follows in which the chorus show their sympathy and try to console her. They are interrupted by the entrance of Chrysothemis who has not heard the news brought by the old slave. She is elated because she had found on her father's grave offerings and a lock of hair, and had at once concluded that Orestes must have been the one to leave them there. Electra quickly shows her that this is impossible, for Orestes is dead and the offerings were probably brought by some friend in memory of him.

Electra now has a bold idea. She no longer has hope of being saved by Orestes. She will, therefore, try to kill Aegisthus herself if Chrysothemis will help her. Chrysothemis, however, is appalled at the thought, for she feels sure that such an attempt could result only in their own death. The members of the chorus, too, think that such a step would be imprudent, but Electra is not to be deterred. She reproaches her sister with cowardice and declares that she will make the attempt alone. It will be noticed that in this scene there is no suggestion that the slaying of Clytaemnestra is contemplated. It is Aegisthus whom Electra wishes to kill.

The scene ends and the chorus come forward and sing the

second stasimon. They comment on the course which each of the sisters will follow, praise Electra and express the hope that she may be successful.

Orestes and Pylades now enter with attendants bearing the funerary urn. Orestes inquires of the chorus if this is the home of Aegisthus, and upon learning that it is asks that word be carried in that they have come from Phocis and desire to see him. Electra realizes that here is confirmation of the messenger's report, and the disguised Orestes assures her that her brother is dead and that the urn which they have with them contains his ashes. Electra asks that it be given to her that she may take it in her hands and bewail the fortunes of her house (PLATE II). She speaks as follows as she holds the urn (ll. 1126–1170):

Memorial of Orestes, dearest one,
How far removed from those fond hopes with which
I sent thee forth do I receive in turn
This relic of thy life. For now I hold
Mere nothing in my hands; and yet, my child,
I sent thee glorious from our home. I would
That I had died before these hands of mine
Stole thee away and to a foreign land
Sent thee and rescued thee from death, for then
Thou wouldst have died that day and shared the tomb
Of thy dead father. Now away from home
An exile in another land hast thou
Met thy unhappy end apart from me,
Thy sister. For with these fond hands of mine
I, wretched, have not bathed thee nor arranged
Thy body, nor from off the blazing pyre
Removed that grievous burden, as was meet.
But thou, unhappy one, by strangers' hands
Wast cared for, and to us thou comest now
A little heap of ashes in an urn.
Alas, poor me! my care of long ago
How useless! care I often gave to thee,

PLATE II

ORESTES GIVES THE URN TO ELECTRA

From a Crater in Vienna

And happy was my task, for never thou
Wast dearer to thy mother than to me.
I was thy nurse, not those within the house,
And "Sister" I was always called by thee.
But now all this has vanished with thy death,
For like a whirlwind thou hast gone thy way
And taken all things with thee. Now our sire
Is gone, and I am dead to thee, and thou
Thyself art dead and gone. Our enemies
Exult; while she, our mother though in truth
No mother to us two, is mad with joy.
About her thou didst often send me word
In secret that as an avenger thou
Wouldst show thyself; but bad luck, thine and mine,
Has robbed us of this plan and sent thee here
In place of thy dear self a useless shade
And ashes. Woe! Oh, woe is me!
Alas! alas! unhappy form!
Ah, me! most dreaded of journeys thou
Hast gone upon and caused my downfall here.
My downfall, darling brother, thou hast caused.
Receive me, therefore, in that same abode
That in the future I may dwell with thee
Beneath the earth, my nothingness with thine.
For when thou wast alive I shared with thee
The selfsame fortunes. Now I long in death
To share thy tomb. The dead are free from pain.

The chorus try to console Electra with the commonplace remark that we are all mortals and must expect to die. Orestes, however, is deeply moved by his sister's pathetic words and by her forlorn appearance. He cannot help questioning her, dangerous as his position is, and at length gently takes the urn from her, telling her that the story is false, that Orestes lives and that he is that very man. In proof he shows her his father's signet ring. Electra undergoes a sudden revulsion of feeling from grief to joy, in which the chorus share. In her happiness she throws her arms about her brother; but Orestes cautions her to keep silent lest they be overheard, and above all not to let her mother perceive her joy. Electra restrains herself and tells him that Clytaemnestra is in the house, but Aegisthus is away.

This passage in which Electra suddenly realizes that her brother is before her is much like the scene in the *Iphigenia in Tauris* of Euripides in which Orestes convinces Iphigenia of his identity. Electra and Iphigenia are both overcome by their emotions. The inference, however, could not be safely drawn that either author was influenced by the other. Similar situations naturally call for similar treatment. The use of the ring as a means of identification is rare in Greek tragedy, no other example occurring in the extant plays. It was, however, a frequent device of the writers of the new comedy.

The old slave enters and cautions them to be quiet. His careful watching at the door alone has saved them from being detected. When Electra learns that he is the very man to whom she had entrusted the young Orestes there is another outburst of joy on her part and she hails him as "Father." But the old man tells them that now is the time to act, for Clytaemnestra is alone. Orestes and Pylades together with him enter the palace and Electra, after a prayer to Apollo for the success of their plot, follows them. The chorus sing a short song. The deed of vengeance is about to be done and it is Hermes who guides the avengers.

Electra now returns. She has come out to give warning of the approach of Aegisthus. She tells the chorus that Clytaemnestra is adorning the funeral urn for burial while Orestes and Pylades stand near her. A moment later a shriek is heard within the house and Clytaemnestra calls for Aegisthus. She is heard beseeching Orestes for pity. Electra comments on her cries and, when she shrieks that she has been struck, calls out, (l. 1415)

> A second blow strike if thou hast the strength.

Again Clytaemnestra screams,

Oh! Oh! once more!

and Electra,

Shriek for Aegisthus, too.

A moment later Orestes and Pylades enter with blood-stained hands, and Orestes briefly informs Electra that her mother is dead. But Aegisthus is seen approaching and the two young men hasten back into the palace. Aegisthus has heard the story of the chariot race and is eager to meet the men who have brought the news. He is told that they are in the house.

In this passage Sophocles indulges in a practice common on the Greek stage and apparently enjoyed by an Athenian audience, that of using words which have one meaning to the speaker and quite a different meaning to the person addressed. It is an example of his so-called irony.[1]

Aegisthus enters and asks Electra where the strangers are who have brought the report of the death of her brother. She tells him they are in the house, and when he asks if he can see the dead body assures him that he can. He then proclaims silence and orders the doors to be opened so that all who might be looking to Orestes for the restoration of the ancient line may behold his dead body and submit to his own authority. The doors are thrown back and the interior of the room shown by means of the *eccyclema*. A dead body is revealed completely covered and Orestes and Pylades standing beside it. Aegisthus asks that the face be shown, and Orestes tells him to remove the covering himself. He proceeds to do so; but first orders Electra to call Clytaemnestra. He then lifts the cloth and beholds the face of the dead queen. He knows then that he has been deceived and that he is in the power of his enemies. He asks permission to speak; but Electra begs her brother not to grant

[1] See p. 19.

it but to kill him and cast out his body. He is then driven into the house to die where he had slain Agamemnon. The *eccyclema* is withdrawn and the death of Aegisthus is supposed to take place behind the scenes.

With this dramatic scene the play comes to an end; while the chorus comment on the successful outcome of the plot and the restoration of the family.

The *Electra* is a powerful play and is distinctly a play for a great actor. It is rightly named for Electra, since she is throughout the most important character in it. This is in contrast with the *Choephoroe* of Aeschylus, where Orestes plays the most important part. A brief summary of the earlier tragedy will make that clear.

The scene is laid at the tomb of Agamemnon, to which Orestes and Pylades have brought offerings. Electra is seen approaching with a band of attendants, that is, the chorus, who are slave women but devoted to their mistress. She has been sent by Clytaemnestra to the tomb with offerings because of a bad dream which she has had. Electra laments her own condition and prays that punishment may come upon her father's slayers. She then discovers the lock of hair left on the tomb by Orestes and thinks that he may have returned. Orestes then steps forth from the place where he had concealed himself and convinces her that he really is her brother. A long lament then follows in lyric verse in which Orestes, Electra, and the chorus take part.

The scene now changes to the space in front of the palace. Orestes and Pylades enter disguised as Phocians and knock at the door, which is opened by a servant. Orestes declares that he has a message for Clytaemnestra, and when she comes out tells her that while on his way from Daulis to Argos a stranger called Strophius had asked him to take the news to her that her son Orestes was dead. He wished to know whether the dead body should be sent home or not. Clytaemnestra pretends to be distressed, but gives orders to entertain the strangers. She then sends the old nurse of Orestes to summon Aegisthus. The old woman enters weeping and is persuaded by the chorus to change Clytaemnestra's message so that Aegisthus should come alone, without his body-guard. A few moments later he hurries in and enters the house eager to question the messengers. A cry is heard and a slave rushes out telling of the death of his master and calling for Clytaemnestra. When the queen hears what has happened she knows that her hour has come and calls for a battle-axe. Orestes appears and tells her that she must die. She begs for mercy and he wavers; but when Pylades impresses upon him that the oracle of Apollo must be obeyed, he drags her off and kills her behind the scenes.

The *eccyclema* is then pushed out showing the dead bodies of Aegisthus and Clytaemnestra side by side and Orestes standing near them. He justifies his deed and says he will go to Delphi as a suppliant, as Apollo had bidden him. The chorus approve of what he has done. Suddenly he sees the Furies and hurries away, while the chorus comment on the misfortunes of the house.

This summary, short as it is, shows how far Sophocles has gone beyond Aeschylus in the development of this theme. The earlier play has all the essentials of the later plot, but Sophocles has made of it a great tragedy largely because he saw the possibilities of Electra as a great tragic character and developed them. In the *Electra* of Euripides again Electra has the longest part, but she is not the strong personality which Sophocles portrays.[1] One cannot help feeling that Sophocles wishes us to think of his heroine as possessing something of her mother's strength of mind. Electra is embittered by the treatment which she has received from her mother and Aegisthus. But this is not all. She hates Aegisthus as the murderer of her father, and she hates her mother because of her shameless life with Aegisthus. The natural modesty of a noble young girl is shocked and

[1] See Bates, *Euripides*, pp. 85 ff.

horrified at her mother's conduct. Even so she feels that she must justify herself for she says (ll. 307 ff.):

> In such misfortunes, friends, one cannot be
> Discreet and pious; but there is great need
> To practise evil when in evil plight.

The poet certainly does not wish us to think of her as incapable of tender feeling. That is clear from her devotion to her brother; and her long soliloquy over the funeral urn is full of pathos. In fact in his portrayal of Electra Sophocles has created one of the most interesting characters of the Greek stage. It is, therefore, not surprising that the tragedy is often played today in Athens, both in ancient Greek and in modern Greek translation.

Next in importance to Electra is Clytaemnestra. She is depicted as the wicked queen whose conscience does not trouble her for her crimes; but she is apprehensive lest she be punished for them. She is superstitious, for she is moved by her dream to send an offering to the tomb of her murdered husband. She pretends to be distressed at the news of her son's death, and yet acknowledges that she is relieved. In fact Clytaemnestra conforms to the usual conception of her by the tragic poets. She is, however, not as bloodthirsty as she is represented in the *Agamemnon*, although she acknowledges her part in the murder of her husband (ll. 525 ff., 558, 588, etc.) without any feeling of remorse, and attempts to justify the deed. In the older version of the story found in Homer,[1] Aegisthus is the actual slayer and Clytaemnestra merely his helper.

Orestes is not particularly noteworthy. He carries out a long-meditated act of vengeance to which he has been ordered by the oracle of Apollo, and after the deed is done he shows no sign of regret.

The other characters call for little comment. Chrysothemis does not appear in the *Choephoroe*, or in the *Electra* of Euripides,

[1] *Odyssey*, XI, 409 ff.

but she is mentioned by Homer[1] as one of the three daughters of Agamemnon. Sophocles represents her as sympathizing with Electra but unwilling to help her from fear of her mother. Her part in the play is not unlike that of Ismene in the *Antigone*. The weaker sister is a foil to the stronger.

Aegisthus is very much of a poltroon. He is eager to obtain confirmation of the death of the one man of whom he is afraid, and, when he finds he is tricked, tamely submits to be driven into the house to meet his death.

The *paidagogos*, the old slave who had rescued the boy Orestes, is a real character. He is a type that Sophocles liked to portray.

Pylades has no speaking part, although he is on the stage much of the time and is addressed by Orestes twice (ll. 16 and 1373).

The story of Electra was not only a favorite with the ancient tragic poets, but several modern writers have been attracted by it as well. Most recent of these are Strauss in his opera *Electra* and O'Neill in his trilogy *Mourning becomes Electra*. Neither of these works, however, is Greek in character. The shrieking mad woman of Strauss has nothing in common with the heroine of Sophocles; and the sordid and debased characters which O'Neill portrays are as far removed from those of Aeschylus, Sophocles, and Euripides as his prose is from their splendid verse.

The legend itself is one of the oldest in Greek. One scene in the tragic story, the death of Clytaemnestra and Aegisthus at the hands of Orestes, may, perhaps, be represented on one of the gold seals found in the Mycenaean rock tomb near Thisbe in Boeotia already mentioned. It dates from about 1500 B.C.[2]

[1] *Iliad*, IX, 142 ff. Laodice and Iphianassa are given as the names of her sisters.

[2] *Jour. of Hel. Studies*, XLV, 1925 p. 38 fig. 38.

VI

The Trachiniae

In six of the extant tragedies of Sophocles we find one outstanding personage who dominates the action and gives his name to the play. With the *Trachiniae* the case is different. Here there are two important characters, one appearing in the first part of the play and the other in the second; and the tragedy takes its name not from either of them, but from the chorus. Deianeira who speaks the prologue is not seen after line 812, although the report of her death extends to line 946. Heracles is brought in on a litter at line 974, and the rest of the play is concerned with him. There are thus two separate actions and parts for two leading actors, unless one man could fill successfully two such different rôles as those of Deianeira and Heracles. The date of the play is unknown, but it is usually assumed that it was one of the dramatist's later works. Jebb[1] would date it tentatively between 420 and 410 B.C.

For his plot Sophocles went back to the old epic poem the *Capture of Oechalia* (Οἰχαλίας ἅλωσις); but apparently, following his usual practice, he made such innovations in the story as he saw fit. Thus he caused Deianeira to send the robe to her husband of her own accord, not at the request of Heracles; and he made Heracles capture Iole for himself, not for Hyllus. There are also a few other variations from the usual story; but the loss of the epic poem makes it impossible to determine with any degree of certainty just what modifications are due to the dramatist.

The scene is laid before the house of Heracles at Trachis in northern Greece. Here the mighty hero had been dwelling since he was driven from Tiryns because of his murder of Iphitus. Deianeira, the wife of Heracles, enters and speaks the prologue. She is accompanied by her nurse whom she is supposed to be addressing, although in reality her speech of forty-eight lines

[1] *Trachiniae*, p. xxiii.

is a soliloquy in which she tells the story of her life. One cannot help feeling that those writers who see in this prologue Euripidean influence are justified in their opinion. Jebb, to be sure, finds differences between the speech of Deianeira and the typical prologue of Euripides;[1] but even so in their principal features they are essentially the same. It is certainly hard to avoid the conclusion that Sophocles saw the practical advantages of the Euripidean prologue and in this play decided to take advantage of them.

Deianeira begins by telling what an unhappy life she had led. While in her father's house at Pleuron she had to her terror been wooed by the river-god Achelous, who appeared now as a bull, now as a serpent, now as a man with a bull's head. Then Heracles had come and conquered him and made her his bride. But ever since her marriage her life had been one full of worry because of the frequent absences of her husband. When he had left home the last time he had given her a tablet in which, as we learn later on, he had told her that if he did not return in fifteen months she should consider him dead. Her old nurse advises her to send her son Hyllus in search of his father. At this moment Hyllus enters and Deianeira tells him the nurse's advice. Hyllus has heard that his father is in Euboea, or about to go there. When she hears this Deianeira remembers an oracle which said that when Heracles had completed this work he would either meet death or have peace for the rest of his life, and she declares that Hyllus must go to assist him.

The chorus, consisting of maidens of Trachis, friends of Deianeira, now enter and sing the parodos. They are the Trachiniae. They pray to Helius to tell them where Heracles is, for they know that Deianeira is worried about him. They try to console and reassure her. Life, they say, has its ups and downs. She understands their object and tells them of the oracle and her own anxiety. An old man now enters and quickly informs her that Lichas, the herald, has arrived with the news that Heracles

[1] *Trachiniae*, pp. xlix f.

will soon be home. Lichas himself is detained by the joyful people. The chorus sing a short song of rejoicing, at the conclusion of which Lichas comes in accompanied by a band of women and confirms the old messenger's news. Heracles is alive and in Euboea. The women are his captives taken in war. His long absence was partly due to the fact that he had been compelled by Zeus to serve Omphale as a slave for a year in atonement for his treacherous murder of Iphitus. After his release he had slain Eurytus, king of Oechalia, whom he blamed for his troubles, and captured his city. Deianeira notices that one of the captives is especially beautiful, and asks about her. This is Iole, the daughter of Eurytus, though Lichas professes not to know who she is. She remains silent and Deianeira pities her and sends her without further question into the house. As she goes in, the messenger, who has been listening, calls Deianeira aside and tells her that Lichas has deceived her. Heracles had really captured Oechalia because of his love for Iole when her father Eurytus refused to give her to him. Deianeira is naturally much distressed and she decides to question Lichas, who at that moment enters from the house. He has come to learn what message he shall carry back to Heracles. She asks him about the captive, but he professes not to know, even though the messenger boldly declares that he has heard him say publicly that she was Iole and the wife of Heracles. Deianeira in a long speech begs Lichas to tell her the truth, and he then acknowledges that things are as the old man said. Heracles had been overcome by love for Iole. He had himself concealed the truth from a wish to spare her feelings. Deianeira says she will bow to the will of the gods and she enters the house, for she means to send back to Heracles a gift as well as a message.

The chorus now sing the first stasimon. They comment on the power of Love and briefly tell the story of the combat between Achelous and Heracles for the hand of Deianeira.

Deianeira now returns from the house. She wishes to confide in the chorus while Lichas is bidding farewell to the captives, and, at the same time, to obtain their sympathy. It is clear that Iole is a rival and likely to supersede her in her husband's affections since she is much younger, and to have her under the same roof is unbearable. She is not angry with Heracles, but she means to win back his love. Once, when she was traveling with him as his bride, the centaur Nessus while conveying her across the river Euenus attempted violence and Heracles, turning back, shot him. As he lay dying, the centaur told her that if she collected the blood gathered about the wound where the arrow tinged with the hydra's blood had entered, it would be a charm to prevent her husband from loving any woman more than he loved her. She has kept this carefully hidden away in a bronze vessel and now, as Nessus had directed, she has anointed a garment with it and is going to send it to Heracles. The chorus approve her plan. When, therefore, Lichas enters and asks for orders she gives him a garment which she had woven herself, in a box sealed with her seal, and asks him to tell her husband to let no one put it on before himself; and not to expose it to the sunshine or to heat from the fire, and to put it on when he is about to sacrifice. This, she says, is in accord with a vow which she had made. Such, as the audience in the theatre knows, were the instructions of Nessus. Lichas promises to do as he is told, and leaves with his followers.

The second stasimon follows. The music of the flute will soon be heard, the chorus sing, for Heracles is returning after his long absence. May he come full of longing.

Deianeira now enters. She is somewhat alarmed and fears that she may not have acted altogether wisely in sending the gift to her husband. When questioned by the chorus she explains that she has seen the flock of wool which she had used in anointing the robe suddenly waste away self-consumed; and where it had been lying in the sunshine there appeared thick clots of foam. She tells them how she had followed the commands of the centaur and kept the substance which he gave her safely preserved from heat ever since she received it. She had placed her gift to Heracles in a box, but on her way to the house just now she saw the bit of wool disappear in this strange fashion. She is frightened for fear that her gift may injure her husband. She realizes, now that it is too late, that Nessus could have no motive for doing her good, but a very strong one for injuring Heracles. And, what is more, the poison from the hydra on his arrows destroys whatever it touches. It, then, will kill Heracles. But if she has harmed him she is determined that she will not live. The chorus point out that even if there is ground for apprehension she should not worry until she knows what has happened. Even then if evil has resulted she is innocent in intent.

Hyllus now enters in great haste and assails his mother with bitter words. He tells her she has murdered her husband. She is deeply distressed and Hyllus when questioned tells his story thus (ll. 749–812):

If thou must learn, then I must tell thee all.
He sacked the famous town of Eurytus
And went away with trophies and with spoil
Of victory. Now there's a jutting crag
Within Euboea, Cape Cenaeum, where
The waves surge round about and here for Zeus
Patroös he established altars and
A precinct set with trees. Here filled with joy
I saw him first. Then, as he was about
To offer an abundant sacrifice,
His herald Lichas came from home and brought
Thy gift, the fatal robe, which he put on
As was directed, and began to slay
Twelve perfect bulls, first victims from his spoil,
For he had brought a hundred head all told.
Now he, poor man, with cheerful mind at first
And happy in his gay attire prayed.
But when the flame of solemn sacrifice
And from the pitchy wood blazed midst the blood,
The sweat burst forth upon him and the robe

Clung to his sides at every joint as if
An artisan had glued it fast; and through
His frame there darted a convulsive pain,
And like the poison of a deadly snake
It was consuming him. And then he called
The wretched Lichas who was not to blame
For thy misdeed and asked with what intent
He brought the robe; and he, ill-fated man,
Not knowing, said it was thy gift alone
And just as it was sent. Then, when he heard,
And as a torturing spasm gripped his lungs,
He grasped the man's foot where the socket turns
And hurled him at a sea-surrounded rock,
And from his hair he made the white brains ooze
And blood together with them, when the skull
Was split in two. And all the people cried
Aloud with anguish seeing that the one
Was sore afflicted and the other slain.
And no one dared to face the man, for he
Was drawn down to the ground, then leaping high
With shouts and shrieks; and round about the rocks
Resounded and the Locrian headlands, too,
And the Euboean cliffs. But when that poor
Unfortunate grew weary, many times
His body hurling on the ground with cries
Of sore distress, and thy ill-fated couch
Reviling and the marriage brought about
By Oeneus, how it had destroyed his life,
Then, from the murky smoke surrounding him,
He raised his rolling eyes and saw me there
Among the crowd bewailing, and he called
Upon me, gazing at me, "Boy, come here,
Keep not away from my calamity,
Nay, even if it is thy fate to die
Together with me. Take me far away
And place me where no man shall see me more.
But if thou feelest pity take me hence
From out this land as quickly as thou canst

And let me not die here." When he had thus
Commanded, in a ship we set him down
And barely brought him groaning to this land
In dire convulsions. Soon ye shall behold
The man still living, or but just now dead.
Such, Mother, are the things thou hast been caught
Devising, yes, and doing to my sire.
Now may avenging Justice punish thee
For this, and may the Furies, too, I pray,
If it is right, and right it is, since thou
Hast scorned the right by slaying the best man
Of all upon the earth; and never such
Another shalt thou see.

Deianeira makes no reply, though the chorus urge her to do so; but slowly moves off the stage in silence and enters the palace, while Hyllus utters bitter words about her.

The chorus comment on the oracle given twelve years before which declared that at the expiration of that time Heracles would be free from his labors, and now they see that he will be freed by death. This has been brought about by the wiles of the centaur Nessus, for the chorus feel certain that Deianeira is innocent of evil intent. They imagine her lamenting all by herself.

At this moment a cry of wailing is heard within the house, and a little later Deianeira's nurse enters in great distress and tells them that her mistress is dead. When they question her she tells how the unhappy woman had moved about the house weeping; and how she had, after a time, gone into the bed-chamber of Heracles and thrown herself upon his couch. Then she had bared her left side and arm. The nurse, alarmed at this, had run to tell Hyllus, but before she could get back Deianeira had driven a sword into her heart. Hyllus had thrown himself down beside her, weeping and reproaching himself for his former words, for he had learned that it was due to the instigation of the dying Nessus that she had sent the fatal robe.

Now he has lost mother as well as father, and the old woman moralizes that one cannot tell what the morrow will bring forth.

A short lament by the chorus follows, and then Heracles is brought in lying upon a litter. Hyllus and an aged man walk beside it, and the latter urges Hyllus to be quiet and not disturb his father, who is still alive. But Heracles awakes, cries out in agony and begs for death. Hyllus, the aged man, and the members of the chorus are all deeply moved, but they are unable to help him. After this outburst, which is in lyric verse, a long speech by Heracles in the usual metre of the dialogue follows. This passage is famous, and a translation of the greater part of it by Cicero is still preserved.[1] It runs as follows (ll. 1046–1111):

Ah me! the many dreadful ills I've borne
With toiling hands and back, and not by word.
But never has the wife of Zeus, nor yet
Eurystheus, hateful that he is to me,
Brought on me such distress as Oeneus' child,
Deceitful one, and fastened round my arms
This Furies' woven net by which I die.
For stuck close to my sides it has consumed
My flesh deep down, and resting where it is
It drains the tubes within my lungs and now
Has drunk my fresh life-blood; and I, held fast
By dreadful fetters, wholly waste away.
No spear upon the battle-field, no host
Of earth-born giants, no wild creature's might,
Nor Greece, nor foreign land which I approached
And cleansed, has ever done such things; but she,
A woman born, no man, has laid me low
Without a sword. Oh! son, now prove thyself
My true-born son and do not honor more

[1] Cicero in *Tusc. Disp.* II, 8 ff. translates lines 1046 to 1102, or fifty-seven lines, which become forty-five lines in his rendering which begins:

O multa dictu gravia, perpessu aspera,
quae corpore exanclata atque animo pertuli!

A mother's name than mine. Do thou thyself
With thine own hands bring hither from the house
Thy mother now and place her in my hands,
That I may know if thou art more distressed
At seeing my poor tortured form or hers
When she is justly made to suffer harm.
Come, son, be bold, have pity on me who
Am pitied now by many, since I weep
And groan as if I were a girl; and this
No man could say he saw me do before,
But always I have followed my ill fate
Without complaint. But now, unhappy man,
I have been found a woman all because
Of this. Approach and stand close by thy sire,
And see from what ill fate I suffered thus
For when uncovered I shall make all plain.
Come, all of ye see this afflicted man,
Behold this wretch, how piteous I am.
Alas! ah, wretched me! alas! once more.
A raging pang again has tortured me
And darted through my sides. It seems as if
This terrible devouring pain could not
Leave me untried. Oh! ruler of the dead,
Oh! Hades, take me!
Oh! fire of Zeus, strike!
Release thy thunderbolt upon me, lord;
Let it crash down, Oh! Father. For once more
The pain consumes me. It has started up
And now bursts forth again. Oh! hands, my hands,
Oh! back and chest and these dear arms of mine,
To this state have ye come, who in the past
Did once the Nemean lion slay by force—
That bane of herdsmen, unapproachable,
A beast that none could meet. The Hydra, too,
Of Lerna ye subdued, and that fierce throng
Of double-natured creatures, partly man
Part horse, rough, lawless, and endowed with strength
Surpassing; and the Erymanthian boar.

The triple-headed dog of Hades, too,
Beneath the earth, invincible, the dread
Echidna's offspring ye once overcame;
The dragon also in those distant lands,
The guardian of the golden apples there.
And countless other labors I have tried,
And no man ever brought defeat upon
These hands of mine. But now with shattered joints
And tattered flesh I am destroyed, alas!
By some black fate, I who was called the child
Of a most noble mother and the son
Of Zeus among the stars. But know this well,
Though I am nothing and I cannot move,
That I shall punish her who did this deed.
Just let her come here that she may be taught
To make it plain to all that I alive
Or dead chastised the wicked.

After the chorus has expressed its distress at the condition of Heracles, Hyllus timidly addresses his father, and when Heracles permits him to speak tells him of the suicide of Deianeira. He explains that she had no evil intent when she sent the fatal garment; that the centaur Nessus had given her a supposed love charm and she was trying to win back her husband's love.

Heracles knows now that his end is near; for it had been foretold that no living creature would cause his death, but one that had already passed away. Furthermore the oracle at Dodona had predicted his release from trouble at this time, and that, he sees, really meant his death. He now makes Hyllus promise to convey him to Mount Oeta and to heap up a great pyre and place his body upon it. Hyllus agrees to do so, but refuses to light the pyre in spite of his father's command. One other thing Heracles directs him to do, and that is to marry Iole. Hyllus objects strenuously, but at length consents. Attendants then raise the litter and carry out the afflicted hero, while Hyllus comments on the cruelty of the gods to their own children.

Such is the *Trachiniae*. It is apparent at once that the most interesting parts of it are the narrative portions, not the dialogue, as is the case with the *Oedipus Tyrannus*, for example. It has been very much discussed, and the most diverse opinions expressed about it by various writers at different times. On the one hand there is the much-quoted statement of A. W. Schlegel,[1] who thought it so far inferior to the other tragedies of Sophocles that he wished to attribute it to some other writer, perhaps Iophon. On the other hand we have Campbell's declaration[2] that "it may be confidently asserted that in point of dramatic structure the *Trachiniae* will bear comparison with the greatest of Sophoclean tragedies." Between these two extremes may be found a great variety of opinions. Jebb[3] agrees with Campbell, though he finds a serious defect in the inferiority in dramatic interest of the part of Heracles to that of Deianeira. M. Croiset[4] calls the *Trachiniae* the weakest of the extant plays of Sophocles; while Christ[5] finds it the most difficult of the poet's tragedies to understand. Christ also calls attention to various features in the play for which Sophocles was indebted to the *Heracles Furens* of Euripides, and he thinks that in it Sophocles deliberately undertook to outdo Euripides in his style of tragedy. Wilamowitz-Moellendorf,[6] too, recognizes the indebtedness of Sophocles to Euripides in the *Trachiniae*, and he declares that Sophocles knew the *Heracles Furens* and had read it carefully. I do not see how anyone who reads the *Trachiniae* with care can fail to see the influence of Euripides in it.[7] I find this most striking at the beginning and at the end of the play; but in spite of this the tragedy remains essentially Sophoclean. In my opinion it is not a great play, but its authorship is not to be questioned.

[1] *Vorlesungen über dram. Kunst und Literatur*, pp. 32 f.; English translation by Black, pp. 76 f.

[2] *Sophocles*, II, p. 237.

[3] *Trachiniae*, p. xlii.

[4] *Histoire de la littérature grecque*, III, p. 244.

[5] *Geschichte der griech. Literatur*, 6th ed. by Schmid, p. 335.

[6] *Euripides Herakles*, 2d. ed. I, p. 153; also n. 63.

[7] For the influence of the *Alcestis* and the *Medea* on the *Trachiniae* see M. L. Earle, *Trans. Amer. Philol. Assoc.* 1902, pp. 5 ff.

Of the various characters in the tragedy Deianeira is outstanding. The critics generally agree in praising her gentleness, her anxiety for Heracles, and her devotion to him in spite of his shortcomings; her sympathy for Iole, even though she has come as a rival; her innocent attempt to win back her husband's love; her apprehension when the flock of wool is consumed; and, finally, when she learns of the terrible disaster caused by her gift, her silence under the provocation of the bitter words of her son. Her suicide forms a dramatic climax to the first part of the play and serves to increase still further our sympathy for her. Her simplicity in believing the centaur's story about the love-charm might, perhaps, be criticized, but in the theatre that would be overlooked or excused.

In contrast with Deianeira is the character of Heracles, with whom the last third of the tragedy is chiefly concerned. He is anything but admirable. It is true that he is represented as suffering terrible agony; but his deliberate murder of Lichas and his constant desire for vengeance upon Deianeira show him in a very unfavorable light. In the *Heracles Furens* of Euripides he is insane when he kills his wife and children, and after he has recovered his reason he wishes to kill himself. In the *Trachiniae* he is in full possession of his senses even in the most dreadful of his torments; but he is so firmly convinced that Deianeira has deliberately plotted his ruin that he is unwilling to admit any other possibility. He would like to get his hands on her and strangle her. It is only with difficulty that Hyllus obtains permission to explain what really happened, and even then Heracles is unmoved. There is no trace here of the good-natured hero usually represented on the Attic stage. From a dramatic point of view his sufferings might be effective in arousing a feeling of pity among the spectators, but they would certainly not excite their admiration for him.

The minor characters in the *Trachiniae* call for little comment. Hyllus wishes to do his mother's bidding, but he takes her guilt for granted when he has beheld his father's sufferings. He curses her, though later, when he has learned of her death, he tries to defend her before his father. He is devoted to Heracles and promises to obey his last commands much as he dislikes to do so. He is on the whole a rather colorless character.

Lichas is the devoted follower of his master, just as the nurse is the devoted slave of Deianeira. The introduction of the latter as a messenger to tell the story of the death of her mistress is an unusual feature, for in the Greek drama the messenger is almost always represented as a man. Both characters are typical faithful servants. The old man who brings Deianeira the news that Heracles is alive, and afterwards reveals to her the true position of Iole, brief as his part is, is well set forth, as we have seen such characters usually are by Sophocles.

The chorus, as has been generally recognized, are not as closely connected with the development of the plot as in some of the other tragedies. As young women, friends and confidantes of Deianeira, they naturally are of most importance in the early part of the play. After her death they have little to do with the action.

In looking back upon the *Trachiniae* after reading it, one cannot help feeling that there is a break between the two parts of the plot. Some admirers of the poet are not disturbed by this. Thus Jebb thinks unity is effected by the love of Heracles for Iole which caused him to destroy Oechalia and caused Deianeira to send the robe; but the tie is certainly not a strong one. In this respect we must conclude that this tragedy in the development of its plot falls far short of that perfection which we find in the *Oedipus Tyrannus*.

VII

The Philoctetes

THE *Philoctetes* was one of the latest of the tragedies of Sophocles. It was brought out in the spring of 409 B.C., as we learn from the prose notice of it which has come down from antiquity, and it won first prize.[1] The poet was then eighty-seven years old. What the titles of the other plays were which accompanied it to complete the tetralogy is unknown. The subject was a favorite with the Greek tragic poets. Aeschylus and Euripides had both previously made use of it, the *Philoctetes* of Euripides being produced in 431 B.C. along with the *Medea* and the *Dictys*.[2] Sophocles himself used it also in his *Philoctetes at Troy*, the date of which is unknown. That play, as the title implies, had to do with the exploits of the hero after his return to Troy and the healing of the sore on his leg. Its action was thus subsequent to that of the extant tragedy, but there is no reason to believe that it was composed later. The seven little fragments of it still preserved give little help for its plot.[3] Among the minor tragic poets Achaeus and the elder Philocles in the fifth century B.C. and Antiphon and Theodectes in the fourth are known to have written plays entitled *Philoctetes*.[4]

The scene of the tragedy is laid on the barren shore of the island of Lemnos in front of the cave in which the unfortunate Philoctetes has been living alone for ten years. He had been marooned in this desolate spot by his companions because of an offensive sore which had developed on his leg after he had been bitten by a serpent;[5] and also because of his dreadful cries caused by the excruciating pain. The poet wishes us to imagine the island uninhabited, at least in that part of it where Philoctetes was, as he tells us at the beginning of the play.[6] Odysseus and Neoptolemus enter stealthily. They have been sent to

[1] The notice reads *ἐδιδάχθη ἐπὶ Γλαυκίππου· πρῶτος ἦν Σοφοκλῆς*. It is preserved in the Laurentian manuscript (Laurentianus xxxii, 9), in Parisinus 2712 and in some later manuscripts.

[2] See Bates, *Euripides*, p. 280.

[3] See pp. 251.

[4] See Haigh, *Tragic Drama of the Greeks*, pp. 477 ff.

[5] This is the version of the story followed by Sophocles (l. 267). According to another version the wound was caused by one of the poisoned arrows of Heracles which he had inadvertently dropped.

[6] Line 2 *βροτοῖς ἄστιπτος οὐδ' οἰκουμένη*. The scholiast explains this as *ἐν ἐρήμῳ γὰρ μέρει τῆς Λήμνου ἐξετέθη ὑπὸ τῶν Ἑλλήνων*.

Lemnos to obtain the bow and arrows of Heracles which the unfortunate Philoctetes possesses.[1] Odysseus explains to his young companion that he had put the sick man ashore at this place ten years before by direction of the leaders, but he is not quite sure where the cave is located. Neoptolemus discovers it and goes forward and inspects it, but finds it empty. There is, however, evidence of its occupation in the foul rags put out to dry. It is clear that the man cannot be far away and, at the suggestion of Odysseus, a man is sent to watch the path, for if Philoctetes should discover Odysseus he would surely kill him. Odysseus now explains the plan which he has in mind. Neoptolemus must win the confidence of the sick man with a story that he had left the Greek camp and is going home because his father's arms had been given to Odysseus instead of to himself. When Philoctetes trusts him it will be possible for him to get possession of the bow and arrows, without which they now know Troy cannot be taken. It was the possession of these infallible weapons which had enabled Philoctetes to support himself on the island. Neoptolemus is a noble youth and is very unwilling to undertake the disgraceful part he is asked to play, but at length he yields to the arguments presented to him by the older man and agrees to do as he is told. Odysseus now withdraws, having first arranged to send a man disguised as a ship-captain to aid Neoptolemus if he does not hear from him in a reasonable time.

This prologue in the form of a dialogue sets forth the facts which it was essential that the audience should know in advance. In this respect the result achieved by the poet is similar to that brought about in the prologues of Euripides, whose influence upon Sophocles in this play has been generally acknowledged. The ancient commentator notes the resemblance, but points out

[1] Philoctetes had received the bow and arrows of Heracles in return for his service in lighting the hero's funeral pyre, cp. ll. 801 ff. The arrows never missed their mark.

that in the *Philoctetes* of Euripides Odysseus alone was the speaker.[1]

The chorus, consisting of sailors from the ship of Neoptolemus,[2] now enter and engage in a lyric dialogue with him. They are aware of the prowess of Philoctetes and ask what part they are to play. They are told to come forward and help when the sign is given. They express their pity for the marooned man. The cries of Philoctetes are heard, and a few moments later he comes stumbling in. He inquires who the strangers are and why they have come there. Neoptolemus replies that he is the son of Achilles and is sailing home from Troy. He pretends that he has never heard of Philoctetes, who tells him his story as follows (ll. 254–316):

> Most wretched I, and hateful to the gods!
> Of my condition word has never gone
> Unto my home, nor anywhere in Greece.
> But they who cast me out smile secretly
> While my affliction ever grows the worse.
> Thou, boy, who hast Achilles for thy sire,
> I am that man whom thou hast heard about
> Perchance, who owns the arms of Heracles—
> The son of Poas, Philoctetes, whom
> That pair of chieftains and with them the king
> Of Cephallenia shamefully cast out
> And left abandoned, wasting with disease,
> A dread affliction caused by cruel bite
> Of that man-slaying viper. Thus alone
> They left me here, my boy, and went away.
> For this is where they put in with their fleet
> From sea-girt Chryse, when with joy they saw
> Me lulled to sleep by motion of the waves;
> And on the shore beneath a hanging rock

[1] Scholium on *Philoctetes* l. 1 καὶ παρὰ τούτῳ προλογίζει Ὀδυσσεὺς καθὰ καὶ παρ' Εὐριπίδῃ, ἐκεῖνο μέντοι διαφέρει παρ' ὅσον ὁ μὲν Εὐριπίδης πάντα τῷ Ὀδυσσεῖ περιτίθησιν, οὗτος δὲ τὸν Νεοπτόλεμον παρεισάγων διὰ τούτου οἰκονομεῖται.

[2] The writer of the prose Hypothesis calls them aged. ὁ δὲ χορὸς ἐκ γερόντων τῶν τῷ Νεοπτολέμῳ συμπλεόντων.

They left me, after setting down a few
Such rags as an ill-fated man might have,
And just a little food to help. May they
Have such a fate! What dost thou think, my boy,
Was my awakening after they had gone?
What tears I wept, what cries of dire lament
I uttered when I saw the ships all gone,
The ships with which I sailed, and no man near
To help, to give a sick man aid in his
Affliction! When I looked about I found
Naught there except distress, but much of that.
Then season after season passed while I
Alone beneath my slender shelter had
To serve myself. My stomach's needs this bow
Supplied by striking down the fluttering doves.
And what the arrow by my bowstring sent
Brought down, to that I, wretched one, would crawl
And drag my poor afflicted foot; and if
I must get drinking water, or break up
Some wood, as in the winter, when the frost
Was spread around, I would accomplish this,
Ah me! by creeping out. Then, there would be
No fire; but rubbing stone on stone at length
I'd make the hidden flame appear—the thing
Which always saved my life; for sheltering roof
And fire provide all things except relief
From my affliction. Come, my boy, do thou
Now learn about this island. Here no man
Who sails the seas approaches willingly,
For there is here no haven; no place where
A profit can be made or welcome found.
No voyages do prudent men make here.
Mayhap a man has come against his will;
For such a thing might happen many times
In the long stretch of years. And when they come,
They show compassion for me, boy, with words
And in their pity give me food or clothes.
But there is one thing, when I mention it,

No one consents to do—to take me home
In safety; but, unhappy that I am,
In this my tenth year I am perishing
From hunger and misfortune while I feed
That greedy sore of mine. Such things, my boy,
The sons of Atreus and that man of might,
Odysseus, have done to me. May the gods
Who hold Olympus grant them in return
Sometime to suffer just such things as these.

The leader of the chorus speaks up and in ambiguous words expresses sympathy for Philoctetes. Neoptolemus is not to be outdone. He declares his hatred for Agamemnon and Menelaus and for Odysseus; and when Philoctetes asks him why, explains at some length. After his father Achilles had been slain by Apollo, he says, Odysseus and Phoenix came to Scyros and told him that now that his father was dead Troy could not be taken without his assistance. He had readily consented to go with them, for he wished to see his father's body before its burial. Philoctetes had not heard of the death of Achilles, and expresses his sorrow. Neoptolemus continues with his story. When he reached Troy he had wept for his father and then asked for his arms, but was told that they had been given to Odysseus. No heed was paid to his remonstrances and in anger he had left Troy and started for home. At the conclusion of this story the chorus of sailors, who are in the plot, address the great Mother Goddess of the land whom they pretend they had asked for vengeance in behalf of their youthful leader.

Philoctetes is completely deceived by this tale, confirmed as it seems to be by the sailors, but he expresses surprise that Ajax should have permitted the injustice. Ajax, he is told, is dead, and so are the other heroes about whom he inquires; and he comments rather bitterly that the gods seem to take a peculiar pleasure in sending the good to Hades and in sparing the bad.

Neoptolemus now bids Philoctetes farewell, for he must be on his way. But the latter makes a piteous appeal to take him, too

—anywhere away from the island, so that he may have a chance to get home. The sailors intercede for him, and Neoptolemus, after warning them not to change their minds when they have him on board, agrees to take him along. Philoctetes is overjoyed and is about to show under what dreadful conditions he has been living in the cave when two men are seen approaching, a sailor from the ship and a stranger. The latter, who is the man Odysseus had promised to send, enters in the guise of a merchant. He pretends that he had put into Lemnos by chance, and finding that Neoptolemus was there had brought him news from Troy in the hope of receiving a reward. When questioned he explains that Phoenix and the sons of Theseus have set out in pursuit of Neoptolemus; and, furthermore, that Odysseus had sworn to bring back Philoctetes from Lemnos when the army had learned that Troy could not be taken without his aid.

The disguised merchant now leaves, and Philoctetes, alarmed at his news, begs Neoptolemus to sail at once, for he will never go to Troy willingly. Neoptolemus assents, though the wind is not favorable. Philoctetes wishes to go into the cave first in order to get an herb which he used to relieve the pain in his foot, and to pick up any of his arrows which he may have dropped. This leads Neoptolemus to ask if the bow which he is carrying is the famous one and, when assured that it is, expresses the desire to handle it. Philoctetes is willing, and the scene comes to an end as the two enter the cave.

The chorus now come forward for their formal song and dance. They moralize on the unhappy life of Philoctetes. No man they can think of except Ixion has suffered so dreadfully. Then, as they see Philoctetes coming from the cave, they add that rescue has come at last and he will return to his Malian home.

As Neoptolemus and Philoctetes reënter the latter is suddenly seized with a violent attack of pain. The agony is so excruciating that he shrieks and begs Neoptolemus to cut off his foot with his sword. He gives him his precious bow, cautioning him to let no one have it. He would gladly die if he only could, and wishes he might be cast into the fire of the volcano. At length the attack becomes less violent, a stream of blood bursts from his foot, and the afflicted man falls asleep from sheer exhaustion; but before that he exacts a promise from Neoptolemus to remain by him.

A lyric passage follows consisting of strophe, antistrophe, and epode sung by the chorus, the strophe and antistrophe being separated by four dactylic hexameter lines chanted by Neoptolemus. It begins with an address to Sleep (ll. 827 ff.):

> Sleep who knowest no pain, Sleep who art free from care,
> Come for us now with a favoring breeze,
> Come bringing happiness, happiness, lord.
> Cast on his eyes such a glimmering light
> As is spread over them now.
> Come, come thou healer for me.

Then they hint that it is well to make the most of their opportunity and get away while Philoctetes is still asleep; but Neoptolemus is unwilling. He says (ll. 839 ff.):

> Nothing he hears; but I see that in vain we have captured his weapon,
> Made ourselves sure of his bow, if we sail on our voyage without him.
> His is the crown, and it's he that the god gave orders to bring back.
> Boasting a task unfinished with fraud is foul and disgraceful.

The chorus warn him to speak quietly so as not to arouse the sleeper, and they urge him more strongly to take the bow and be gone.

Philoctetes now opens his eyes and raises his head. He sees Neoptolemus and his sailors and expresses his gratitude to them. He realizes the offensive nature of his affliction, but finds that the son of Achilles has a noble character in keeping with his birth. He asks to be helped up now that he has a temporary relief from pain, so that when he has somewhat recovered they may go to the ship. Neoptolemus assents and the afflicted man is set on his feet. But at this moment his conscience gets the better of Neoptolemus and he falters. He knows he is doing a disreputable deed, wholly contrary to his real nature, and, when Philoctetes observes his hesitation, tells him plainly that he is going to take him to Troy. The sick man sees that he has been tricked and demands back his bow; and then in an agony of despair takes Neoptolemus to task for the disgraceful part he has played. He says (ll. 927–962):

Thou fire, thou utter monster, most abhorred
Contriver of this dreadful villainy,
What things hast thou done to me, what deceits
Hast thou engaged in! Art thou not ashamed
When thou dost look on me, thy suppliant,
The one who begged thy aid, thou wretched man?
When thou didst take away from me my bow
Thou didst deprive me of my means of life.
I beg thee, I beseech thee, give it back.
Now by thy fathers' gods, my boy, do not
Thus rob me of my life. Oh, wretched me!
He does not any longer speak to me
But looks as though he would not let it go.
Oh! harbors, headlands, Oh! ye jagged rocks,
And companies of mountain-roving beasts,
To ye I utter my laments, for ye
Are here as is your wont, and no one else
I know to whom to speak; such are the deeds
Achilles' son has done me. Though he swore
That he would take me home, he takes me now
To Troy; and though he pledged me his right hand,
He took my sacred bow which once belonged
To Heracles, the son of Zeus, and he
Desires to show it to those Argive men.
As if he'd captured a strong man by force
He leads me hence and does not recognize
That he is slaying a dead man—mere smoke
And shadow, just a ghost. If I had had

My strength he never would have captured me;
Nor would he even as I am except
By guile. But now, ill-fated that I am,
I've been deceived. What, then, ought I to do?
Come, give it back; be thine own self again.
What dost thou say? Art silent? Then I die,
Ill-fated. Oh! ye outlines of the rock
With double entrance ways, I now come back,
Stripped of my arms, with no means of support,
To ye again. And I shall waste away
Alone, in this cave, for no winged bird
Nor mountain-roving beast shall I destroy
With those famed arrows, but myself, alas!
Shall die and furnish food to those by whom
I fed myself; and they that I did hunt
Will now hunt me. And I, unhappy man,
Shall in requital pay for blood with blood.
And this from one who seemed to know no wrong!
Now may'st thou perish—though not yet, until
I learn if thou wilt change thy mind again.
If thou wilt not, then may'st thou die accursed.

The sailors are deeply moved by the words of Philoctetes, who urges Neoptolemus still further when he sees the young man wavering in his purpose. But at this moment Odysseus appears and demands the bow. Philoctetes sees that he is lost and threatens to kill himself by leaping from the cliffs rather than go with Odysseus; but the latter quickly orders his men to seize him. Philoctetes is now in despair. He laments his helpless condition and calls down the vengeance of the gods on Odysseus and those with him. Odysseus is not disturbed. He sees no need of defending his actions and, since he has the bow, tells the sailors to release the man and leave him where he is. Philoctetes appeals to Neoptolemus and to the sailors who are ordered to remain with him until the ship is ready to sail. Neoptolemus and Odysseus then leave the stage.

A long lyric dialogue follows between Philoctetes and the

chorus. The former sees nothing before him but misery and death, while the chorus try to convince him that it is for his advantage to go with them to Troy. Neoptolemus and Odysseus are seen approaching and a moment later enter in conversation. Odysseus addresses his companion (ll. 1222 ff.):

ODYSSEUS

Wilt thou not tell me why thou goest back
Along this path and that so hastily?

NEOPTOLEMUS

That I may right the wrong that I have done.

ODYSSEUS

A dread thing thou dost say. What was the wrong?

NEOPTOLEMUS

In which obeying thee and all the host—

ODYSSEUS

Thou didst what deed that was not fitting thee?

NEOPTOLEMUS

By shameful wiles and tricks I caught a man.

ODYSSEUS

What man? Ah me! Thou dost not plan some wrong?

NEOPTOLEMUS

No wrong; but to the son of Poas here—

ODYSSEUS

What wilt thou do? A fear steals over me.

NEOPTOLEMUS

From whom I took the bow I will again—

ODYSSEUS

Oh Zeus! what wilt thou say? Not give it back?

NEOPTOLEMUS

Unjustly did I win it, and with shame.

ODYSSEUS

Now by the gods! dost thou say this in jest?

NEOPTOLEMUS

If jesting is to speak the truth I do.

ODYSSEUS

What dost thou say, Achilles' son; what word?

NEOPTOLEMUS

Must I repeat the same words twice or thrice?

ODYSSEUS

I wish I had not heard them even once.

NEOPTOLEMUS

Thou hast the whole tale now, be well assured.

ODYSSEUS

There is some one who will prevent thy deed.

NEOPTOLEMUS

What dost thou say? What man will hinder me?

ODYSSEUS

The whole Achaean army and myself.

NEOPTOLEMUS

Wise though thou art thou sayest nothing wise.

ODYSSEUS

Thou dost not say nor wish to do things wise.

NEOPTOLEMUS

If they are just then they surpass what's wise.

ODYSSEUS

How is it just to give back that which thou
Didst gain by plans of mine?

NEOPTOLEMUS

I shall attempt
To make up for the shameful wrong I did.

ODYSSEUS

Dost thou not fear the army doing this?

NEOPTOLEMUS

With right on my side I have not thy fear.

ODYSSEUS

* * * * * * * * [1]

NEOPTOLEMUS

I yield not to thy hand in what I do.

ODYSSEUS

Then we shall not fight Trojans, but fight thee.

NEOPTOLEMUS

Let what the future has in store come on.

ODYSSEUS

Dost thou see my right hand rest on my sword?

NEOPTOLEMUS

Thou shalt see mine do that same thing at once.

[1] The reply of Odysseus is lost.

ODYSSEUS

I will, then, leave thee, and go tell these things
To all the army which will punish thee.

NEOPTOLEMUS

Thou hast become discreet; and if thou art
As wise in future time perhaps thou wilt
Keep thy foot out of trouble. But do thou, (*Exit Odysseus*)
I speak to Philoctetes, Poas' son,
Come forth and leave thy shelter in the rocks.

PHILOCTETES (*from within the cave*)

What noisy cries arise beside my cave?
Why do ye call me out? What do ye want? (*He looks out*)
Ah me! an evil thing! It cannot be
That ye are present adding woes to woes.

NEOPTOLEMUS

Be of good cheer and hear the words I bring.

PHILOCTETES

I am afraid. Thou spakest fair before
And I fared ill, persuaded by thy words.

NEOPTOLEMUS

Is it not possible to change one's mind?

PHILOCTETES

Such was thy speech when thou didst steal my bow,
Persuasive, but with ruin underneath.

NEOPTOLEMUS

But not so now. I wish to hear from thee
If thy determination is to stay
Or sail with us.

PHILOCTETES

Stop there! Say nothing more,
For all thou sayest will be said in vain.

NEOPTOLEMUS

Does it seem so?

PHILOCTETES

Aye, more than I can tell.

NEOPTOLEMUS

I wish I had convinced thee with my words.
But if I speak untimely I am done.

PHILOCTETES

Thou wilt say all in vain. Thou wilt not win
My mind to friendly thoughts, since by a trick
Thou didst deprive me of my means of life;
And then thou comest here with thy advice,
Most hateful son of a most noble sire.
Perdition take ye—the Atridae first,
And then Laertes' son and thee!

NEOPTOLEMUS

Curse not;
But rather take these weapons from my hand.

PHILOCTETES

What dost thou say? Am I tricked once again?

NEOPTOLEMUS

Nay, by the sanctity of holy Zeus
Most high, I swear.

PHILOCTETES

If thou dost speak the truth
Thou sayest what is dearest to my heart.

NEOPTOLEMUS (*holding out the bow*)

My act shall make this clear. Stretch forth thy hand
And make thyself the master of thy arms.

ODYSSEUS (*who has been watching hastens forward*)

But I forbid, the gods be witnesses,
I speak for the Atridae and the host.

PHILOCTETES

My son, whose voice was that? It cannot be
That I have heard Odysseus.

ODYSSEUS

Rest assured.
And what is more, thou seest him close by
Who will convey thee to the plains of Troy
By force, no matter if Achilles' son
Is willing or is not.

PHILOCTETES

Thou sayest this
To thy misfortune if this shaft goes straight. (*He aims the bow*)

NEOPTOLEMUS (*grasping his arm*)

Ah! Do not shoot the arrow, by the gods!

PHILOCTETES

Let go my hand, I beg thee, dearest boy.

NEOPTOLEMUS

I will not let thee go.

PHILOCTETES

Alas! Why hast
Thou hindered me from slaying with my bow
A hateful enemy?

NEOPTOLEMUS

It is not well
For me, nor yet for thee, to do this thing.

PHILOCTETES (*as Odysseus withdraws*)

But know so much at least, the leaders of
The army, lying heralds of the Greeks,
Are cowards with the spear, though bold in words.

NEOPTOLEMUS

Ah well! Thou hast the bow and thou canst not
Have anger towards myself, nor even blame.

PHILOCTETES

I do agree; and thou hast shown, my boy,
Thy native stock, not sprung from Sisyphus[1]
But from Achilles who, when still alive,
Had fairest fame, as now among the dead.

Neoptolemus is pleased at these words, but he takes Philoctetes to task for his attitude towards the army. The only cure for his affliction is to go to Troy which, as Helenus prophesied, is doomed to be taken with the help of the arrows of Heracles. But Philoctetes is not to be persuaded. He cannot forget what he has been made to suffer by the leaders of the army, and he can see only further ill-treatment at their hands if he goes to Troy. He asks Neoptolemus to keep his word and take him home. Neoptolemus, seeing that he cannot influence him, agrees and they start for the ship.

At this moment Heracles is made to appear on high as the *deus ex machina*. He explains that he has won immortality and

[1] Sophocles follows the version of the story that makes Odysseus really the son of Sisyphus. Cf. l. 417.

fame after his life of toil, and he has come to make known the will of Zeus. He directs Philoctetes to go to Troy, and promises to send Asclepius to heal the sore on his leg; for he is destined to slay Paris with one of his arrows, and he will sack Troy and return home with honor and spoil. He must, however, reverence the gods. Philoctetes recognizes the hero and promises to obey, as does Neoptolemus. The vision fades away. Philoctetes bids farewell to the place where he had spent so many wretched years. The sailors urge the whole company to start after praying to the sea nymphs for a safe return; and thus the play ends.

The *Philoctetes* is a well-constructed tragedy with a plot which moves steadily forward from the beginning. It will be noticed at once that there is no female character in it, and in this respect it differs from the other extant tragedies of Sophocles; but there is none in the traditional story which the dramatist was following. What he has undertaken to do is to set forth the character of two men under certain conditions, and in this he is most successful. In Philoctetes he has given us a thoroughly natural and human character consistently represented throughout. He is a man of determined will tortured not only by the pain of his physical injury, but tortured still more and embittered by his sense of the injustice which he has suffered at the hands of those who should have befriended him. The poet makes no attempt to minimize the disgusting nature of his wound, but rather impresses his hearers with the horror of it. Philoctetes was one of the great leaders of the expedition. He had as much right to expect as his just due the coöperation and help of the other Achaean chiefs in his affliction as Agamemnon or any of the rest of them. The fact that he did not get it burns him to the very soul. If because of the pain from the sore on his leg he weakens temporarily, he does what any other man would do under the circumstances. Philoctetes is not an Oedipus; but he has a strong personality, and in depicting him Sophocles has shown how truly he understood man. A weaker character would have yielded quickly to the overwhelming misfortunes which had come upon him. Philoctetes does not do so. He maintains to the end his unyielding determination to resist his enemies, and it is only through the supernatural that he is finally induced to bow to the inevitable. On the other hand he is not wholly lost to better thoughts, as is shown by his expressions of joy when he thinks he is to be taken home (ll. 530 ff.); and by his gratitude to Neoptolemus when he recovers from his fainting fit (ll. 867 ff.).

With Neoptolemus the problem is different, but here, too, the great dramatist has given us a natural and in some respects a lovable character. The young warrior tries to do what he is told to do by his elders and superiors; but the essential nobility of his nature rebels at his own acts and forces him to show the character that he really is. It would have been impossible for the Neoptolemus of Sophocles to continue with the treachery into which he had been enticed and be a true son of Achilles. He, too, is thoroughly human.

Odysseus is the traditional Odysseus of the tragic stage, not the Homeric hero. He is the villain of the play, utterly unscrupulous, one for whom the end justifies the means. He has no pity for Philoctetes. His object is to capture Troy, and to accomplish that he must have the bow and arrows of Heracles. It is immaterial to him by what device he acquires them.

There is nothing particularly noteworthy about the other speaking characters. The "Merchant" is introduced for the purpose of misleading Philoctetes and allaying any suspicion which he might harbor against Neoptolemus. He fills his rôle satisfactorily.

Heracles appears as the typical *deus ex machina*. Here, as is generally agreed, Sophocles was influenced by Euripides. The spectacular effect of a divinity appearing on high had been repeatedly demonstrated by the younger dramatist; and Sophocles evidently felt that he might well avail himself of a practice which had become popular and which pleased the audience in the theatre.

The duty of the chorus of sailors is set forth early (ll. 144 ff.). They are to assist their master Neoptolemus in the rôle he is to play. They thus have a definite part in the development of the plot. In representing them as Greek sailors Sophocles differed from both Aeschylus and Euripides, each of whom made the chorus in his *Philoctetes* to consist of Lemnians. This we know from Dion Chrysostom[1] who has left us a discussion of the three plays. But a chorus of Lemnians would have been out of place in the *Philoctetes* of Sophocles in which the barren and deserted nature of the place where the scene is laid is emphasized. They perform the task assigned to them satisfactorily.

[1] Dion Chrysostom, *Or.* LII, 7 *ἄμφω γὰρ* (i.e. Aeschylus and Euripides) *ἐκ τῶν Λημνίων ἐποίησαν τὸν χορόν*. For the *Philoctetes* of Euripides see Bates, *Euripides*, pp. 278 ff.

Chapter V

THE LOST PLAYS

We have already seen that Suidas in his brief notice of the poet says that he wrote 123 plays or, according to some authorities, more; and that the anonymous writer of the *Life* which has come down to modern times quotes Aristophanes of Byzantium as authority for the statement that there were 130 plays current under the name of Sophocles, but that seventeen of them were spurious. In addition to the seven extant dramas, fragments of at least 109 others are actually preserved. These are discussed in the pages which follow under 107 headings. It has seemed advisable to treat together the two tragedies entitled *Athamas* as *Athamas A* and *B*, and similarly *Phineus A* and *B*, and *Tyro A* and *B*; and likewise under one heading the three plays entitled *Thyestes*. There has also been included what may be said for a possible *Oeneus*.[1]

In general the fragments are short, sometimes consisting of single words quoted either because they are rare or because of some peculiarity in the meaning given to them. As a consequence it is often impossible to show step by step how the plot of a play developed; but the general outlines can usually be determined, for the stories upon which the plots were based are nearly all known. Like Aeschylus, Sophocles made extensive use of the poems of the Trojan Cycle as sources, so that he might well have said with the older poet that his tragedies were "slices of meat from the great banquets of Homer."[2] But he also drew widely from the other epic poems and from various local tales as we have already seen. In fact his knowledge of the legendary

[1] For other doubtful plays see p. 7, n. 3.

[2] Athenaeus, VIII, p. 347e . . . *τοῦ καλοῦ καὶ λαμπροῦ Αἰσχύλου, ὃς τὰς αὑτοῦ τραγῳδίας τεμάχη εἶναι ἔλεγεν τῶν Ὁμήρου μεγάλων δείπνων.*

history of Greece was very extensive, and there were few of the mythological stories current in his day that he did not use at one time or another. A study of these fragments, therefore, short as they are, is of great importance for anyone who would have a better appreciation of the poet's genius and the extent of his dramatic work than can be obtained from the seven extant masterpieces.

The *Ichneutae* papyrus[1] furnishes a notable exception to the brevity of the fragments, for some four hundred lines of it can be restored. Unfortunately most of the papyrus fragments of Sophocles are neither as long nor as numerous as those of Euripides, but there is no good reason to believe that the sands of Egypt have given us all the Greek writing concealed beneath their surface.

In addition to the fragments which can be definitely assigned to known dramas there are 386 miscellaneous quotations from Sophocles in the literature where the names of the plays from which they were taken are not preserved. It has not seemed necessary to give an account of them. The known plays are discussed in alphabetical order.

I

The Acrisius

THERE are seventeen fragments of the *Acrisius* extant, all of them short. The longest consists of four lines, four are of two lines each, three of single lines, three of two words, and six of single words.[2] Unfortunately no one of them gives a clue as to the part of the story with which the play dealt. Some of the older commentators (e.g., Jacobs and Welcker and more recently Zielinski) thought that the *Acrisius* was identical with the *Danaë*,[3]

[1] See p. 211.

[2] Pearson, *Fragments of Sophocles*, I, pp. 38 ff.; Welcker, *Die griechischen Tragödien*, I, pp. 348 f.

[3] For the *Danaë* see p. 192.

but that is not likely, as Pearson points out. Furthermore there are six fragments quoted from the *Danaë*, though one of these (Frag. 165) may possibly have come from the *Danaë* of Euripides, as the name of Sophocles is not actually mentioned with it. It is found in a scholium on line 1 of the *Ajax*. It has also been argued that the *Acrisius* was identical with the *Larisaeans*[1] which had to do with the latter part of the story of Acrisius and Danaë. In that play Acrisius, who had fled to Larisa to escape death at the hands of Perseus as foretold by the oracle, was hit by a discus thrown by Perseus in an athletic contest and died as a result of his injury. But there is no satisfactory evidence for regarding the two titles as belonging to one tragedy.

It is not unlikely that the *Acrisius* had to do with the early part of the Danaë story in which the death of Acrisius at the hands of a son who should be born to Danaë was foretold, and that the plot set forth the means taken by him to prevent this. Fragments 66 and 67 seem to have been spoken by Acrisius to his daughter in justification of his shutting her up in a bronze-walled room. How the plot was developed it is impossible to say. It may have reached a climax with the birth of Perseus and his condemnation to be exposed with his mother. The plot would then apparently cover part of the same ground as the *Danaë*. It is not at all likely, however, that the poet would use the same incidents in two different tragedies, but what means he took to avoid overlapping cannot be told.

II

The Aegeus

THERE are seven fragments of the *Aegeus* extant, amounting altogether to about seventeen lines.[2] The longest consists of six and a half lines; one has three lines, two a line and a half, two

[1] See p. 229.

[2] Pearson, *op. cit.*, I, pp. 15 ff.; Welcker, *op. cit.*, I, pp. 393 ff.

one line and one two words. This is rather meager material from which to recover the plot of the tragedy; but enough can be made out to show that the story of the journey of the young Theseus from Troezen to Athens in search of his father and his adventures on the way was included in it. One fragment refers to the capture of the Marathonian bull, as Photius who quotes it explains. It seems likely that the plot resembled that of the *Aegeus* of Euripides.[1] It may have been something like this: The youthful Theseus comes to Athens bringing with him the sword and sandals deposited under the rock by his father Aegeus. He is probably plotted against by Medea who is living with Aegeus, made to perform certain feats, including the capture of the Marathonian bull, and then at the critical moment is recognized by Aegeus, perhaps by means of the sword, as in Euripides.

III

The Aegisthus

Two doubtful fragments, one of two words and the other of one, are assigned by Pearson with hesitation to the *Aegisthus* of Sophocles.[2] There is no other evidence for a play with this title by him. Aegisthus as the paramour of Clytaemnestra was one of the best-known characters of the tragic stage. The Greek poets, however, do not seem to have made him the central figure in any of their tragedies, but to have given him a secondary position. Hence it is not surprising that no tragedy entitled *Aegisthus*, with the possible exception of this one, is known in Greek literature. On the Roman stage Livius Andronicus and Attius are both said to have produced plays with this title.[3] If Sophocles did write an *Aegisthus* nothing can be inferred from the two fragments as to its plot. Aegisthus could hardly have been made the hero in a tragedy leading up to the murder of Agamemnon.

[1] See Bates, *Euripides*, p. 204.
[2] Pearson, *op. cit.*, I, pp. 21 f.
[3] See Ribbeck, *op. cit.* I, pp. 1 f. and 138 f.

IV

The Ajax the Locrian

BESIDES his extant play dealing with the madness of Ajax the son of Telamon, Sophocles wrote another tragedy, *Ajax the Locrian*, in which the son of Oïleus was the hero. Eight small fragments of this play are preserved, but they are without significance for the plot.[1] How Sophocles handled his material and what part of the story of Ajax he included in his tragedy can only be conjectured. The one outstanding incident in the story of the lesser Ajax as we know it from various sources is his sacrilegious attack upon Cassandra, whom he dragged away from the image of Athena. The story was told in the *Iliupersis* and was a common subject with the Greek vase-painters.[2] Proclus in his summary of the *Iliupersis* (p. 239, 30, ed. Westphal) states further that the Greeks, angered at the offense of Ajax, wished to stone him to death, but that he took refuge at the altar of Athena and so was saved from the danger that threatened him. In the great painting of Polygnotus in the Lesche of the Cnidians at Delphi depicting scenes after the fall of Troy, Ajax was represented standing beside an altar and taking an oath in regard to Cassandra.[3] So, too, in the painting by Polygnotus in the Stoa Poecile at Athens he was depicted before the Greek chiefs to answer for his sacrilegious act.[4] Presumably, then, this great crime of Ajax formed the background for the tragedy.[5] In the *Odyssey* (IV, 499 ff.) there is an account of his death by shipwreck. It is possible that the plot of the tragedy centered around the trial and acquittal of Ajax. In that case the story

[1] Pearson, *op. cit.*, I, pp. 8 ff.; Welcker, *op. cit.*, I, pp. 161 ff.

[2] See Reinach, *Répertoire des Vases*, I, pp. 221, 338, 365, 366, 367, 380, 496; II, p. 226.

[3] See Pausanias, X, 26, 3 and the reconstruction of the painting by Robert, *Hallisches Winckelmannsprogramm*, 1893.

[4] Pausanias, I, 15, 2.

[5] For Zielinski's theory that the *Ajax the Locrian* and the *Captives* are different titles for the same play see p. 186.

of his death might be foretold, perhaps by Athena as *deus ex machina*.

Of the eight fragments of the play extant four consist of single lines, two of single words, one of two lines and one of a line and a half.

V

The Alcmaeon

THE *Alcmaeon*[1] is represented today by three scanty fragments, one consisting of a line and a half and the others of single words.[2] From the first of these (Frag. 108) we can infer that the hero was still afflicted with madness. There has been much discussion about the play as well as about the *Epigoni* and the *Eriphyle*, which have to do with other parts of the story. Pearson may well be right in his opinion that the *Alcmaeon* was based on the events which occurred after the death of Eriphyle, but while Alcmaeon was still mad. Hence it is likely that it covered much the same ground as the *Alcmaeon at Psophis* of Euripides.

After Alcmaeon had slain his mother to avenge the death of his father Amphiaraus, he became insane and fled to Psophis in Arcadia where he married Alphesiboea, daughter of the king, Phegeus. He gave his bride the famous necklace of Harmonia. Later on, because the land was afflicted with barrenness, the oracle at Delphi directed Alcmaeon, as the cause of the trouble, to go to the newest land which the sea had uncovered since he slew his mother. In that way alone could he escape the avenging fury of Eriphyle. He, therefore, went to the alluvial land formed by the river Achelous and married Callirrhoë, the daughter of the river god. She had heard of the necklace and robe of Harmonia, and demanded that Alcmaeon obtain them for her. He

[1] For the spelling of the name see Bates, *Euripides*, p. 207, n. 3; and Meisterhans, *Grammatik der Attisch. Inschrift.* 3d ed. p. 35, 11.

[2] Pearson, *op. cit.*, I, pp. 68 ff.; 129 ff.; Welcker, *op. cit.*, I, pp. 278 ff.

returned to Psophis to recover them from his former wife; but Phegeus learned of his purpose and ordered his sons to waylay and kill him. This they did. Such, then, was the story which Euripides used in his *Alcmaeon at Psophis* and presumably Sophocles in his *Alcmaeon.*

The Alcmaeon story was one of the most famous in Greek mythology, and it was used repeatedly by the Greek tragic poets. No fewer than eight *Alcmaeons* are known by title.[1] The tragedy of Sophocles does not seem to have enjoyed the same fame as his *Epigoni.*[2]

VI

The Aleadae

The *Aleadae* is represented today by fifteen fragments with a total of about thirty-six lines.[3] One fragment (No. 88) consists of twelve lines and is in praise of wealth. Very little can be inferred in regard to the plot and the way in which it was developed; but it is clear that it had to do with that part of the Telephus story in which the hero slew his mother's brothers. So much may be inferred from the title; the rest must be left to conjecture.

According to Alcidamas,[4] Aleos, king of Tegea, received an oracle that if his daughter Auge had a son his own sons would be killed by him. He, therefore, made her priestess of Athena, forbidding her marriage under pain of death. But Heracles met her secretly, and when Aleos discovered that she was about to become a mother he gave her to Nauplius, king of Euboea, to drown. On Mount Parthenion Auge gave birth to Telephus, and Nauplius, instead of following his instructions, sold her and her baby to Teuthras, king of Mysia, who married her and

[1] See Bates, *Euripides*, p. 208, n. 1.

[2] See p. 195.

[3] Pearson, *op. cit.*, I, pp. 46 ff.; Welcker, *op. cit.*, I, pp. 406 ff.

[4] *Odysseus*, 13–16.

adopted her son. One version of the story relates that Telephus was exposed on Mount Parthenion and suckled by a hind, and this incident was mentioned by Sophocles in the *Aleadae*, as may be inferred from Fragment 89.[1] Euripides in his *Auge* followed another version according to which Auge and her baby were put into a chest and cast into the sea.[2] But Telephus reached Mysia, either as an infant or as a young man, and was there when the Greeks on their way to Troy landed and ravaged the country. He fought with them and was wounded by Achilles. His wound did not heal, and an oracle declared that it could be cured only by the spear which caused the wound. He, therefore, set out in disguise for Argos. His various adventures and the way in which his cure was brought about formed the plot of the *Telephus* of Euripides,[3] and apparently of the *Muster of the Achaeans* of Sophocles.[4] Where in this story there was an opportunity for Telephus to slay his uncles is not clear. If Sophocles followed the version that brought Telephus to Mysia after he had grown to manhood, as seems likely, it is possible that the death of his uncles at his hands may have been the reason for his departure from Greece.[5] At the same time the possibility cannot be excluded that he slew them at the time of the invasion of Mysia by the Greeks; or, perhaps, on his journey in disguise to Argos.

The discovery of an inscription in 1929 between the towns of Voulas and Vari, in the ancient deme of Halae Aexonides,[6] suggests interesting possibilities in this connection. It is cut on a circular base which presumably once supported a statue, and

[1] *νομὰς δέ τις κεροῦσσ' ἀπ' ὀρθίων πάγων*
καθεῖρπεν ἔλαφος . . . . . .
ἄρασα μύξας . . καὶ κερασφόρους
στόρθυγγας εἶρφ' ἕκηλος

[2] See Bates, *Euripides*, p. 228.

[3] The first fifteen and one half lines of this tragedy have been recovered from a papyrus in Milan. See *Aegyptus*, 1935, pp. 239 ff.

[4] See p. 236.

[5] So Arvanitopoulos, *Polemon*, I, 1929, pp. 182 ff.

[6] See M. Fromhold-Treu, *Hermes*, LXIX, p. 324.

records victories of two choregi with various plays, both tragedies and comedies. It was first published by A. A. Palaios in *Polemon* (I, 1929, pp. 161 ff.).[1] The stone is broken at the top and at the bottom, but in the last line occurs the statement that a certain Epichares was the victorious choregus when Sophocles brought out his *Telepheia.* We have no other mention of a *Telepheia* by Sophocles, but the word can hardly mean anything else than a trilogy on the story of Telephus, just as the *Oresteia* of Aeschylus is a trilogy dealing with the Orestes story.[2] A single play with such a title is unthinkable. It is known from a statement of Suidas[3] that Sophocles at least sometimes competed with trilogies in which the different plays were not related; but it is in the highest degree probable that in his earlier tragedies he followed the practice of Aeschylus in composing three tragedies on one subject.

The *Aleadae* may well have been the first play of this *Telepheia.* The second play would probably be the *Mysians,* of which scanty fragments remain. The third play was probably the *Muster of the Achaeans* (Ἀχαιῶν Σύλλογος).[4] Arvanitopoulos[5] thinks a *Telephus* was the third play and a *Telephus Sphaltes* the satyr drama. There is but one reference to a *Telephus* by Sophocles, and that is in the *Lexicon* of Hesychius. It is impossible to learn from it whether the play was a tragedy or a satyr drama;

[1] The whole inscription reads:

Ἐ[πιχάρης χορηγῶν ἐνίκα] κωμῳδοῖς
Ἐκφαντίδης ἐδίδασκε Πεῖρας.
Θρασύβολος χορηγῶν ἐνίκα κωμῳδοῖς
Κρατῖνος ἐδίδασκε Βουκόλος.
Θρασύβολος χορη[γ]ῶν ἐνίκα τραγῳδοῖς
Τιμόθεος ἐδίδασκε Ἀλκμέωνα, Ἀλφεσίβο[ιαν
Ἐπιχάρης χ ͻρηγῶν ἐνίκα τραγῳδοῖ[ς
Σοφοκλῆς ἐδίδασκε Τηλέφεια[ν.

[2] In the Hypothesis to the *Seven against Thebes* of Aeschylus there is mention of a tetralogy by Polyphradmon entitled *Lycurgeia.*

[3] S. v. Σοφοκλῆς.

[4] In *Philologus,* XCIII, 1939, A. Szantyr argues that the first play was an *Auge,* entirely unknown, the second the *Aleadae,* and the third the *Mysians.*

[5] *Polemon,* I, 1929, pp. 185 ff.

but the question seems to be settled by the mention of a σατυρικὸν Τήλεφ[[1] by Sophocles in a fragmentary Rhodian inscription. It does not, however, prove the existence of a *Telephus Sphaltes.*

The inscription in which the *Telepheia* is mentioned has been discussed by various writers[2] both from the point of view of its date and the purpose for which it was set up. M. Guarducci's contention[3] that it is to be placed as far back as 420 B.C. and that both Cratinus and Sophocles were alive at the time I find untenable. The forms of the letters indicate a later date, near the end of the fifth or beginning of the fourth century. I should date it for epigraphical reasons about 405 B.C.

The purpose for which the inscription was written can be inferred, though not definitely proved. It seems to have been carved on the base for a statue[4] erected to commemorate the victories of certain choregi with tragedies and comedies. The idea that the plays mentioned were all brought out at one time, either for their first appearance or at a later date, at Aexone or elsewhere, seems very improbable. It is more likely that Epichares and Thrasybulus, citizens of Aexone, had been choregi in Athens in the years when the plays mentioned were brought out and won victories; and that at a later time their relatives or friends, wishing to commemorate their victories, erected a statue in their native town with the inscription recording their successes.

VII

The Aletes

THERE are seven fragments of the *Aletes* with a total of twenty-four lines all preserved by Stobaeus, who is the only author to mention the play. One is of ten lines, three of three lines each,

[1] So read by Kaibel. See p. 211, n. 2.

[2] For a general account of it see A. W. Pickard-Cambridge in Powell, *New Chapters in Greek Literature*, Third Series, pp. 69 ff.

[3] *Rivista di Filologia*, 1930, pp. 202 ff.

[4] *Polemon*, I, 1929, p. 161.

two of two lines, and one a single line.[1] They give little information as to the plot, which had to do with Aletes, the son of Aegisthus and Clytaemnestra. The story upon which it was based is preserved by Hyginus (*Fab.* 122), as was recognized by Welcker long ago. It is this:

A messenger came to Electra with false news telling her that Orestes and his friend Pylades while among the Taurians had been sacrificed to Artemis. When Aletes learned this he determined to seize the sovereignty of Mycenae. Electra then went to Delphi for advice, and the messenger pointed out Iphigenia, who on the same day had arrived at Delphi in company with Orestes, as his slayer. Electra, not knowing who she was, seized a burning brand from the altar to blind her, but was stopped by Orestes. A recognition followed and all returned to Mycenae, where Orestes slew Aletes. Erigone, the sister of Aletes, was saved by Artemis, who made her a priestess in Attica. After the death of Neoptolemus Orestes married Hermione and Pylades, Electra.

This is the tale told by Hyginus. How much of it Sophocles used in his tragedy and how he developed his plot must be left to conjecture. Welcker thought that the *Aletes* should be identified with the *Erigone*, and Ribbeck[2] that the *Agamemnonidae* of Attius and the *Erigone* had the same plot; but for any real knowledge of it we must await the discovery of new fragments.

VIII

The Alexander

NINE fragments of the *Alexander* remain, no one of them longer than a single line and six consisting of single words.[3] One line (Frag. 93) refers to a herdsman defeating men from the city; and

[1] Pearson, *op. cit.*, I, pp. 62 ff.; Welcker, *op. cit.*, I, pp. 215 ff.
[2] *Op. cit.*, I, p. 141.
[3] Pearson, *op. cit.*, I, pp. 57 ff.; Welcker, *op. cit.*, I, p. 100.

on the strength of that the plot has been supposed to have been similar to that of the *Alexander* of Euripides. The story is told by Hyginus (*Fab*. 91) as follows:

Hecuba dreamed that she gave birth to a burning torch from which several serpents came forth. This seemed to indicate that her unborn child would cause the destruction of his country. When, therefore, Alexander (Paris) was born he was given to certain attendants to put to death, but they left him to die in a certain spot where herdsmen found him. They named him Paris and brought him up. When he had grown to manhood among the herdsmen, slaves of Priam appeared one day and carried off a favorite bull of his to be a prize at certain funeral games to be held in honor of the dead child Alexander. Paris in anger went to the city, entered the contest and won the bull, defeating his own brothers. Deïphobus in a rage tried to kill him, but he took refuge at the altar of Zeus Herceus and was declared by Cassandra to be Alexander, long supposed to be dead. Priam then identified him and took him to the palace.

So much for Hyginus. How far Sophocles followed this story and in what respects his plot differed from that of the *Alexander* of Euripides[1] we have no means of knowing. There are about fifty lines of the latter play preserved and this may, perhaps, be regarded as evidence that it was the more popular of the two. Ennius seems to have followed Euripides in his *Alexander*.[2]

IX

The Amphiaraus

Amphiaraus was used as a title for both tragedies and comedies by ancient dramatists and, as it is distinctly stated, by Sophocles for a satyr drama. Eight fragments of it are preserved of which five are single words and the others single lines.[3] Not one of

[1] Bates, *Euripides*, pp. 213 ff.
[2] Ribbeck, *op. cit.*, I, pp. 19 ff.
[3] Pearson, *op. cit.*, I, pp. 72 ff.

them gives a hint as to what part of the story of Amphiaraus was used by the poet in this play. Pearson suggests that an incident related by Hyginus (*Fab.* 73) may have been the subject. It is this: Amphiaraus, knowing that he would not come back from Thebes alive, hid himself with the help of Eriphyle. She, however, was bribed by Adrastus and betrayed him. Perhaps a search for Amphiaraus, in which somehow the satyrs had a part, was introduced and made ridiculous. But neither this, nor another suggestion that the plot had to do with the death of Opheltes and the founding of the Nemean Games seems especially suitable for a satyr drama. With such scanty evidence available no plausible conjecture can be brought forward.

X

The Amphitryon

THE *Amphitryon* is known from three quotations, one of a line and a half and two of one word each.[1] These give no hint as to the part of the story which Sophocles used for his plot. The most familiar incident in the history of Amphitryon and his wife Alcmena is the visit of Zeus to the latter in the guise of her husband; but this could hardly have been a suitable subject for tragedy. The attempted punishment of Alcmena by Amphitryon for her apparent unfaithfulness played an important part in the *Alcmena* of Euripides;[2] but there is no evidence that this was even mentioned by Sophocles. Perhaps one might conjecture that the play had to do with the accidental killing of Electryon by Amphitryon, his subsequent adventures, and death in battle. There is no evidence that the *Amphitryon* was a satyr drama, as has sometimes been imagined.

[1] Pearson, *op. cit.*, I, pp. 76 ff.; Welcker, *op. cit.*, I, pp. 371 ff.
[2] See Bates, *Euripides*, pp. 211 ff.

XI

The Amycus

Two lines are all that remain today of the satyr drama *Amycus*,[1] but the story upon which the plot was based is related by several authors. Thus Apollonius Rhodius gives it at considerable length in the beginning of the second book of his *Argonautica*, and it is told more briefly by Apollodorus[2] and by Hyginus.[3] There are some slight differences in the details, but in general it is this:

After the Argonauts left Mysia they came to the land of the Bebrycians in Bithynia where Amycus, the king, compelled all strangers who landed there to box with him. Being the son of Poseidon he was very powerful and had no difficulty in killing his opponents. Following his usual custom he challenged anybody on the Argo to a boxing match. Pollux accepted the challenge and killed him with a blow on the side of the head, as Apollonius says. Theocritus,[4] however, says that Pollux spared his life, but made him swear that he would not molest strangers in the future. As Pearson points out, this would be a more suitable ending for a satyr drama.

It is easy to see the possibilities for fun in a plot based upon such a tale, for the satyrs must have been in the service of Amycus and manifested a lively interest in the contest. There is, however, no hint of such a thing in the narrative of Apollonius.

[1] Pearson, *op. cit.*, I, pp. 71 ff.

[2] *Bibl.* I, 9, 20. For a full list of references see Frazer, *Apollodorus*, Vol. I, p. 102, n. 2.

[3] *Fab.* 17.

[4] *Idyls*, XXII, 131 ff.

XII

The Andromache

IN THE *Etymologicum Magnum*[1] the word *παρασάγγης* is quoted as being found in the *Andromache* of Sophocles. There is no other quotation from the play. This word is, however, mentioned as being found in the *Shepherds*,[2] in which play Andromache may have been a character. Hence Welcker[3] argued that there was no *Andromache* by Sophocles; and Pearson[4] is inclined to agree with him. On the other hand, Andromache was a fitting subject for tragedy, as the extant play of Euripides proves. With the very slender evidence that exists it can neither be affirmed or denied that Sophocles wrote a play with this title.

XIII

The Andromeda

THE *Andromeda* of Sophocles brought before an Athenian audience a familiar tale in Greek mythology, but however well the plot may have been constructed the play seems never to have attained the fame of the *Andromeda* of Euripides.[5] It is known today from eleven scanty fragments of which five consist of single words, two of two words, three of single lines, and one of three lines.[6] The story which has come down to us with several variants[7] is briefly as follows:

Cassiepea, wife of Cepheus king of Ethiopia, had boasted that she, or her daughter (for there are different versions) was more beautiful than the Nereids. This excited the wrath of Poseidon, who sent a flood upon the country and a sea-monster to ravage

[1] S. v. *παρασάγγαι: παρὰ δὲ Σοφοκλεῖ ἐν Ἀνδρομάχῃ ἐπὶ τοῦ ἀγγέλου εἴρηται.*
[2] Frag. 520.
[3] *Op. cit.*, I, pp. 113 ff.
[4] *Op. cit.*, I, p. 78 and II, p. 161, Frag. 520.
[5] See Bates, *Euripides*, pp. 216 ff.
[6] Pearson, *op. cit.*, I, pp. 78 ff.; Welcker, *op. cit.*, I, pp. 349 ff.
[7] For the sources see Frazer, *Apollodorus*, Vol. I, p. 158 n. 3.

it. The oracle was consulted and replied that relief could be had only by exposing the king's daughter to be devoured by the monster. Andromeda was, therefore, fastened to a rock on the seashore to await her end. Perseus, who was returning from his expedition against the Gorgons, arrived at this time and was promised the maiden's hand if he would save the country by slaying the monster. This he did; but the king declined to give him Andromeda, either because she had previously been betrothed to her uncle, named Pheneus or Agenor, or for some other reason. This led to a fight. But Perseus by exposing the head of Medusa, which he was bringing back with him, turned his enemies to stone and departed with Andromeda.

How much of this tale Sophocles used and how he developed his plot we have no way of knowing. The main outlines of the story as given above must have been included in it, and, in fact, there is literary evidence to that effect;[1] but further than this we cannot go. So little, indeed, is known about it that some scholars have thought it may have been a satyr drama.[2] E. Petersen,[3] on the evidence of a red-figured hydria painted before the *Andromeda* of Euripides was written, thinks that Sophocles in the early part of his tragedy emphasized the contrast between the heroic Perseus and the cowardly Phineus. He argues further that in the tragedy Phineus renewed his claim to Andromeda after her rescue and so brought on the quarrel which ended in the triumph of Perseus. This may have been the case, but it cannot be proved. One fact, however, seems to be established, that Sophocles mentioned Cassiepea as being transported to the sky and becoming a constellation.[4]

The Roman poets Ennius and Attius both wrote *Andromedas*

[1] See Eratosthenes, Καταστερισμοί, 16 and 36. (A. Olivier, *Mythographi Graeci*).

[2] See Pearson, *op. cit.*, I, p. 79.

[3] *Jour. of Hel. Stud.* XXIV, 1904, pp. 99 ff. and *Die Attische Tragödie als Bild- und Bühnenkunst*, pp. 610 ff. See also L. Séchan, *Études sur la tragédie grecque*, pp. 148 ff.

[4] See the passages quoted by Pearson.

of which a few lines are preserved.[1] Ennius undoubtedly followed the more famous tragedy of Euripides, and, perhaps, Attius did, too; though Petersen thinks the latter followed Sophocles.

XIV

The Antenoridae

THREE fragments, one consisting of a trimeter line and two of single words are quoted from the *Antenoridae.*[2] From such scanty evidence it is impossible to obtain an idea of the plot, but a hint as to part of it may probably be found in a passage of Strabo. He makes the statement[3] that Sophocles says that at the time of the capture of Troy a leopard skin was placed in front of the door of Antenor as an indication that his house was to be spared; that Antenor and his sons together with the surviving Heneti escaped to Thrace and from there to the land called Henetica on the Adriatic. It would seem as if Strabo must have had the *Antenoridae* in mind in writing the passage, though he does not say so.

That Antenor and his sons were saved after the fall of Troy is part of the regular tradition. It was their reward for their hospitable treatment of Odysseus and Menelaus when the latter came to Troy to demand back Helen;[4] and, furthermore, Antenor had been in favor of returning Helen with her property to the Greeks.[5] The incident of the leopard skin was an acknowledged part of the story. It was introduced by Polygnotus in

[1] Ten lines of the *Andromeda* of Ennius are preserved, and seventeen of the *Andromeda* of Attius. See Ribbeck, *op. cit.*, I, pp. 27 f. and 148 ff.

[2] Pearson, *op. cit.*, I, pp. 86 ff.; Welcker, *op. cit.*, I, pp. 166 ff.

[3] XIII, 1, 53, Σοφοκλῆς γοῦν ἐν τῇ ἁλώσει τοῦ Ἰλίου παρδαλέαν φησὶ πρὸ τῆς θύρας τοῦ Ἀντήνορος προτεθῆναι σύμβολον τοῦ ἀπόρθητον ἐαθῆναι τὴν οἰκίαν. τὸν μὲν οὖν Ἀντήνορα καὶ τοὺς παῖδας μετὰ τῶν περιγενομένων Ἑνετῶν εἰς τὴν Θρᾴκην περισωθῆναι κἀκεῖθεν διαπεσεῖν εἰς τὴν λεγομένην κατὰ τὸν Ἀδρίαν Ἑνετικήν, κ.τ.λ.

[4] *Iliad*, III, 203–297.

[5] *Iliad*, VII, 347–353.

his great painting in the Lesche of the Cnidians at Delphi representing Troy after its fall.[1] It might be added that a scholium on *Iliad* XXIV, 496 relates that Bacchylides said that Antenor had fifty children, though the unknown writer would correct the number to nineteen.

The fourteenth ode of Bacchylides is entitled Ἀντηνορίδαι ἢ Ἑλένης Ἀπαίτησις. This led Blass and Wilamowitz-Moellendorf[2] to conclude that Ἀντηνορίδαι and Ἑλένης Ἀπαίτησις were names for the same tragedy, for fragments of Sophocles are preserved under both titles. Perhaps this is possible; but one would naturally expect the *Demand for Helen* to precede, and the *Antenoridae* to follow, the Trojan war.

Attius may have followed Sophocles in his *Antenoridae*, of which about five lines survive.[3]

XV

The Athamas A and B

SOPHOCLES wrote two tragedies entitled *Athamas*, as we learn from a scholium to the *Clouds* of Aristophanes, line 257. In the text of the play Strepsiades says to Socrates "Don't sacrifice me like Athamas." Whereupon the scholiast[4] explains that the reference is to the second *Athamas* of Sophocles, who had represented the hero garlanded standing by the altar ready to be sacrificed when Heracles appeared and rescued him. This statement gives us a clue to the plot of one of the two plays. It is not, however, the familiar story which has to do with his attempted sacrifice of his son Phrixus. As told by Apollodorus,[5]

[1] Pausanias, X, 27, 2.

[2] See Jebb, *Bacchylides*, p. 220, n. 1.

[3] See Ribbeck, *op. cit.*, I, pp. 151 f.

[4] τοῦτο πρὸς τὸν ἕτερον Ἀθάμαντα Σοφοκλέους ἀποτεινόμενος λέγει. ὁ γάρ τοι Σοφοκλῆς πεποίηκε τὸν Ἀθάμαντα ἐστεφανωμένον καὶ παρεστῶτα τῷ βωμῷ τοῦ Διὸς ὡς σφαγιασθησόμενον καὶ μέλλοντος ἀποσφάττεσθαι αὐτοῦ παραγενόμενον Ἡρακλέα καὶ τοῦτον θανάτου ῥυόμενον.

[5] *Bibl.* I, 9, 1.

Ino, the second wife of Athamas, jealous of his children by his first wife, Nephele, persuaded the women of Boeotia without the knowledge of the men to parch the seed grain so that the earth did not bear its usual crop. Athamas sent messengers to Delphi to inquire the cause, and Ino bribed them to say that the barrenness would cease if he sacrificed his son Phrixus to Zeus. The people forced Athamas to bring the youth to the altar, when his mother, Nephele, rescued him and gave him a ram with a golden fleece which she had received from Hermes. By means of it he and his sister Helle were transported through the air; but Helle fell off and was drowned in the sea called for that reason the Hellespont. Phrixus came to the land of the Colchians, where he sacrificed the ram to Zeus. Presumably the first *Athamas* dealt with the earlier part of this story, but Sophocles also wrote a *Phrixus* which may have been concerned with the latter part of it. The extant fragments of all three plays are so meager that little can be inferred from them.[1]

The story of the mad Athamas is also told by Apollodorus[2] thus: After the birth of Dionysus from the thigh of Zeus, Hermes carried the child to Athamas and Ino and commanded them to rear him as a girl. Hera, however, drove them both mad. Athamas hunted his eldest son by Ino thinking him to be a deer, and slew him; while Ino threw Melicertes into a boiling cauldron and then leaped with him into the sea.

Just how Athamas was brought to the altar for sacrifice is not clear. Pearson[3] points out that according to the later scholia on the passage in the *Clouds* referred to above, Nephele was responsible; but that he was saved from sacrifice by Heracles, who announced that Phrixus was alive. Herodotus[4] in mentioning a local custom at Alos in Thessaly also refers to the sacri-

[1] See Pearson, *op. cit.*, I, pp. 1 ff.; Welcker, *op. cit.*, I, pp. 319 ff.

[2] *Bibl.* III, 4, 3.

[3] *Op. cit.*, I, p. 2.

[4] VII, 197 . . .*διότι καθαρμὸν τῆς χώρης ποιευμένων Ἀχαιῶν ἐκ θεοπροπίου Ἀθάμαντα τὸν Αἰόλου καὶ μελλόντων μιν θύειν ἀπικόμενος οὗτος ὁ Κυτίσσωρος ἐξ Αἴης τῆς Κολχίδος ἐρρύσατο, κ.τ.λ.*

Plate III

The Mad Athamas with his Bonds Broken

From a Column Crater in Chicago

fice which, he says, was prevented by Cytissorus, the son of Phrixus.

Part of the story of the sacrifice of Athamas is depicted on a red-figured column crater in Chicago published by Professor Ernest Gardner.[1] Here Athamas is represented garlanded with his bonds broken and apparently mad (PLATE III).

Ten fragments of the two plays, all very short, are preserved. In fact seven of the ten consist of a single word each. It is not surprising, therefore, that they give us almost no help in reconstructing the plots. R. J. Walker[2] has advanced the theory that *Athamas* I and II, *Phrixus*, and *Dionysiscus* together formed a tetralogy and were all brought out at the same time. His evidence is, however, very slight and far from convincing.

XVI

The Atreus

IN A scholium to the *Hippolytus* of Euripides, line 307, two iambic trimeter lines are quoted as coming from the *Mycenaean Women* of Sophocles.[3] The lexicographer Hesychius (s. v. ἐπισπάσει) refers to Sophocles Ἀτρεῖ ἢ Μυκήναις. The last word is evidently a mistake for Μυκηναίαις, that is *Mycenaean Women.*[4] This implies that the *Atreus* had an alternative title. There are no other references to an *Atreus* by Sophocles in the literature. There is, however, good evidence for three tragedies by him entitled *Thyestes*,[5] and it has been conjectured that the *Atreus* is to be identified with one of these. Atreus was certainly a suitable character for tragedy, and an *Atreus* of which twenty fragments are preserved was written by the Roman poet Attius.[6]

[1] *Am. Jour. Arch.* III, 1899, pp. 331 ff.
[2] *Ichneutae*, p. 611.
[3] Σοφοκλῆς ἐν Μυκηναίαις.
[4] Pearson, *op. cit.*, I, pp. 91 ff.; Welcker, *op. cit.*, I, pp. 357 ff.
[5] See p. 273.
[6] See Ribbeck, *op. cit.*, I, pp. 161 ff.

It may be that the latter play was based upon the *Atreus* of Sophocles. The plot of this tragedy would naturally be concerned with the early part of the Thyestes story—the seduction of Aërope, wife of Atreus, by Thyestes; the golden lamb; the slaughter of the children of Thyestes by Atreus and the serving of their flesh at a banquet to their father. There is also the possibility that it had to do with another part of the story leading to the slaying of Atreus by Aegisthus. Much of this must have been included in the plays called *Thyestes.*

In the light of the very slender evidence which we have we are, perhaps, justified in concluding that Sophocles wrote an *Atreus or the Mycenaean Women* which was sometimes referred to as the *First Thyestes,* but we can only guess as to the nature of its plot.

XVII

The Banqueters

THERE are extant nine fragments of the *Banqueters* (Σύνδειπνοι, also quoted, probably erroneously, as Σύνδειπνον[1]), and, in addition, three lines which may with great probability be assigned to the play. Two of the fragments are of four lines each, two of three lines, one of two lines, one of a line and a half, and three are single words.[2]

Enough is known about the play to determine the subject with which it dealt. The banquet was held on the island of Tenedos by the Greek chieftains before the fleet reached the land of Troy. It was on this occasion that Philoctetes was bitten by the serpent. Achilles seems to have received a late invitation, or not to have been invited at all, and this led to a quarrel between him and Agamemnon. Achilles threatened to return home. The story was found in the *Cypria.*[3]

[1] Athenaeus in one place (I, p. 17d) refers to it as Ἀχαιῶν σύνδειπνον, though elsewhere he calls it Σύνδειπνοι.

[2] Pearson, *op. cit.*, II, pp. 198 ff.; Welcker, *op. cit.*, I, pp. 232 ff.

[3] Proclus, *Chrestomathia*, p. 235, ll. 32 ff., ed. Westphal.

How the plot was developed is not at all clear. One passage of four lines (Frag. 565) preserved by Athenaeus is of so remarkable a character that it seems hardly possible that it could have had a place in any Greek tragedy. In it the speaker, who is unidentified, complains that some one who is not named had broken a *pot de chambre* over his head, and that he had fled in consequence. Athenaeus points out that almost the same words were to be found in a play of Aeschylus,[1] which modern scholars have usually assumed was a satyr drama. It has, therefore, been argued that the *Banqueters* was a satyr drama, though it is nowhere mentioned as such. Pearson takes a different view of it. He finds no place for a satyr chorus in the story and concludes that the *Banqueters*, like the *Alcestis* of Euripides, was the fourth play of a tetralogy, taking the place of a satyr drama. But even then it is hard to see how there could have been a place for such lines as those referred to. It seems more likely that the play was a satyr drama. The satyrs may be imagined to have been found on the island by the Achaeans and to have made themselves known when they discovered preparations for the banquet going on. Satyrs seem to have been associated with islands in the popular imagination.[2]

XVIII

The Captives

THE *Captives* (Αἰχμαλωτίδες) is known to us from twenty-six different quotations, but of these thirteen consist of single words and no one of the others is longer than a single line.[3] It is not possible to gather from any one of them a definite clue to the nature of the plot. Various conjectures have been made and are duly recorded by Pearson. Thus Welcker thought that the

[1] Athenaeus, I, p. 17c. The play was probably the Ὀστολόγοι or *Bone Gatherers*, in which Odysseus was made to suffer the indignity at the hands of one of the suitors.

[2] See Pausanias, I, 23, 6.

[3] Pearson, *op. cit.*, I, pp. 25 ff.; Welcker, *op. cit.*, I, pp. 171 ff.

death of Astyanax was the chief incident; Ahrens, that the plot had to do with the story of Polydorus and Polymestor as told by Hyginus (*Fab.* 109). There the Greeks bribe Polymestor, king of Thrace, to kill Priam's son Polydorus, who had been brought up by his sister Iliona, wife of Polymestor. But Polymestor kills his own son Deïphilus by mistake and is afterwards blinded by Polydorus. Schoell and Bergk thought that the plot was to be found in the First Book of the *Iliad* and had to do with the return of Chryseis.

More interesting, however, than any of these conjectures is the ingenious theory of T. Zielinski[1] that the *Captives* is an alternative title for the *Ajax the Locrian*. He notes that in the description of the painting of Polygnotus in the Stoa Poecile at Athens as given by Pausanias, Ajax was represented with Cassandra and other captive women.[2] He thinks that these captives composed the chorus of the tragedy in which the trial of Ajax was the principal incident. He finds confirmation of his theory in some of the fragments. The chief objection to it would seem to be that the *Captives* is quoted under that title twenty-six times and the *Ajax the Locrian* quoted as such eight times, and that if these were two titles for the same play we should expect some one of these thirty-four references to give us that information. That the captives were Trojan women and that they made up the chorus is certainly likely. The writer of the Hypothesis to the extant *Ajax* definitely states (l. 2) that the *Captives* had to do with the story of Troy. One might, perhaps, imagine a plot not unlike that of the *Troades* of Euripides, that is that it was concerned with the unhappy fate of the captured women after the fall of Troy.

[1] *Eos*, XXVIII, 1925, pp. 37 ff.

[2] Pausanias, I, 15, 2 . . . καὶ αὐτὸν ἡ γραφὴ τὸν Αἴαντα ἔχει καὶ γυναῖκας τῶν αἰχμαλώτων ἄλλας τε καὶ Κασσάνδραν.

XIX

The Cedalion

FIVE fragments of the satyr drama *Cedalion* exist, the longest consisting of two lines. Two are single lines, one a line and a half, and one of two words. In addition there are two words which Pearson, following a conjecture of Gaisford, prints with the other fragments.[1] They give no clue to the plot, but there are various references in the literature to the story on which it was based. The outlines of it are these:

Orion, the son of the daughter of Minos, Euryale, by Poseidon had from his father the power of walking over the sea. He came to Chios and while drunk attempted to assault Merope, the daughter of Oenopion, who blinded him as a punishment. But an oracle declared that he would be cured if he walked towards the rising sun. He, therefore, took upon his shoulders Cedalion, one of the servants of Hephaestus, to guide him, and upon meeting the Sun recovered his sight. There is nothing in the story so far to suggest a plot for a satyr drama; but Servius on Vergil's *Aeneid* (X, 763) adds that Dionysus and the satyrs helped Oenopion blind Orion. Here there seems to be a hint as to the way in which Sophocles treated the myth. Furthermore, if we may conjecture that he represented Cedalion as one of the satyrs (which the name might well suggest), gave him an important part in the blinding, and then had Orion seize him and hold him by force upon his shoulders to guide him, various ridiculous scenes might be imagined.

There are some variants in the story such as that of Vergil (*Aeneid* X, 763 ff.), who makes Orion wade through the sea instead of walking upon it.

[1] Pearson, *op. cit.*, II, pp. 8 ff.

XX

The Chryses

FOUR single lines and a single word are cited from the *Chryses*,[1] but no one of them is of special significance. The outlines of the plot may, perhaps, be found in Hyginus, *Fab.* 120. There it is stated that Chryseis, after she had been returned to her father, gave birth to a son named Chryses, claiming that Apollo was his father. When Orestes and Iphigenia escaped from the land of the Taurians with the statue of Artemis they came first to the island of Sminthe where Chryses was living. He was about to surrender them to Thoas, king of the Taurians, when he learned that he himself was the son of Agamemnon and half brother of Orestes and Iphigenia. He then assisted Orestes in killing Thoas. In consequence Orestes and Iphigenia continued their flight with the image safely to Greece.

There is not enough in the extant fragments to prove that such was the nature of the plot. Wilamowitz-Moellendorf[2] doubted it; and Pearson even thought that there were hints that the *Chryses* might have been a satyr drama—something which can neither be confirmed nor denied.

The Roman dramatist Pacuvius wrote a *Chryses* which may have been based upon this play of Sophocles. Twenty-one fragments of it with a total of about thirty lines are preserved.[3]

XXI

The Clytaemnestra

A *Clytaemnestra* by Sophocles is referred to once, though perhaps the quotation belongs to two passages, as Pearson[4] thought. No hint exists as to the plot, and Welcker[5] conjectured that the

[1] Pearson, *op. cit.*, II, pp. 327 ff.; Welcker, *op. cit.*, I, pp. 210 ff.
[2] *Hermes*, XVIII, pp. 257 f.
[3] Ribbeck, *op. cit.*, I, pp. 86 ff.
[4] *Op. cit.*, II, pp. 13 f.
[5] *Op. cit.*, I, p. 108.

reference was really to the *Iphigenia.* Pearson thought it more likely to belong to the *Aegisthus*; but in the absence of evidence nothing satisfactory can be conjectured about it. It would seem probable that if Sophocles had written a tragedy with *Clytaemnestra* as the title we should have heard more about it.

XXII

The Colchian Women

AT LEAST ten, and possibly fourteen fragments with a total of about fifteen lines are preserved of the *Colchian Women* (Κολχίδες), quoted four times as the *Colchians* (Κόλχοι).[1] Little can be gathered from them as to the plot of the play. That the Colchian Women were the attendants or friends of Medea, and that they made up the chorus, may be regarded as certain.

The plot evidently dealt with the stay of Jason in Colchis, where the scene was laid, his successful performance of the tasks set him by king Aeetes, his getting possession of the Golden Fleece, and his flight with Medea. The story is briefly told in the *Fourth Pythian* ode of Pindar (ll. 212 ff.), and at length by Apollonius Rhodius in the *Argonautica* (III, 576 ff.), and is familiar from other sources.[2] A note by the scholiast to the *Argonautica* (III, 1040) makes it clear that the interview between Medea and Jason in which she instructed him how to overcome the fire-breathing bulls, and to sow the dragon's teeth, occurred on the stage. Fragment 336 seems to refer to the first of these tasks, though it cannot definitely be proved to come from the *Colchian Women*; and Fragment 341 refers to the second. How the plot was developed can only be conjectured, but it must have ended with the flight of Medea and Jason with the Golden Fleece, no doubt with the active assistance of the chorus. The title of the play would seem to be evidence of the important part they had in the action.

[1] Pearson, *op. cit.*, II, pp. 15 ff.; Welcker, *op. cit.*, I, pp. 333 ff.

[2] See, for example, the references in Frazer's *Apollodorus*, Vol. I, p. 109, n. 4.

XXIII

The Creusa

THE *Creusa* is better represented by quotations than most of the lost tragedies of Sophocles. There is one fragment of seven lines, one of four, two of three, two of two, two single lines, and a single word. Altogether these make nine fragments with a total of about twenty-two lines. Unfortunately none of the fragments gives a clue to the plot. Presumably it dealt with the story used by Euripides in his *Ion*, that is, the discovery that the boy Ion was Creusa's own son by the god Apollo.[1] Whether Sophocles made Creusa attempt the murder of Ion when she learned that the oracle had declared him to be the son of Xuthus cannot be told. If he did, the plot would probably include the discovery of Creusa's guilt, her condemnation to death and escape through the discovery of the identity of the boy, as in the play of Euripides.[2]

Two fragments—perhaps four—are quoted from an *Ion* by Sophocles,[3] and these make it clear that Sophocles made this local myth the subject of a drama. They are, however, not otherwise significant. It has been suggested that they really belong to the *Creusa*, that is, that there was no play by Sophocles entitled *Ion*. This is very probable, for it does not seem likely that Sophocles would write two tragedies on this old Attic legend. The story apparently does not furnish sufficient material for that. It should be noted, however, that two other Creusas besides the daughter of Erechtheus are known in Greek mythology. One was the daughter of Creon for whom Jason forsook Medea; the other was the wife of Aeneas; but neither of these is known to have been of sufficient importance to have her name selected as the title of a tragedy.

[1] Pearson, *op. cit.*, II, pp. 23 ff.; Welcker, *op. cit.*, I, pp. 391 ff.
[2] See Bates, *Euripides*, pp. 117 ff.
[3] Pearson, *op. cit.*, II, pp. 1 ff.

XXIV

The Daedalus

THERE are six references to the *Daedalus* in ancient literature, but no one of them gives any hint as to the plot. The quotations consist of two single lines, two single words, and there are two of two words each. The subject is entirely unknown. Pearson[1] inclines to the view that the destruction of Talos, the bronze giant who guarded Crete, as told in the *Argonautica* of Apollonius Rhodius,[2] was an important incident in the play. In a scholium on the passage the *Talos* of Sophocles is referred to, and this is supposed to be an error for the *Daedalus*. The story was that Talos was given by Hephaestus to Minos (or by Zeus to Europa[3]) to protect the island of Crete, and he made the circuit of it three times a day. He was entirely of bronze, but had an artery in his ankle covered with thin skin. He prevented the Argonauts from landing by hurling rocks at them. Medea, however, by her magic arts caused him to hit his ankle against a sharp rock. The artery was broken and the *ichor*, or vital fluid, ran out and so caused his death.

At the same time it should be noted that Talos[4] was also the name of the nephew and pupil of Daedalus, who murdered him by throwing him over the cliffs of the Acropolis at Athens because of jealousy for his skill. Daedalus was tried for murder before the Areopagus; he was condemned and fled to Crete.[5] This would seem to be a more fitting subject for a tragic plot than the story of the brazen monster. But in the absence of definite information nothing further can be said.

There is no evidence that the *Daedalus* was a satyr drama.

[1] *Op. cit.*, I, pp. 110 ff.

[2] IV, 1638–1688.

[3] Apollonius Rhodius, *Argonautica*, IV, 1643.

[4] The name is also given as Calos by Pausanias, I, 21, 4. His tomb was shown on the south side of the Acropolis.

[5] Apollodorus, *Bibl.* III, 15, 8. For other sources see Frazer, *Apollodorus*, Vol. II, p. 121, n. 3.

XXV

The Danaë

THE *Danaë* of Sophocles is known from six quotations,[1] three of which consist of single words, one of part of a line, one of a single line, and one of two lines. The last of these is found in a scholium on the *Ajax* (l. 1) but without mention of the name of Sophocles. There is, therefore, only presumptive evidence for assigning the fragment to him. There is the possibility that it may have come from the *Danaë* of Euripides. If we could be sure of the attribution of these two lines to Sophocles we could say that his *Danaë* had to do with the earlier part of the story. This is not unlikely. The plot, then, would include an account of the oracle foretelling the death of Acrisius at the hands of a child of his daughter Danaë; his attempts to prevent her from having offspring; the discovery of the birth of Perseus; and the punishment of Danaë. The climax may have come with the removal of Danaë and her baby to be placed in the chest and cast into the sea. This was the traditional story, and it affords sufficient material for a good tragic plot. Sophocles appears to have used it again, at least in part, in his *Acrisius*,[2] and this fact led some scholars (e.g., Welcker) to the conclusion that there was but one play called the *Acrisius or the Danaë*. The evidence, however, seems to be sufficient to establish two tragedies, but not to permit an attempt to reconstruct the plot of either of them.

Besides the *Acrisius*, the *Danaë*, and the *Larisaeans* of Sophocles, the *Danaë* and the *Dictys* of Euripides[3] had for their plots parts of the story, and apparently also the *Polydectes* and the *Dictyoulkoi*[4] of Aeschylus. It was, too, the subject of a famous

[1] Pearson, *op. cit.*, I, pp. 115 ff.; Welcker, *op. cit.*, I, pp. 348 f.

[2] See p. 165.

[3] See Bates, *Euripides*, pp. 243–245.

[4] The *Dictyoulkoi* is now known to have been a satyr drama. In 1932 fragments of four plays of Aeschylus were found at Oxyrhynchus. There were twenty-one lines of his *Niobe*, twenty-one of the *Dictyoulkoi*, six lines of the *Glaucus Potnieus* and fourteen lines of the *Myrmidons*, all partly broken. They are published in

poem by Simonides of which a beautiful fragment is still preserved.[1]

XXVI

The Demand for Helen

THERE are four references in Greek authors to a play by Sophocles entitled the *Demand for Helen* (Ἑλένης Ἀπαίτησις).[2] Two consist of quotations of two lines each, one is a single word, and one a statement by Strabo that in this play Sophocles transferred the death of Calchas to Cilicia, which he poetically (τραγικῶς) called Pamphylia.[3] In addition there are two lines quoted from a *Helen* and assigned by Dindorf and others to this play.

The subject can hardly have been anything else than the embassy of Menelaus and Odysseus to Troy before the Trojan War began, demanding that Helen be given back to them. There are references to this embassy in two passages in the *Iliad*,[4] and it is known that an account of it was given in the *Cypria*.[5] The demand for the death of the ambassadors by the Trojan Antimachus, who had been bribed by Paris, and their rescue by Antenor provided the poet with a tragic theme. It is not hard to imagine that this incident played an important part in the plot.

Papiri Greci e Latini, XI, pp. 92 ff. A brief account of the discovery may be conveniently found in *Hermes*, LXVIII, 1933, p. 249, where A. Körte discusses the text of the *Niobe* and the *Dictyoulkoi*. See also R. Pfeiffer, *Sitzb. Bayer. Akad. der Wissenschaft*, Phil. Hist. Abt. 1938, Heft 2, pp. 1–22.

[1] See Smyth, *Greek Melic Poets*, p. 59.

[2] Pearson, *op. cit.*, I, pp. 121 ff.; Welcker, *op. cit.*, I, pp. 117 ff.; Séchan, *op. cit.*, pp. 181 ff.

[3] XIV, 5, 16, ταύτην τε γὰρ τὴν ἔριν (i.e., between Calchas and Mopsus) μεταφέρουσιν ἔνιοι, καθάπερ καὶ Σοφοκλῆς, εἰς Κιλικίαν, καλέσας ἐκεῖνος αὐτὴν Παμφυλίαν τραγικῶς, κ.τ.λ. See also XVI, 1, 27.

[4] III, 205 ff., with scholium, and XI, 139 ff.

[5] See Proclus, *Chrestomathia*, p. 236, ed. Westphal. For a list of the sources see Frazer, *Apollodorus*, Vol. II, p. 197 n. 1.

On the other hand it is difficult to see how the death of Calchas could be connected with it. The story was that Calchas, knowing the disasters which would befall the Greeks on their return home after the sack of Troy, refused to go back but journeyed to Pamphylia where, in accordance with a prophecy, he died after a contest with Mopsus, who proved himself a greater prophet.[1] It may be that the return of the Greeks and his own end were foretold by the seer in some passage. Such a prediction, however, would seem to be more appropriate to a tragedy having to do with the fall of Troy; and this has been used as an argument for identifying the *Demand for Helen* with the *Antenoridae*.[2]

In the Hypothesis to the *Ajax*, mention is made of a play entitled Ἑλένης Ἁρπαγή which, together with the *Antenoridae*, the *Aechmalotides*, and the *Memnon*, had to do with a Trojan subject. Nothing more is known of this play and it is generally assumed that ἁρπαγή is an error for ἀπαίτησις. At all events the statement shows that it was not the same as the *Antenoridae*.

XXVII

The Dionysiscus

The *Dionysiscus* is known from three fragments, one of three iambic trimeter lines, one of two short lyric lines, and one of one word.[3] One of the three expressly states that it is a satyr play; but even without such evidence the same inference would be drawn from the title. The form Διονυσιακός which is found in two of the three quotations is a manifest error.

The plot was evidently woven about the divine infant Dionysus who created wine and gave it to the satyrs. The three-line fragment seems to have been spoken by Silenus, and tells how the baby felt of his nose and touched his bald head, laughing. It is

[1] See Immisch, *Jhb. für Phil. Suppl.* XVII, p. 160. The story of the death of Calchas is told with some difference of detail by different authors.

[2] See p. 180.

[3] Pearson, *op. cit.*, I, pp. 117 ff.

easy to see how the play could be made very funny. One has only to imagine the delight of the satyrs at the marvelous new drink which the child had given them, and the amusing effects which it produced.

Pearson suggests that the scene was laid at the mythical Nysa on the shore of the Ocean, home of the nymphs who nursed the infant Dionysus.[1] Very likely this was the case. The plot, however, cannot be recovered from the references now preserved.

XXVIII

The Dolopians

Two fragments, one of one line and one of a single word, alone remain from the lost *Dolopians*.[2] Nothing is known about the play and there is not sufficient evidence even to make a plausible conjecture as to its subject. The Dolopians, as Pearson points out, played no important part in Greek legend. In the *Iliad* (IX, 484) Phoenix is mentioned as ruling them; and Thucydides (I, 98, 2) says that Dolopians inhabited the island of Scyros. It has been argued on the basis of these two passages that the play had to do with the story of Achilles. Whether or not this was the case there is no means of knowing. It does not seem likely that the *Dolopians* was another title for the *Phoenix*[3] as Welcker thought.

XXIX

The Epigoni

THE *Epigoni* of Sophocles presents problems which, with our present evidence, it is impossible to solve. There can be no

[1] Homeric *Hymn to Dionysus*, XXVI.
[2] Pearson, *op. cit.*, I, pp. 119 f.; Welcker, *op. cit.*, I, pp. 140 ff.
[3] See p. 254.

question that it dealt with the second expedition against Thebes in which Alcmaeon took part. The title alone shows that. The story forms part of one of the famous legends of Greece, the outlines of which are in brief these:[1]

Polynices, son of Oedipus, deprived of the throne at Thebes by his brother Eteocles, with the help of Adrastus organized against him a great expedition in which seven heroes took part. The *Seven against Thebes* of Aeschylus deals with this part of this story. One of the seven was the seer Amphiaraus, who could forsee his own death if he joined the others in their attack on Thebes. He, therefore, declined to go; but Polynices bribed his wife Eriphyle by the gift of the famous necklace of Harmonia to send him. For when he married her Amphiaraus had promised that if he and her brother Adrastus ever disagreed he would abide by whatever she should decide between them. She then decided against him, and true to his pledge Amphiaraus accompanied the other heroes to Thebes. Like the six others, this one righteous man did not survive the expedition. He was swallowed up by the earth. Before leaving home, however, he directed his son Alcmaeon to slay his mother Eriphyle as a punishment for her treachery. According to another version it was Apollo who ordered Alcmaeon to kill his mother. At least Alcmaeon did the dreadful deed and, in consequence, was pursued by the Furies.

But ten years after the first expedition the sons of the seven heroes organized a second expedition against Thebes which was successful. The city was captured and destroyed. Alcmaeon did not want to go on this, but was persuaded to by his mother, who was bribed a second time, Thersander the son of Polynices giving her the robe of Harmonia.

Such are the main outlines of the story. When we try to discover just how much of it was included in the plot of the *Epigoni* we at once encounter difficulties. There are extant only three quotations from the play having a total of six lines; and

[1] See e.g., Apollodorus, *Bibl.*, III, 6, 1 ff. and 7, 2 ff.

three other references which seem to have to do with it. One passage seems to refer to Eriphyle. There is not enough here to suggest how the plot was constructed.

But besides the references to the *Epigoni* there are seven quotations which are explicitly stated to have come from the *Eriphyle* of Sophocles. These amount to eleven lines in all. One line seems to hint at the madness of Alcmaeon after he had committed the crime. A tragedy entitled *Eriphyle* would naturally have as the crisis in the plot her murder at the hands of her son; although the possibility must be admitted that it might be concerned with the earlier part of her story, that is, her acceptance of the bribe from Polynices and sending her husband to his death.

Welcker[1] many years ago argued that the *Eriphyle* was simply another name for the *Epigoni*, in other words that the name of the chief character was substituted for the name of the play. Pearson[2] takes this view and argues persuasively in support of it. If the death of Eriphyle could be proved to have been included in the plot of the *Epigoni* the evidence would be strong for such an identification, but it cannot. Again, if the real name of the tragedy was *Eriphyle* it is hard to see how it could ever have been referred to as the *Epigoni*; and, on the other hand, if the correct title was *Epigoni* it is astonishing that we should have seven passages in which it is called *Eriphyle*. Nowhere do we find the title Οἱ Ἐπίγονοι ἢ Ἐριφύλη. With the evidence in the unsatisfactory condition in which we find it, it would seem that there were two different plays. There was surely enough material in the story for two. But whether Sophocles made Alcmaeon slay his mother before or after the expedition, or as to any other detail of the plot, it is idle to speculate.

The story in all its parts was a favorite with the tragic poets. Aeschylus wrote the extant *Seven against Thebes* and an *Epigoni*; Sophocles also an *Alcmaeon* and a satyr drama *Amphiaraus*; and

[1] *Op. cit.*, I, pp. 296 ff.
[2] *Op. cit.*, I, pp. 129 ff.

Euripides an *Alcmaeon at Corinth*, an *Alcmaeon at Psophis*, and the extant *Suppliants*. The Roman poet Attius wrote an *Epigoni*, perhaps based upon the *Epigoni* of Sophocles;[1] and one line is quoted from an *Eriphyla*.[2] Here the same question as to the identity of the two plays comes up.

In his *Electra* (ll. 836 ff.) Sophocles refers to the bribe given to Eriphyle, the death of Amphiaraus, and the vengeance of Alcmaeon.

XXX

The Erigone

Two quotations, one of two lines and the other of one, are all that remain of the *Erigone*.[3] They give no hint as to the nature of the play. Two different stories exist, according to either of which Erigone might be made the chief character in a tragedy. One relates that she was the daughter of Aegisthus and Clytaemnestra and that she went to Athens to prosecute Orestes for the murder of her father. Such, for example, is the statement recorded in the Parian Marble (l. 40).[4] According to the other story she was the daughter of Icarius. When her father had learned from Dionysus the art of making wine and had given some to certain shepherds, they killed him, thinking that they had been poisoned. The next day they buried him; but his dog brought Erigone to the place where his body was concealed and she, in grief, hanged herself.[5] There is no means of knowing which of these stories Sophocles utilized for his tragedy. The Athenians had an ancient festival known as the Aeora (Αἰώρα) supposed to commemorate the death of Erigone.[6]

[1] Ribbeck, *op. cit.*, I, pp. 173 ff.
[2] *Ibid.*, p. 176.
[3] Pearson, *op. cit.*, I, pp. 173 ff.
[4] See also *Etymologicum Magnum*, 42, 1.3; and Apollodorus, *Epit.*, VI, 25.
[5] Apollodorus, *Bibl.*, III, 14, 7.
[6] See Frazer, *Apollodorus* Vol. II, p. 96, n. 2.

The Roman poet Attius wrote an *Erigona* of which seven small fragments are preserved.[1] This was concerned with Erigone, daughter of Aegisthus, and the trial of Orestes; but there is no proof that Attius was following Sophocles. Tragedies with the same title are known to have been written by several of the less well known tragic poets. Welcker[2] thought that the *Erigone* and the *Aletes* were the same, but little can be said for that conjecture.

XXXI

The Eriphyle

SEVEN passages with a total of eleven lines are quoted as coming from the *Eriphyle* of Sophocles. Whether this was a separate tragedy or was the same as the *Epigoni* has already been considered. The evidence as it now stands seems to be a little stronger in favor of regarding the *Eriphyle* as a different play. For a discussion of the problem see under *Epigoni*, p. 195.

XXXII

The Eris

THREE fragments, one a single iambic trimeter line and the others consisting of two words each, are all that remain of the *Eris* of Sophocles.[3] Nothing is known of the plot, though the suggestion of Pearson and others that it was concerned with the story of the marriage of Peleus and Thetis and the strife of the three goddesses caused by the Golden Apple tossed into their midst by Eris is a natural conjecture. In fact, it is hard to see with what else a play with such a title could be concerned. Pearson is inclined to think that it was a satyr drama; but there

[1] Ribbeck, *op. cit.*, I, pp. 142 f.
[2] *Op. cit.*, I, pp. 215 ff.
[3] Pearson, *op. cit.*, I, pp. 139 f.

is at present no means of knowing definitely whether or not that was the case. When satyr dramas are quoted by ancient authors the fact that they were such is usually noted along with the title; but, on the other hand, the *Inachus* is quoted twenty-six times without any such mention, and yet the new fragments of that play from Tebtunis seem to prove that it was a satyr play.[1] The single line of the *Eris* which is preserved,[2] in which a female character says

> With hungry eyes I gaze upon the cakes

certainly seems more likely to have come from a satyr drama than from a tragedy. Furthermore a contest between Hera, Athena, and Aphrodite for the Golden Apple can hardly have been a suitable subject for a tragedy. If we imagine a chorus of satyrs present at the marriage of Peleus and Thetis, or at the subsequent judgment of the three goddesses the possibilities for fun are apparent. The evidence at present is decidedly in favor of a satyr play.

Sophocles is known to have written another play, the *Krisis* (see p. 226), expressly mentioned as a satyr drama, and this was certainly concerned with the Judgment of Paris. Pearson suggests that this was a sequel to the *Eris*.[3]

XXXIII

The Ethiopians

Six fragments of the *Ethiopians* (Αἰθίοπες) are known, four of them consisting of single words. Three lines are quoted by Athenaeus, and a line and a half by Photius.[4] With such scanty material it is impossible to recover the plot, but it is almost

[1] *Tebtunis Papyri*, III, Pt. 1, pp. 3 ff.

[2] ἐγὼ δὲ πεινῶσ' αὖ πρὸς ἴτρια βλέπω.

[3] It might be pointed out that Walker, *Ichneutae*, pp. 353 ff., argues against the existence of a play by Sophocles with this title.

[4] Pearson, *op. cit.*, I, pp. 22 ff.; Welcker, *op. cit.*, I, p. 138.

certain that it was concerned with the exploits and death of Memnon. In the Hypothesis to the *Ajax* (l. 2) it is stated that that play has to do with a Trojan subject, like the *Antenoridae*, the *Captives*, the *Rape of Helen*, and the *Memnon*. There is no other allusion to the last-named play, and it was long ago conjectured that it was identical with the *Ethiopians*.

The exploits of Memnon were related in the *Aethiopis*, the epic poem attributed to Arctinus of Miletus, in which the story of Troy was carried on from the place where the *Iliad* left off. In the brief summary of it preserved by Proclus (pp. 237 f., ed. Westphal) we are told of the arrival of Memnon and his Ethiopians at Troy; his encounter with Antilochus, the son of Nestor, whom he slew; his own death at the hands of Achilles; and finally that his mother the Dawn (Ἠώς) begged immortality for him from Zeus. The story is told at greater length by Quintus of Smyrna in the Second Book of his *Posthomerica*.

The deaths of Antilochus and of Memnon in battle are tragic incidents in themselves, but it is not easy to see how they could be given dramatic unity. It might be conjectured that the climax of the tragedy came with the death of Memnon, and that the rest of the play was largely devoted to the lament of the Dawn for her son. The Ethiopians must have been soldiers in Memnon's army, that is, they formed the chorus, and they may well have had an important part in the action.

XXXIV

The Eumelus

The *Eumelus* is known only from two quotations of single words by lexicographers, and about one of these there is some doubt. Harpocration[1] says that the word καθελών was used to mean "having slain" (ἀνελὼν ἢ ἀποκτείνας) by Sophocles in the *Eumelus*; and Hesychius (p. 59, l. 30 ed. minor) in a corrupt

[1] S. v. καθελών.

passage quotes Sophocles' ἀμήλῳ, which is supposed to stand for Εὐμήλῳ. No other references to the play are known.

Our information about the character for whom the play was named is not much more extensive than that about the play itself. We do not know of any tragic hero of that name. Pearson[1] points out that Admetus and Alcestis had a son Eumelus who took part in the Trojan War and was famous for his horses. He was one of the little band of warriors who hid in the Wooden Horse[2] and so got access to the city. This is about all that is known concerning him, and it is not at all clear how he could have been the principal character in a tragic plot. If the references to the play are correct it is probable that some story that has not come down to modern times was associated with his name.

XXXV

The Euryalus

No fragment of the *Euryalus* is known to exist; but Eustathius in his *Commentary on the Odyssey* (p. 1796, line 52) says that Sophocles tells the story of Euryalus, son of Euippe, whom Telemachus slew.[3] This is the only evidence for a play with this name by Sophocles. The name Euryalus was not uncommon in Greek legend. Thus one of the suitors of Penelope from Dulichium and another from Zacynthus[4] bore this name. But the reference in Eustathius evidently has to do with the story told in the *Erotica* of Parthenius (ch. III). Here it is related that Odysseus had a son named Euryalus by the Thesprotian Euippe; that the youth when grown to manhood was sent to Ithaca by his mother with tokens which would serve to identify him (σύμβολά τινα δοῦσα ἐν δέλτῳ κατεσφραγισμένα); that Penel-

[1] *Op. cit.*, I, p. 144.
[2] Quintus of Smyrna, XII, 324.
[3] Pearson, *op. cit.*, I, pp. 145 f.; Welcker, *op. cit.*, I, pp. 248 f.
[4] Apollodorus, *Epit.*, VII, 27 and 29.

ope discovered who he was and contrived his death at the hands of Odysseus.

There is here material for a good tragic plot, whether the youth were slain by his father or, as Eustathius says, by Telemachus; but how Sophocles handled it can only be conjectured.[1]

XXXVI

The Eurypylus

AT THE time the papyrus containing the long fragments of the *Ichneutae* was discovered there were found many small pieces of another papyrus which had apparently been a companion piece. Both manuscripts are in the same handwriting and both date from late in the second century A.D. This second play was a tragedy and its title was not preserved, but it can be identified as the *Eurypylus*.[2] Sophocles was not previously known to have written such a play, although that had been suspected. Aristotle in the *Poetics* (p. 1459b 6) mentions a *Eurypylus* as a tragedy drawing its plot from the *Little Iliad*. He does not, however, give the author's name, and there is no other reference to the play in the literature. But the style of the newly found fragments and the apparent agreement of an unassigned line of Sophocles with a broken line in the papyrus make the writer's identity practically certain.[3]

The story of Eurypylus was this. He was the son of Telephus and Astyoche, sister of Priam, and came to Troy, as the city neared its fall, with an army to help the Trojans. According to

[1] In a discussion of the *Telegonia* of Eugammon, J. Vürtheim (*Mnemosyne*, XXIX, pp. 56 f.) takes up the question of the plot of the *Euryalus* and concludes that Parthenius has preserved the outline of it.

[2] See Hunt, *Oxyrhynchus Papyri*, IX, pp. 86 ff.; and Pearson, *op. cit.*, I, pp. 146 ff.

[3] See Plutarch, *Moralia*, p. 458 e (*De cohib. ira*, ch. 10) *καὶ τὸν Νεοπτόλεμον ὁ Σοφοκλῆς καὶ τὸν Εὐρύπυλον ὁπλίσας* "*Ἐκόμπασ' ἀλοιδόρητα, φησίν, ἐρρηξάτην ἐς κύκλα χαλκέων ὅπλων." In the papyrus Frag. 5, line 9 ends χ]αλκέων ὅπλων. The line fits in well at this place.

one version Priam bribed Astyoche to send her son to Troy by giving her the golden vine which Zeus had bestowed upon Laomedon in return for Ganymede. This story was evidently known to Homer, as a passage in the *Odyssey*[1] shows. After performing brilliant exploits and slaying many Achaeans, Eurypylus was killed by Neoptolemus, the son of Achilles. Quintus of Smyrna tells of his arrival at Troy (VI, ll. 119 ff.), his numerous deeds of valor (VI and VII *passim*), and finally his death (VIII, ll. 199 ff.). He makes no mention of the golden vine which, however, must have formed part of the story as it was related in the *Little Iliad*.[2]

Just how these incidents could be combined to form a tragic plot is not clear, and little help can be obtained from the papyrus, it is so badly mutilated. With our present evidence a reconstruction of the plot is out of the question; and little more than a hint can be obtained as to the manner in which the poet treated the myth. We can make out that the scene was laid at Troy. In one of the best-preserved fragments (col. ii, ll. 1–22) there is a commatic passage in which a woman laments the death of some one and is consoled by the chorus. She feels that she is meeting her just deserts. This can hardly have been anyone else than Astyoche, and the reference would seem to be to her part in sending her son to Troy. Before and after this passage there seems to have been the report of a messenger. The only other well-preserved lines tell of the grief of Priam at the death of Eurypylus. The division of the messenger's speech into two parts is peculiar. The crisis in the play no doubt came with the death of the hero.

Altogether there are preserved parts of about two hundred lines of the *Eurypylus*, many of them consisting of little more than a single word. About forty lines can be restored.

[1] XI, ll. 519 ff. ἀλλ' οἷον τὸν Τηλεφίδην κατενήρατο χαλκῷ,
ἥρω' Εὐρύπυλον· πολλοὶ δ' ἀμφ' αὐτὸν ἑταῖροι
Κήτειοι κτείνοντο γυναίων εἵνεκα δώρων.

[2] See Pearson, *op. cit.*, I, p. 147.

XXXVII

The Eurysaces

One word (*ἀδόξαστον*) is quoted by Hesychius[1] as coming from the *Eurysaces* of Sophocles.[2] There is no other reference to the play. The Roman poet Attius, however, is known to have written a tragedy with this title, and twenty-three fragments of it are preserved.[3] On the ground that this was based on the tragedy of Sophocles, Welcker[4] tried to reconstruct the plot of the latter play, using as further evidence a passage in Justin (XLIV, 3, 2).

Eurysaces was the son of Ajax and Tecmessa, and is so mentioned in the extant *Ajax* (e.g. l. 575) where he has a silent part. According to Justin he prevented Teucer from landing at Salamis when he tried to return to his native land from Cyprus upon hearing of the death of his father, Telamon. Justin goes on to say that Teucer then withdrew and made a settlement in Spain. Pearson points out the improbability that this part of the story had any connection with the plot of the *Eurysaces*; but what that was the evidence at present available does not permit us to say.

XXXVIII

The Heracleïscus

The two quotations, each of a single line (Fragments 228 and 229), of a satyr drama *Heracleïscus* clearly have to do with a subject that was very different from that treated in the *Heracles at Taenarum.* The diminutive form of the hero's name shows that he must have been represented as a boy, if not as a baby.

We are familiar with the exploits of the infant Hermes in the

[1] S. v. *ἀδόξαστον*.
[2] See Pearson, *op. cit.*, I, pp. 165 ff.
[3] Ribbeck, *op. cit.*, I, pp. 179 ff.
[4] *Op. cit.*, I, pp. 197 ff.

Ichneutae; and in the *Dionysiscus* we have further evidence that Sophocles could find material for the plot of a satyr drama in the marvelous deeds of an infant divinity. In the case of Heracles one thinks first of his exploit in strangling the serpents sent against him by Hera; but just how this incident could be introduced into a satyr play, and where the satyrs would come in is not clear. The plot may have been constructed somewhat after the fashion of the plot of the *Ichneutae*, but in the absence of definite information nothing more can be said about it.

XXXIX

The Heracles at Taenarum

HERACLES belonged to the comic rather than to the tragic stage, but the *Heracles* of Euripides is sufficient proof that the life of the mighty hero furnished ample material for a tragic plot. The *Trachiniae*, too, may be cited to show how Sophocles likewise made use of the tragic element in his history. But the burly hero with his big stick and his astounding adventures was an ideal character for a satyr drama. It is not surprising, therefore, to find Sophocles mentioned as the author of satyr dramas variously referred to as *Heracles*, Ἐπιταιναρίοις, ἐπὶ Ταινάρῳ, *Heracleïscus* and *Cerberus*. Ἐπιταιναρίοις and ἐπὶ Ταινάρῳ must be intended for one and the same play, which, as Pearson points out,[1] was very likely the *Heracles*. The correct title would then probably be *Heracles at Taenarum*, a satyr drama.

Apollodorus[2] tells the story of the descent of Heracles into Hades at Taenarum in Laconia to perform his Twelfth Labor. This was to carry off Cerberus, the watchdog of the Lower World. The assigned task was successfully performed, and after showing the monster to Eurystheus the hero took him back again. The painters of vases found a congenial theme in the

[1] *Op. cit.*, I, pp. 167 ff.
[2] *Bibl.*, II, 5, 12.

scene where Heracles presents himself with Cerberus before the frightened Eurystheus.[1] It is easy to see that such a scene might be made very amusing. The early part of the play might not be so very different from the beginning of the *Frogs* of Aristophanes if one makes due allowance for the difference between Heracles and Dionysus; and the latter part with the terrified Eurystheus taking refuge from Cerberus in a huge jar might be made uproariously funny. Euripides wrote a satyr drama entitled *Eurystheus* on this same subject.[2]

The single reference in a scholium (Fragment 224) to a *Cerberus* by Sophocles, as Pearson points out, almost certainly belongs to the *Heracles at Taenarum*. One cannot well imagine Sophocles writing two satyr dramas on the Twelfth Labor of Heracles.

XL

The Hermione

Two quotations, one of a single line and the other of one word, are all that remains of the *Hermione*.[3] These are not enough to give any help towards the reconstruction of the plot; but there is a passage in the *Commentary* of Eustathius on the *Odyssey* (p. 1479, lines 11 ff.) that is of assistance. There it is stated that Sophocles in the *Hermione* related that while Menelaus was still at Troy his daughter Hermione was given to Orestes by Tyndareus; that later on she was taken away from him and given to Neoptolemus in accordance with a promise made at Troy. When the latter was slain by Machaereus at Delphi she was returned to Orestes. A son was afterwards born to them named Tisamenus because of the vengeance inflicted by Orestes on the murderers of his father.

In a scholium on the *Orestes* of Euripides (l. 1655) the story of the death of Neoptolemus at Delphi is told on the authority of

[1] See e.g., Reinach, *Répertoire des vases*, I, p. 153.
[2] See Bates, *Euripides*, pp. 247 ff.
[3] Pearson, *op. cit.*, I, pp. 141 ff.

Pherecydes, and it is added further that Sophocles told this part of the family history (ταῦτα γενεαλογεῖ καὶ Σοφοκλῆς). The reference is apparently to the *Hermione*.

In the *Andromache* of Euripides (ll. 967 ff.) we are told that Hermione had been given Orestes as his wife by Menelaus, who afterwards promised her to Neoptolemus if he should sack Troy. After the fall of the city Orestes was obliged to give Hermione up; but he contrived the death of Neoptolemus at Delphi and so recovered her.

There is here surely sufficient material for a tragic plot,[1] and, in the light of the passage in Eustathius, it would seem to be safe to conclude that it was the struggle between Orestes and Neoptolemus for the possession of Hermione with which the action of the play was chiefly concerned. Whether Andromache had a part in the tragedy as in the *Andromache* of Euripides[2] cannot be determined. So, too, we cannot be sure whether in the play Hermione was represented as actually married to Orestes before she was given to Neoptolemus; whether Neoptolemus was killed by the devices of Orestes or by the Delphians; or, in short, which of the other variants in the story Sophocles may have followed.[3] Such matters and the way in which the plot was worked out must be left to conjecture.

In Roman times the poets Livius Andronicus[4] and Pacuvius[5] each wrote a tragedy entitled *Hermiona*, and some fragments of these are preserved.

[1] See Welcker (*op. cit.*, I, pp. 319 ff.) who thinks that the scene was laid at Delphi and that the chorus consisted of priests.

[2] For a discussion of this play see Bates, *Euripides*, pp. 65 ff.

[3] A brief discussion of the different versions of the story may be found in Frazer, *Apollodorus*, Vol. II, p. 252, note.

[4] Ribbeck, *op. cit.*, I, p. 3.

[5] *Ibid.*, I, pp. 96 ff.

XLI

The Hipponous

Two fragments of two lines each, one a single line, and two single words make up what exists of the lost *Hipponous*.[1] Naturally little can be inferred from them as to the nature of the plot, but the story on which it was based was this. Hipponous, king of Olenus in Achaea, finding that his daughter Periboea was about to become a mother, sent her to Oeneus at Calydon with orders to put her to death. But Oeneus spared her and, according to Diodorus (IV, 35), married her and became the father of Tydeus. There are, however, certain variants in the tale, and it is impossible to determine just how Sophocles handled it. The title seems to imply that Hipponous had a more important part in the play than would have been the case if the plot dealt chiefly with the latter part of the story. On the other hand the line

From Olenus, my native land, I come[2]

seems to imply, as Pearson suggests, that the words were spoken by Periboea after her arrival in Calydon.

Whether Oeneus proved to be the father of the unborn child, as Welcker thought,[3] and this fact was revealed as the tragedy developed, can only be conjectured. As it is, not enough information remains to permit anything like a plausible restoration of the plot. A reference to the *Hipponous* in Pollux (IV, 111) gives no help.

Euripides wrote an *Oeneus* which dealt with a later portion of the story, that is, with the banishment of the aged king by the sons of his brother Agrius, and his subsequent restoration to his throne by his grandson Diomedes.[4]

[1] Pearson, *op. cit.*, I, pp. 216 ff.
[2] Frag. 300.
[3] *Op. cit.*, I, p. 428.
[4] Bates, *Euripides*, pp. 267 ff.

XLII

The Hybris

NOTHING more is known about the *Hybris* of Sophocles than is furnished by the two extant quotations from it.[1] One of these consists of a single line and the other of a line and a half. In the latter quotation it is designated as a satyr drama. Hybris is known to have been the name of the mother of Pan,[2] and here, perhaps, we have a clue to the plot. It is possible that Pan may have been represented in it as a precocious infant performing marvelous feats somewhat after the fashion of Hermes in the *Ichneutae*. But with such meager evidence as we have, no safe conjecture can be made as to the subject of this satyr play.

XLIII

The Hydrophori

THE *Water Carriers* (Ὑδροφόροι) is known from three little quotations,[3] the longest consisting of one line, which give no hint as to what the play was about. Aeschylus wrote a *Semele or the Water Carriers*, and it has been conjectured from that title that the *Hydrophori* of Sophocles may have had to do with the story of the birth of Dionysus. The evidence is, however, so slight that it is not safe even to venture a conjecture as to what tale Sophocles used for the construction of his plot.

XLIV

The Iberians

THE *Iberians* of Sophocles is known from a single reference, and that in a fragmentary inscription from Rhodes copied many

[1] Pearson, *op. cit.*, II, p. 291.
[2] Apollodorus, *Bibl.* I, 4, 1.
[3] Pearson, *op. cit.*, II, pp. 292 f.; Welcker, *op. cit.*, I, p. 286.

years ago by P. Bonarroti. The inscription is discussed at length by G. Kaibel[1] who combines three (*a*, *e*, and *g*) of the seven pieces belonging to it. From these we learn that a certain Alcimachus, an Athenian, acted plays of Sophocles at Rhodes in the third or fourth century B.C. Mention is made of the *Odysseus*, the *Iberians*, and the satyr drama *Telephus*. Another play preceded the *Odysseus*, but only two letters of the name remain. Kaibel conjectures that this was the *Peleus*.[2]

What the *Iberians* was about must be left to the imagination. Pearson[3] suggests that the story of Geryon is the most likely subject for a play with such a title. The Tenth Labor of Heracles was to bring from Erythia, or Gadira, the cattle of the triple-bodied Geryon.[4] After various adventures, in the course of which he slew Geryon, the hero successfully accomplished the task. Pearson thinks such a story more suitable for a satyr drama than for a tragedy. That is evident; but the text of the inscription implies that the *Iberians* was a tragedy.

XLV

The Ichneutae

THE *Ichneutae*, or *Trackers*, was known to modern scholars from three little fragments only down to the year 1907, when a papyrus containing about four hundred lines of the play, more or less broken, was found at Oxyrhynchus in the Fayum. There are in all considerable portions of seventeen columns of writing besides numerous small pieces. The papyrus, which dates from the latter part of the second century A.D., was published by A. S.

[1] *Hermes*, XXIII, 1888, pp. 268 ff.

[2] Kaibel restores the passage thus:

'Αλκίμαχος 'Αθ[ηναῖος Πη-
λ]έα Σοφοκλέους καὶ 'Οδυσσέ[α μαινόμενον
κ]αὶ Ἴβηρας καὶ σατυρικὸν Τήλεφ[ον ἐνίκα
ὑ]ποκρινόμενος ἐν 'Ρόδῳ, δεύ[τερος ἦν κ.τ.λ.

[3] *Op. cit.*, I, p. 197.

[4] Apollodorus, *Bibl.* II, 5, 10; Frazer, *Apollodorus*, Vol. I, p. 210, n. 1.

Hunt in 1912.[1] It has since been much discussed and reëdited so that in his edition published in 1919 R. J. Walker felt that he could restore 473 lines. The play is positively identified by the appearance in the papyrus of a line quoted by Athenaeus as coming from the *Ichneutae*.[2]

The text is carefully written and was corrected by a second hand who sometimes added variant readings in the margin and quoted his authority for them. Thus he quotes Theon, probably a grammarian of the time of Augustus; Αρν or Αρ, who may have been Aristophanes of Byzantium or Aristarchus; and N with a vertical stroke through it which may stand for Nicander or Nicanor.

We seem to have the play from the beginning,[3] though the early lines are rather badly mutilated. Opposite line 94 is the letter ᾱ, evidently intended to record the first 100 lines, and opposite line 197 is a β̄; also γ̄ opposite line 292 and δ̄ opposite 392 but, as Hunt points out,[4] a list of the characters in the play may have preceded; and, again, such stichometric figures are not always accurate.[5]

The scene of the *Ichneutae* is laid on Mount Cyllene in Arcadia in front of the cave of the nymph Cyllene, who is secretly taking care of the infant Hermes, son of Zeus and Maia. Apollo is the speaker as the play opens. He has lost his cattle and can discover no trace of them anywhere. He therefore offers a reward to anyone who will help him find them. Silenus and the satyrs who form the chorus hear his words and agree to undertake the task. They set out on their search, apparently divided into two groups, and look about. At length one group finds tracks of cattle, but they are reversed. They try to follow them up

[1] *Ox. Pap.* IX, pp. 30 ff.

[2] Athenaeus, p. 62 f. Σοφοκλῆς Ἰχνευταῖς κἀξορμενίζει κοὐκ ἐπισχολάζεται βλάστη (Frag. No. 294, Nauck). In the papyrus it reads

[κἀξορ]μενίζει κοὐκέτι σχολάζεται
[βλάστη]

[3] Bethe, *Ber. Sächs. Gesel. der Wiss. zu Leipzig*, 1919, pp. 1 ff. thinks otherwise.

[4] *Ox. Pap.* IX, p. 68.

[5] For the stichometry see Walker, *Ichneutae*, pp. 155 ff.

but find them badly mixed and confused. Then they become alarmed by a strange sound which issues from the cave on the mountain. It is the sound of the lyre. Silenus scolds them but without much effect. They are thoroughly frightened.

The text is well enough preserved here to permit a translation.

CHORUS

Just listen to the thing a little while—
A sound such as no mortal ever heard
By which we have been startled and aroused.

SILENUS

Why fear a noise? Why are ye so alarmed
With your accursed bodies made of wax,
Ye worst of beasts who see a frightful sight
In every shadow, scared at everything?
It's feeble service, slovenly and base
That ye perform, and if one looks at ye
He finds ye tongue and phallus, nothing else;
And, where there's need, quite ready with your tongue
Though deeds ye flee from, creatures that ye are
Most base, though sprung from such a sire as I,
Whose many trophies won through manliness
When I was young rest in my sweethearts' homes.
I never turned to flight, no coward I;
I did not crouch in terror at the noise
Of mountain-nurtured beasts, but with my spear
Did glorious deeds perform which now by ye
Are tarnished by some humbug shepherd's noise.
Ye fear it since ye do not see the cause.
Ye're losing, too, that shining wealth of gold
Which Phoebus mentioned, which he pledged to ye
And offered freedom both to ye and me.
Ye throw this all away; ye are asleep.
Unless ye find the path and track those cows
To see where with their herder they have gone,
Your cowardice itself will be the cause
Of weeping on your part and noise, too.

CHORUS

Oh! father, you just trot along with us
That you may know if there is cowardice.
For when you're there yourself you'll see you're wrong.

SILENUS

Aye, I'll be there; my words will make ye go.
From every side I'll sic ye on like hounds.
Come! leave the crossways and I'll guide ye straight
Intent upon my task.

A lyric passage which was commatic in character follows, but the lines are badly mutilated.

The members of the chorus go sniffing about like hounds trying to find the scent,[1] all the time talking to Silenus and to one another. No doubt there was much horse-play here that might be very amusing to the audience.

The sound of the lyre is heard again, and Silenus, in spite of his bold words, is as much alarmed at it as any of the satyrs, and wants to run away. But at length they all screw up their courage and go to the entrance to the cave. They kick at the door and shout to the inmate to come out. After a time the nymph Cyllene appears and questions them. She asks indignantly why they have come there shouting instead of following Dionysus as they usually do thyrsus in hand attended by a crowd of nymphs. She expresses surprise at the hunting cries which they have uttered.

The chorus assure her that they have no hostile intent, but ask the cause of the sounds they have heard. She explains that that is a secret, and must not come to the knowledge of Hera. One of the daughters of Atlas has borne a son to Zeus and she, Cyllene, is taking care of the baby. He has grown with marvelous speed and although only six days old is as large as a youth. He is concealed in the cave by his father's command.

[1] In *Harv. Stud. in Class. Philol.*, XLVI, 1935, pp. 167 ff. F. R. Walton suggests that they were costumed like dogs.

In a single day he constructed the instrument by which he makes the sounds they have heard. At this place in the manuscript the lines are mutilated, but it is clear from what follows that she explained that it was made from a dead animal. Seven badly broken lines of the chorus then follow, and after them a dozen well-preserved lines of dialogue written in iambic tetrameter verse. This metre is not found elsewhere in Greek drama, though it must have been used in the New Comedy, for it is common enough in the Latin comedies of Plautus and Terence. The passage runs thus:

CYLLENE

Now don't distrust me, for I tell you truthful things to make you smile.

CHORUS

But how shall I believe dead creatures uttered such a dreadful sound?

CYLLENE

Believe it, for the beast, though speechless living, makes a sound when dead.

CHORUS

In form what was it like? Come, tell me. Was it long, or round, or short?

CYLLENE

I say that it was short and pot-like, shriveled, with a mottled skin.

CHORUS

Can it be likened in its nature to a leopard or a cat?

CYLLENE

Between the two—aye, far between them, for it's round and has short legs.

CHORUS

Why, then it must be like a weasel; or can it be like a crab?

CYLLENE

Again I tell you it is nothing of the sort. Guess something else.

CHORUS

Can it be like a horned beetle, one of the Etnean kind?

CYLLENE

Ah! now you have almost discovered what the beast resembles most.

CHORUS

What part of it, within or outside, is it that gives forth the sound?

CYLLENE

It is a mountain-dwelling creature, one of those which have a shell.[1]

CHORUS

If you are able just oblige me, tell me by what name it goes.

CYLLENE

The boy declares the beast a tortoise; that which sounds he calls a lyre.

The lines which immediately follow are too mutilated to make much out of, but the word "hide" (*δέρμα*) evidently gives the chorus a clue to the whereabouts of the lost cattle. After learning a little more about the lyre they accuse Hermes of the theft. Cyllene is indignant and defends him, pointing out that he is a son of Zeus and incapable of stealing; but the chorus refuse to be convinced. From this point on the text is either badly mutilated or entirely gone. Evidently the satyrs find other

[1] In this and the two following lines much is restored.

indications that Hermes is to blame, make known their discovery to Apollo and claim their reward. It seems likely that in the end Apollo got back most of his cattle and was appeased by Hermes who gave him the lyre.[1] It is unfortunate that the last part of the play should not have been preserved.

It is apparent at once that in the *Ichneutae* we have a very different type of drama from the great masterpieces of Sophocles which have come down from antiquity through the usual channels. The lofty plane on which the splendid characters of his tragedies move is gone, and instead we find a composition of very simple type which is far from lofty. The play shows us another side of the poet's genius.

There is no outstanding character which would give a great actor an opportunity to show his ability as in the tragedies. In fact the dramatic element is rather slight. It seems clear that the poet sought to amuse his audience chiefly by the antics of the satyrs. That Athenians could be satisfied with so simple a dramatic composition can be understood only when we remember that three tragedies had preceded it. At the same time it must have enjoyed some fame even as late as the end of the second century A.D. or the copy of it which we have would not have been made.

The *Ichneutae* is especially important for the light which it sheds on the way in which Sophocles handled his material in this type of composition. The only satyr drama previously known, as has been explained, was the *Cyclops* of Euripides. Now Sophocles may be judged in the same field. In the *Ichneutae* he took his plot from the Homeric *Hymn to Hermes*, but he did not hesitate to make such changes in the story as he saw fit in order to enliven the action and bring about certain dramatic situations. Thus in the *Hymn* the theft of the cattle comes after the invention of the lyre. By reversing the order the poet provides a motive for the search carried out by his

[1] In the Homeric *Hymn to Hermes* (IV, 475 ff.) Hermes offers the lyre to Apollo, who accepts it (l. 496) and appoints him keeper of his cattle.

chorus, thus enabling them to find a clue leading to the discovery of the cows. Again, the infant is in charge of Cyllene, not of Maia; and the place of his concealment is located on Mount Cyllene, not at Pylos. The satyrs, too, are naturally an innovation. This evidently means that in his satyr dramas Sophocles felt at liberty to make such changes in the old myths as suited his convenience.

The *Ichneutae* could apparently be presented with two actors only, and this fact together with certain metrical features led Wilamowitz-Moellendorf to conclude that the play was an early one. Other scholars have reached the same conclusion, and this may well have been the case. In its vocabulary, as might be expected, it is closer to tragedy than to comedy; but the lofty diction of the tragic stage is naturally absent. It has many unusual words. Walker enumerates forty-three not found elsewhere.[1] It has been much discussed since its first publication by Hunt. Noteworthy contributions are those of Wilamowitz-Moellendorf,[2] Pearson,[3] Bethe[4] and R. J. Walker.[5]

The story of the theft of Apollo's cattle is not altogether unrepresented in Greek art. On a Caeretan hydria in the Louvre[6] the infant Hermes is depicted in the cave with the cattle (PLATE IV). The vase is, however, earlier than the play, so that it could not have influenced the painter. He probably got his inspiration as Sophocles did from the *Hymn to Hermes*.

XLVI

The Inachus

THE *Inachus* of Sophocles must have enjoyed considerable fame in antiquity, for no less than twenty-six references to it are

[1] The vocabulary is discussed by him at great length, *op. cit.*, pp. 30 ff.
[2] *Neue Jahrbücher*, 1912, pp. 449 ff.
[3] *Op. cit.*, I, pp. 224 ff.
[4] *Op. cit.*
[5] *Op. cit.*
[6] See Pottier, *Catalogue des vases antiques*, II, p. 537 (No. 702).

PLATE IV

THE INFANT HERMES WITH THE CATTLE OF APOLLO

From a Caeretan Hydria in the Louvre

found in the literature.[1] The quotations from it are all short, the longest consisting of seven lines, and four are of one word only. This material is not sufficient to permit a reconstruction of the plot; but there can be no doubt that it concerned Io and her adventures. The story as it has come down to us has several variants in it, but in its main outlines it is this. Zeus had a love affair with Io, daughter of the river-god Inachus. Hera discovered it and Io was transformed into a cow either by Hera or by Zeus himself. The many-eyed Argus was then set to watch her by Hera, but Hermes lulled him to sleep and killed him. Io, driven by a gadfly, subsequently wandered to Egypt, where she gave birth to Epaphus, ancestor of Danaus.

This story has more to do with Io than with her father, Inachus. No doubt she appeared on the stage as a maiden with cow's horns, as she is depicted on Greek vases,[2] and perhaps her transformation was even brought about in the course of the play. Such an incident is hardly suitable for a tragedy and, in fact, the whole story seems unsuited to the tragic stage. Pearson,[3] therefore, and several other scholars before him, concluded that the *Inachus* was a satyr drama. Against this was the fact that in none of the references to it was the play so designated, though satyr plays were usually mentioned as such. This problem has now apparently been settled in favor of a satyr play by the discovery of about forty lines of the *Inachus*, more or less complete, on a papyrus from the cartonnage of a mummy found at Umm el Baragat, the ancient Tebtunis, in the Fayum. The fragments were published by Hunt and Smyly[4] in 1933. It is evident at once that the language and metres are well suited to a satyr play.

The papyrus dates from the second century B.C. In line 20 of column iv Inachus is named, which is good evidence for the

[1] Pearson, *op. cit.*, I, pp. 197 ff.; R. Pfeiffer, *Sitzb. Bayer. Akad. der Wissenschaft*, Phil. Hist. Abt. 1938, Heft 2, pp. 23–63.

[2] See Reinach, *Répertoire des Vases Peints*, I, p. 469; II, p. 16. In the earlier vases she has the form of a cow.

[3] *Op. cit.*, I, pp. 198 f.

[4] *Tebtunis Papyri*, III, Pt. 1, pp. 3 ff.

FIGURE 3.—HERMES IN HADES-CAP AND HOLDING SWORD APPROACHES ARGUS WHO IS WATCHING IO. ABOVE VARIOUS DIVINITIES. BELOW TWO SATYRS.
From a Crater at Naples

identification of the drama. Hermes is seen to have been one of the characters and is referred to as the "messenger of the loves of Zeus" (τὸν Διὸς μὲν οὖν ἐρώτων ἄγγελον). He wore the Hades-cap which made him invisible. It is easy to see that an invisible Hermes, Argus (who is referred to), and a chorus of satyrs suggest all sorts of possibilities for fun. The editors of the papyrus call attention to a late red-figured crater in Naples (Fig. 3) on which Hermes wearing the Hades-cap, Argus, Io, and other figures as well as two satyrs are represented.[1]

The myth does not seem to have been used by Aeschylus or Euripides, but Chaeremon in the fourth century B.C. wrote an *Io*.[2]

XLVII

The Iobates

Two small fragments—one a trimeter line, and the other, two words—and another consisting of a single line, but with the name of the drama corrupt, are all that is left of the *Iobates*.[3] They give no hint of the plot; but the title makes it clear that this tragedy had to do with the story of Bellerophon told in the Sixth Book of the *Iliad*. Welcker[4] many years ago suggested that a passage from Asclepiades (*F. H. G.* III, 303) quoted by the scholiast on *Iliad* VI, 155 contained the gist of the plot. Here we are told that Proetus, not wishing to kill Bellerophon with his own hand, sent him to Lycia to his son-in-law Iobates with a secret message calling for his death. But Bellerophon so distinguished himself in Lycia that Iobates not only spared his life but gave him his daughter Cassandra in marriage and a share in his kingdom. This scholium may or may not have been based on the *Iobates* of Sophocles. There is no way of

[1] J. Overbeck, *Griech. Kunstmyth.* IV (Atlas) pl. VII, No. 16.
[2] See Athenaeus, XIII, p. 608 d.
[3] Pearson, *op. cit.*, I, pp. 214 f.
[4] *Op. cit.*, I, pp. 416 ff.

knowing. It should be remembered, however, that Euripides wrote two famous plays about Bellerophon,[1] the *Bellerophon* and the *Stheneboea*.

XLVIII

The Ion

Two fragments are cited as coming from an *Ion* by Sophocles, and two others may possibly be referred to it, but the text in each case is corrupt and the restoration uncertain. The four fragments amount altogether to about four lines.[2] There are, however, nine fragments of a *Creusa* extant amounting to twenty-two lines, and it has been suggested that the *Ion* is identical with this. The suggestion seems probable, as it does not seem likely that Sophocles would have written two tragedies on this local myth.[3]

XLIX

The Iphigenia

THE *Iphigenia* of Sophocles is represented today by three unrelated trimeter lines, by a fragment of two lines, and by four single words.[4] As one might imagine, little can be inferred from these meager remains in regard to the plot of the play. Photius[5] in quoting the line

Gaining the mightiest son-in-law of all[6]

says that it was spoken by Odysseus to Clytaemnestra with reference to Achilles. This makes it clear that the bringing of

[1] Bates, *Euripides*, pp. 232 ff. and pp. 290 ff.
[2] Pearson, *op. cit.*, II, p. 23.
[3] See p. 190.
[4] Pearson, *op. cit.*, I, pp. 218 ff.
[5] *Lexicon*, p. 410, 13.
[6] Frag. 305, σὺ δ' ὦ μεγίστων τυγχάνουσα πενθερῶν.

Iphigenia to Aulis on the pretext that she was to be married to Achilles was one of the incidents in the play, as it was in the *Iphigenia at Aulis* of Euripides. The fact that Odysseus had an important part in deceiving Clytaemnestra and in enticing Iphigenia to Aulis, as Photius implies, leads Pearson to conclude that Sophocles followed the version of the story in the *Cypria* more closely than Euripides did. Little more can be said of the plot. Like the *Iphigenia* of Aeschylus the play does not seem to have attracted particular attention in antiquity. It certainly did not have the fame enjoyed by the *Iphigenia in Tauris* of Euripides. Welcker[1] thought that *Iphigenia* and *Clytaemnestra* were alternative titles for the same play.

L

The Ixion

Two scholia, one on a passage of the *Argonautica* of Apollonius Rhodius (IV, 14) and the other on the *Iliad* (IV, 171) are the only evidence for an *Ixion* by Sophocles. This is not, however, a sufficient reason for doubting that he composed such a play. Ixion was the subject of tragedies by Aeschylus, Euripides, and some of the minor tragic poets.[2]

There is no hint as to how Sophocles constructed his plot, whether it was concerned with the murder of Eioneus, whom Ixion killed by pushing him into a pit full of fire; or with the story of his attempted intimacy with Hera and his punishment by being attached to a fiery wheel. The last part of the story seems to have been used by Euripides.[3]

[1] *Op. cit.*, I, pp. 107 ff.
[2] Pearson, *op. cit.*, I, pp. 213 f.
[3] Bates, *Euripides*, pp. 255 ff.

LI

The Kamikoi

FOUR fragments amounting in all to six lines remain of the Καμικοί or *Men of Camicus.*[1] With one exception they are without significance; but fortunately the story on which the plot of the play was based is preserved by Apollodorus[2] and, with slight variations, by Zenobius.[3] It is as follows:

After Theseus and his companions had escaped from Crete, Minos shut up Daedalus and his son Icarus in the labyrinth; but Daedalus constructed wings for himself and Icarus and so escaped. Icarus fell into the sea, but Daedalus arrived safely at Camicus in Sicily where he was received by king Cocalus. Minos went in pursuit of him; and in every country to which he came he offered a reward if anyone could run a thread through a spiral shell, hoping by this means to discover the whereabouts of Daedalus. When he came to Camicus, Cocalus undertook to accomplish this for him. He showed the shell to Daedalus, who bored a hole in one end of it, then attached a thread to an ant and allowed it to pass through the interior, thus solving the problem. As no one other than Daedalus was likely to have been clever enough to do this Minos charged Cocalus with harboring the fugitive and demanded that he give him up. Cocalus agreed to do so; but his daughters contrived the death of Minos in his bath, either by means of scalding water as related by Apollodorus, or by boiling pitch as Zenobius states. At least the climax in the play was evidently the death of Minos. There is a reference to the shell in Fragment 324. The men of Camicus from whom the play got its title were evidently the chorus.

R. Wagner[4] suggested that Apollodorus derived his narrative from the Hypothesis of the tragedy—a not improbable conjecture, but one which cannot be proved.

[1] Pearson, *op. cit.*, II, pp. 3 ff.; Welcker, *op. cit.*, I, pp. 431 ff.

[2] *Epit.* I, 13 ff.

[3] *Epitoma proverb. Cent.* IV, 92. See Frazer's *Apollodorus*, Vol. II, pp. 138 ff.

[4] *Epitoma Vaticana ex Apol. Bibl.* p. 132.

LII

The Kophoi

ONLY one fragment of the satyr drama Κωφοί or the *Blockheads* has come down to modern times.[1] It is part of an iambic trimeter line which was preserved because of the peculiar expression ὄνος ἰσόσπριος used for the woodlouse. But in addition to this fragment there are various statements made about the play by ancient authors which make it possible to recover the plot with considerable certainty.[2] It was somewhat like this:

The scene was laid on Mount Ida in the Troad in front of the cave of the Idaean Dactyls, who represented the older race of men. They had been busily engaged in smelting iron with the help of the fire which Prometheus had brought them. The play may have opened with a dialogue between Prometheus and Celmis, one of the Dactyls, in which the story of the gift of fire to mankind was told. The chorus of satyrs, with Silenus mounted on a donkey, then enter. They learn from Celmis about the marvelous new element and agree to take service with the Dactyls in working iron by means of it. They are duly warned about the fire, but at once begin to meddle with it and get singed and burnt. Zeus arrives at that moment and is informed by them of the gift made by Prometheus to the Dactyls. In return for their information Zeus gives them a magic plant which will confer perpetual youth upon its possessor. The satyrs are delighted and put the plant upon the donkey while they celebrate with a dance. The donkey, however, wanders away and gives the plant to a serpent in exchange for a drink of water. The serpent thus won perpetual youth, as evidence of which it sloughs off its skin each year. When the satyrs recover the donkey and find out that they have lost the magic herb they are enraged, and the play may have ended by their venting their wrath on the unfortunate donkey as they pursue him off the stage.

[1] Pearson, *op. cit.*, II, pp. 31 ff.

[2] See Bates, *Am. Jour. of Philol.*, LV, 1934, pp. 167 ff.

Such must have been the general character of the plot. The satyrs are the *blockheads* not only because of their silly meddling with the fire, but also because of their stupidity in losing the plant which would have given them immortality.

The idea of a magic herb having the power to confer perpetual youth upon its possessor is very old. In the old Sumerian epic the hero Gilgamesh after great exertions at length obtains possession of the plant, but on his way home he stops to bathe in a spring when a serpent seizes the plant and makes away with it. Mankind thus loses immortality and the serpent gains it. The story is told in detail in Books IX, X, and XI of the Assyrian version of the Gilgamesh epic.[1] It is thus one of the oldest tales in Greek mythology.[2]

LIII

The Krisis

THERE are two references to the Κρίσις or *Judgment*,[3] one of which expressly designates it as a satyr drama. It is regarded by Pearson as having been a sequel to the *Eris*. It must have been concerned with the Judgment of Paris when the three goddesses Hera, Athena, and Aphrodite led by Hermes appeared before the youthful shepherd for a decision as to their charms. In one of the two fragments (No. 360) there is reference to Aphrodite and Athena. It is not hard to imagine that a ludicrous spectacle might be produced if the goddesses on their way to Mount Ida encountered a chorus of satyrs who decided to accompany them. If, furthermore, the satyrs were present when each goddess set forth her claims to the golden apple, and if they did not hesitate to interrupt and express their opinions the situation might become even more ridiculous.

[1] See Langdon, *Semitic Mythology*, pp. 227 ff.

[2] Nicander, *Theriaca*, 343 ff.

[3] Pearson, *op. cit.*, II, pp. 29 ff.

In this connection it may be well to recall that in the *Dionysalexander* of Cratinus[1] the contest of the three goddesses played an important part; but Dionysus was the judge, not Paris. He decided in favor of Aphrodite when she promised that he would be the most beautiful and best beloved (*κάλλιστόν τε καὶ ἐπέραστον*); and it was he who went to Sparta and carried off Helen. There is no hint that Sophocles went so far, or that he introduced the other absurdities found in that comedy; but it furnishes good evidence for the presence of satyrs at the judgment of the three goddesses.

LIV

The Laconian Women

THREE quotations, one of three lines and two of one each, are made by ancient authors from the *Laconian Women* (*Λάκαιναι*).[2] The tragedy is mentioned by Aristotle[3] as being based upon a story in the *Little Iliad*. The subject was the theft of the Palladium by Odysseus and Diomedes assisted by Helen, and the Laconian women must have been Helen's attendants. They certainly composed the chorus, and no doubt had an important part in the development of the plot. How this was constructed we have no means of knowing. One line (Frag. 367)

> We slipped into a narrow muddy drain[4]

seems to have been spoken by one of the two heroes, explaining how they got into the city.

The scene may well have been laid at Troy and the plot have culminated in the escape of Odysseus and Diomedes with the statue. Suggestions that Antenor and his wife were involved in

[1] *Ox. Pap.* IV, 1904, pp. 69 ff.

[2] Pearson, *op. cit.*, II, pp. 34 ff.; Welcker, *op. cit.*, I, pp. 145 ff.; Séchan, *op. cit.*, pp. 156 ff.

[3] *Poet.*, p. 1459b, 6 . . . . *καὶ τῆς μικρᾶς Ἰλιάδος πλέον ὀκτὼ οἷον . . . Λάκαιναι.*

[4] *στενὴν δ' ἔδυμεν ψαλίδα κοὐκ ἀβόρβορον.*

the theft, and that Odysseus and Diomedes quarreled on their way back to the Greek camp may, perhaps, have been incidents in the play, but there are no means of proving that to have been the case.[1]

LV

The Laocoön

THE *Laocoön* of Sophocles[2] is quoted seven times by ancient authors. One quotation consists of six lines, one of four, one of two, and two of one line each; the others are single words.

The story of Laocoön is familiar especially from Vergil (*Aeneid*, II, 201 ff.), but it is related with some variations by Apollodorus (*Epit.* V, 16 ff.), Hyginus (*Fab.* 135), Quintus of Smyrna (*Posthomerica*, XII, 444 ff.), and others. It was derived from the old epic poem, the *Iliupersis*, attributed to Arctinus. In brief it is this: The Greeks leaving the Wooden Horse behind them retired to Tenedos, and the Trojans thinking that they had returned home held high festival. The Horse was dragged into the city in spite of the warnings of Cassandra and the seer Laocoön, brother of Anchises. But two great serpents sent by Apollo came from the sea and destroyed Laocoön and his two sons; or, according to another version, the sons only.

How Sophocles developed his plot from this material is not at all clear. The climax would naturally come with the death of Laocoön, or his sons; but what motive he introduced to justify the punishment of the seer is uncertain. The fact that Laocoön warned the Trojans against the Wooden Horse does not seem adequate; and the statement of Hyginus that he had offended Apollo by marrying contrary to his wishes seems rather far removed in point of time. A scholium to the *Alexandra* of Lyco-

[1] See R. Wagner, Pauly-Wissowa, *op. cit.*, I, p. 2352.

[2] Pearson, *op. cit.*, II, pp. 38 ff.; Welcker, *op. cit.*, I, pp. 151 ff.; Séchan, *op. cit.*, pp. 160 ff.

phron (l. 347) makes the temple of Thymbraean Apollo the scene of the death of the two sons; and Servius (*Aeneid*, II, 201) states that Laocoön had offended Apollo by sleeping with his wife in his temple. Robert, therefore, suggests that this was the crime committed by Laocoön which Sophocles used as justification for the disaster which befell him. If we could assume that in the play Laocoön himself was spared and his sons slain we might infer that the dramatist devoted himself to portraying the character of Laocoön under misfortune, somewhat as he did that of Ajax in the extant tragedy of that name. This is, however, all conjecture.

LVI

The Larisaeans

THERE are six quotations from the *Larisaeans* in the literature, one of four lines, one of two, two of one, one a line and a half, and one a single word.[1] Two of these (Frags. 378 and 379) give a hint as to the plot, which was based on the story of Danaë.

When Perseus returned to Argos after turning the Seriphians to stone by means of the Gorgon's head he found that his grandfather Acrisius, fearing the death predicted for him at the hands of Danaë's son, had fled to the Pelasgian town of Larisa. He followed him, made himself known, and persuaded him to accompany him back to Argos. Athletic games were held in which Perseus competed, but in throwing the discus he hit the foot of Acrisius and so injured him that he died. This is the story told by the scholiast on the *Argonautica* of Apollonius Rhodius (IV, 1091) on the authority of Pherecydes. There are, however, some variants in it, such as that of Hyginus (*Fab.* 63) that the games were the funeral games of Polydectes in Seriphus, and that the discus of Perseus carried by the wind killed Acrisius by hitting him on the head. Euripides may have followed this

[1] Pearson, *op. cit.*, II, pp. 47 ff.; Welcker, *op. cit.*, I, p. 352.

version of the story in his *Danaë*.[1] Fragment 379 implies that the scene of the *Larisaeans* was laid at Larisa, not on the island of Seriphus, and Fragment 378 that the games were given by Acrisius.

LVII

The Lemnian Women

THE *Lemnian Women* is known from five quotations, three of which are single lines, one a line and a half, and one of two words. In addition there is one reference to it where no words are quoted.[2] The title of the play is thus firmly established, and one statement even implies that Sophocles either wrote more than one play with this title or revised his first version.[3]

The plot seems to have been based upon the account of the stay of the Argonauts on the island of Lemnos where the men, with one exception, had been murdered by the women. Hypsipyle, who was ruling the island, had secretly saved her father Thoas. A scholium on the *Argonautica* of Apollonius Rhodius (I, 769) says that Sophocles in the *Lemnian Women* spoke of the Argonauts engaging in a furious battle with the women.[4] This would seem to prove that the slaying of the men did not form the chief motive in the tragedy, as might be imagined, but that event had taken place before the action of the drama began.

The story was this:[5] that the Argonauts being storm-tossed landed on the island of Lemnos, but were attacked by the women. They, however, made peace with them and remained on the island for several days (Ovid[6] says years) and then departed. As a result of their stay Hypsipyle bore Jason two sons. Pearson

[1] See Bates, *Euripides*, pp. 243 ff.

[2] Pearson, *op. cit.*, II, pp. 51 ff.; Welcker, *op. cit.*, I, pp. 325 ff.

[3] Stephanus of Byzantium, p. 257, 5 quotes Sophocles ἐν Λημνίαις προτέραις.

[4] Σοφοκλῆς δὲ ἐν ταῖς Λημνίαις καὶ μάχην ἰσχυρὰν αὐτοὺς συνάψαι φησίν.

[5] Apollonius Rhodius, *Argonautica*, I, 607 ff.

[6] *Heroides*, VI, 56.

suggests that Sophocles was chiefly interested in the story because it gave him a chance to portray the character of Hypsipyle under trying circumstances, and that the climax came with the departure of Jason. This may well have been the case, though the evidence for it is lacking. There is, in fact, no way of determining how the plot developed.

Nothing can be said for Hermann's conjecture that the *Lemnian Women* was a satyr drama.

LVIII

The Lovers of Achilles

NINE fragments amounting in all to about nineteen lines remain of the satyr drama Ἀχιλλέως Ἐρασταί, or the *Lovers of Achilles*. One fragment of nine lines compares love to a lump of melting ice which boys want to drop and to hold at the same time. Of the other fragments six consist of single lines, one of one and a half, and one of two and a half lines.[1]

There is no hint as to the plot, and the various conjectures that have been made are purely hypothetical. It is not unlikely that, as Pearson suggests, the scene was laid at the cave of Chiron on Mount Pelion, where Achilles was brought up. It is not stated anywhere that the play was a satyr drama, but the title and one of the fragments[2] seem to furnish sufficient evidence that it was. The satyrs must have made up the chorus as in other satyr dramas, but it is hard to see how they could have been brought in unless they were the Lovers.

[1] Pearson, *op. cit.*, I, pp. 103 f.

[2] No. 153 which reads, παπαῖ, τὰ παιδίχ', ὡς ὁρᾷς, ἀπώλεσας.

LIX

The Mad Odysseus

THERE are five fragments of the *Mad Odysseus* (Ὀδυσσεὺς μαινόμενος), one of two lines, one of two words, and three single words.[1] From such meager material, as might be supposed, it is impossible to get any hint as to how Sophocles constructed his plot. The story upon which it was based is well known. According to Hyginus,[2] Odysseus was told by an oracle that if he went to Troy he would return alone and in need, without his comrades. When, therefore, the Greeks came to Ithaca to solicit his aid he pretended madness by harnessing an ox and a horse to his plough. Palamedes saw through the trick and placed the infant Telemachus in front of the plough. Odysseus then acknowledged the ruse and agreed to join the Achaean force. The story has some variants, but the different writers who tell it[3] agree as to its main outlines. Sophocles probably used the *Cypria* as his source.

LX

The Marriage of Helen

THREE single words and a pair of defective iambic trimeter lines are quoted from the *Marriage of Helen* (Ἑλένης γάμος).[4] They furnish no clue to the plot further than may be inferred from the title. A passage in Aristides,[5] as well as the title itself, implies that it was a satyr drama, though this is nowhere stated. The marriage of Menelaus and Helen could not be a suitable subject for a tragedy or a satyr drama; the plot must, therefore,

[1] Pearson, *op. cit.*, II, pp. 115 ff.; Welcker, *op. cit.*, I, pp. 100 ff.

[2] *Fab.* 95.

[3] For a list see Frazer, *Apollodorus*, Vol. II, p. 176, n. 2.

[4] Pearson, *op. cit.*, I, pp. 126 ff.

[5] Vol. II, p. 399 (ed. Dindorf). The passage reads αὐτὴν μὲν γὰρ ἐὰν ἴδωσιν Ἑλένην, Ἑλένην λέγω; θεράπαιναν μὲν οὖν ὁποίαν ἐποίησε Μένανδρος τὴν Φρυγίαν, τῷ ὄντι παιδιὰν ἀποφαίνουσι τοὺς σατύρους τοῦ Σοφοκλέους.

have been concerned with Paris and Helen. How they could be brought into contact with the satyrs is at first sight not apparent; but it may be pointed out that there was an island lying off the coast of Attica near Thoricus which in antiquity was known as the island of Helen. Pausanias[1] says that it was so called because Helen stopped there after the fall of Troy. Strabo, however, identifies it with the Homeric Cranaë where Paris and Helen stopped first on their flight from Sparta.[2] If Sophocles laid the scene of his play there it would have a local coloring; and it would be no more difficult for him to bring the satyrs there than it was for Euripides in the *Cyclops* to bring them to Sicily. It is not at all surprising that the adventures of Paris and Helen should be made the subject of a satyr drama. One has only to look at the plot of the *Dionysalexander* of Cratinus,[3] in which the satyrs had an important part, to see that the Athenians were already familiar with such a treatment of the familiar story.

LXI

The Meleager

THE *Meleager* of Sophocles is quoted five times, but no one of the quotations is a full line in length. Two lines, to be sure, are given by Lucian without naming the play (Frag. 401), where the sense seems to show that they must have come from the *Meleager*.[4]

The story of Meleager is one of the most familiar in Greek mythology. It is related at length by Homer (*Iliad*, IX, 529 ff.), is delightfully told by Bacchylides in his *Fifth Ode*, and in more or less detail by later writers. As might be expected, there are

[1] I, 35, 1.

[2] After quoting *Iliad*, III, 443–445, Strabo says (IX, 22, p. 399) *ταύτην γὰρ λέγει* (i.e., Homer) *Κρανάην τὴν νῦν Ἑλένην ἀπὸ τοῦ ἐκεῖ γενέσθαι τὴν μίξιν.*

[3] See p. 227.

[4] Pearson, *op. cit.*, II, pp. 64 ff.; Welcker, *op. cit.*, I, pp. 403 ff.

variants in the telling. In Homer Meleager kills his mother's brother in a fight between the men of Calydon and the Curetes for the possession of the hide of the Calydonian boar after it had been slain by Meleager and his friends. His mother Althaea then curses him, with the result that, as Homer implies, he was killed in battle. Bacchylides follows the more familiar version that the Fates had told Althaea at the birth of her son that he would live only as long as a brand burning in the fire survived. She had snatched it out of the fire and carefully preserved it, but angered at the death of her two brothers in battle (not one as in Homer) at the hands of Meleager, she burned the fatal brand and caused her son to perish. Whether Sophocles represented Atalanta as the cause of the quarrel cannot be determined. The later version laid the blame on the award of the hide of the boar to her. This seems to have been the story followed by Euripides in his *Meleager*.[1] Pearson[2] adopts the view that Sophocles followed the Homeric story, but in the absence of positive evidence no satisfactory conclusion can be reached.[3]

LXII

The Minos

CLEMENT of Alexandria (*Stromata*, VI, p. 741) quotes a single iambic trimeter line from the *Minos* of Sophocles. Nothing more is known of such a play, and it has been plausibly conjectured[4] that *Minos* was an alternative title for the *Men of Camicus*, for which see p. 224.

[1] See Bates, *Euripides*, pp. 262 ff.
[2] *Op. cit.*, II, p. 66.
[3] For a brief discussion of the myth see Jebb, *Bacchylides*, pp. 468 ff.
[4] Pearson, *op. cit.*, II, pp. 69 and 4; Welcker, *op. cit.*, I, pp. 431 ff.

LXIII

The Momus

SIX single words, one doubtfully, are quoted by ancient writers as coming from the *Momus* of Sophocles.[1] The title itself suggests at once that the play was a satyr drama, though that is nowhere stated. Pearson points out that in Hesiod (*Theog*. 214) Momus is mentioned as one of the children of Night, and Zeus may have taken council with him in his plan to reduce the population of the world by means of the Trojan War.[2] Our information is, however, too meager to permit even a conjecture as to the nature of the plot.

LXIV

The Muses

A SINGLE quotation of two words from Bekker's *Anecdota* (p. 83, 22) is all that remains of the *Muses* of Sophocles,[3] unless, indeed, the manuscripts of Pollux[4] are correct when they quote an iambic trimeter line as coming from that play. The words *ἐν Μούσαις* are usually emended to *ἐν Μυσοῖς*, and the line (Frag. 413) which speaks of bracelets, tiaras, and heavy woolen dress certainly seems more appropriate to a play such as the *Mysians* is supposed to have been. The title *Muses* is, however, confirmed by an inscription[5] which mentions both plays in a list of works by Sophocles.

Perhaps a hint as to the subject of this drama may be found in Pausanias I, 19, 5 where he says that on the bank of the Ilissus there was an altar of the Muses of the Ilissus, and that there was shown the place where the Peloponnesians slew the Athenian

[1] Pearson, *op. cit.*, II, pp. 77 ff.
[2] Schol. on Homer, *Iliad*, I, 5.
[3] Pearson, *op. cit.*, II, pp. 69 f.
[4] X, 186.
[5] *I. G.* II, 992, ll. 24 f. Μυσο[ὶ . . . . . Μ]οῦσαι.

king Codrus. The story was that when the Dorians invaded Attica they were told by an oracle that they would be victorious only if they spared the life of the Attic king. When Codrus learned of this he disguised himself, entered the camp of the enemy, engaged in a fight with the soldiers and was slain. When the Peloponnesians found that they had killed the king they withdrew from the land. Here would seem to be material for a tragic plot based on a local legend; but whether it was used by Sophocles or not for his lost *Muses* can only be conjectured.

LXV

The Muster of the Achaeans

SIX fragments, two of two lines each and four consisting of single words, were all that was known of the *Muster of the Achaeans* (Ἀχαιῶν Σύλλογος)[1] down to the year 1907. In that year part of a papyrus containing twenty-four lines and various small fragments of an unnamed play came to light and were identified by Wilamowitz-Moellendorf[2] as belonging to the Ἀχαιῶν Σύλλογος. The proof is not absolutely certain, but the character of the fragments is such that it is hard to see to what other tragedy they could be assigned; and in line 12 the words *σύλλογος φίλων* actually occur. Ten lines of the large fragment come from the end of a choral ode; the remaining fourteen form the beginning of a dialogue between Achilles and Odysseus. Achilles is disgusted at the slowness of the Greeks in getting started on the expedition to Troy. He calls for action, not words. These lines must have come rather early in the play.[3]

The tragedy dealt with part of the Telephus story, though the way in which the plot was developed is still unknown. When

[1] Pearson, *op. cit.*, I, pp. 94 ff.

[2] *Berliner Klassikertexte*, V, 2, pp. 64 ff.

[3] An unidentified tragic fragment in the John Rylands Library (*Catalogue of Greek and Latin Papyri*, Vol. III, No. 482) has sometimes been thought to belong to the Ἀχαιῶν Σύλλογος, but even its authorship has not yet been established.

the Greeks were on their way to Troy they landed in Mysia, not knowing where they were. They were driven away by Telephus, then king of the country; but Telephus was wounded in the thigh by Achilles. After the Greeks withdrew the wound did not heal, for it was made by a famous spear given by Chiron to Peleus, father of Achilles. When Telephus consulted the oracle about it he was told that he could be cured only by the spear that inflicted the wound. The method by which he went to Argos in disguise and obtained a cure formed the subject of the famous *Telephus* of Euripides.

After their repulse in Mysia the Achaeans returned home, and it was not until eight years later, according to Apollodorus,[1] that they made a second attempt. The gathering for that second expedition probably gave Sophocles the title for his play. In the course of it Telephus must somehow have been cured. It is not unlikely that the oracle which declared that Troy could not be taken without the aid of Telephus was made known, and likewise that he was really an Achaean, son of Heracles and Auge. It may be that Odysseus persuaded Achilles to cure Telephus of his wound, using the oracle and his Greek origin as arguments. It does not seem probable that the seizure of the infant Orestes by Telephus and his threat to kill him if molested was introduced into the plot, although it formed an important scene in the *Telephus*[2] of Euripides. The play must have had a happy ending.

The *Muster of the Achaeans* may well have been the third tragedy in the trilogy known as the *Telepheia*, as shown in the discussion of the *Aleadae*,[3] the second play being the *Mysians*.

[1] *Epit.* III, 19.
[2] See Bates, *Euripides*, pp. 295 f.
[3] See p. 170.

LXVI

The Mysians

TEN small fragments of the *Mysians* survive, amounting in all to about ten lines, though four of them consist of one word only.[1] From one fragment (No. 4) it is clear that the scene of the tragedy was laid in Mysia. It has long been recognized that the plot had to do with the fortunes of Telephus, and it has already been shown (pp. 172 ff.) that there are good grounds for believing the *Mysians* to have been the second tragedy of a trilogy called *Telepheia*. Welcker[2] thought it another name for the *Telephus*.

The main features of the plot are probably preserved by Hyginus.[3] They are as follows: Telephus, either directed by an oracle or, perhaps, because of blood-guiltiness,[4] has come to Mysia, where the aged king Teuthras is in danger of being deprived of his throne by a certain Idas. Teuthras promises Telephus the hand of his adopted daughter Auge in marriage, and declares that he will make him his successor if he will protect him from his enemy. Telephus defeats Idas in battle, and Teuthras is ready to make good his promise in regard to Auge. She, however, conceals a sword in her bedroom, determined to slay her intended husband on her wedding night. When Telephus arrives she is about to kill him, but a monstrous serpent appears and frightens her into a confession. He decides to punish her for her wickedness with death, when in some way not clear—perhaps through an exclamation—her identity becomes known, and Telephus, realizing that she is his own mother, takes her back to her home in Tegea.

Robert[5] argues that incidents in the life of Telephus treated

[1] Pearson, *op. cit.*, II, pp. 70 ff.

[2] *Op. cit.*, I, pp. 414 ff.

[3] Fab. 100; see also Aelian, *Nat. Anim.* III, 47.

[4] Something of this sort seems to be implied in Fragment 410,

> ἄμοχθος γὰρ οὐδείς· ὁ δ'ἥκιστ'
> ἔχων μακάρτατος.

[5] *Jahrbuch Arch. Inst.* II, pp. 246 ff.

in the *Mysians* are represented on the small frieze of the great altar from Pergamon now in Berlin.

LXVII

The Nauplius

THE *Nauplius* has long been a puzzle to students of Sophocles.[1] It is quoted three times as the *Fire-kindling Nauplius* (Ναύπλιος πυρκαεύς), three, perhaps four, times as the *Returning Nauplius* (Ναύπλιος καταπλέων), and five times simply as the *Nauplius*. There are besides two other quotations in which the character Nauplius is mentioned (Frags. 432 and 435) which may have come from the play. Fragment 432 is the longest of any preserved. It contains eleven lines; but there is no way of knowing whether it came from the *Nauplius* or the *Palamedes*. Aside from this fragment all the others together amount to a total of less than ten lines. Two papyrus fragments from Oxyrhynchus, one of six and the other of twenty-three badly mutilated lines[2] were at one time thought to have come from the *Nauplius*, but they are now definitely known to belong to the *Scyrians* (see p. 262). The problem at once arises as to whether Sophocles wrote two tragedies entitled *Nauplius*, and if so what they were about.

Nauplius is best known as the father of Palamedes. He went to Troy to demand the punishment of the murderers of his son and, when he could not get satisfaction, determined on revenge. He bided his time until the Greeks were sailing home after the fall of the city, when he kindled a fire on the rocky coast of southern Euboea so that the ships were wrecked and the men drowned.[3] It is clear that the *Fire-kindling Nauplius* must have been concerned with this part of the story. Whether the *Returning Nauplius* was a different play, and if so, with what

[1] Pearson, *op. cit.*, II, pp. 80 ff.; Welcker, *op. cit.*, I, pp. 184 ff.
[2] *Ox. Pap.* XVII, 1927, No. 2077.
[3] Apollodorus, *Epit.* VI, 8 ff.; Hyginus, *Fab.* 116; etc.

part of the Nauplius legend it had to do, it is impossible to say from the evidence now available. Pearson makes the suggestion that the subject of it was the ruin of the house of Idomeneus through his foster son Leucus, brought about by the intrigues of Nauplius.

LXVIII

The Nausicaa or the Washerwomen

POLLUX (VII, 45) quotes an iambic trimeter line as coming from the *Washerwomen* (Πλύντριαι) of Sophocles, and in another passage (X, 52) quotes a single word from the *Nausicaa* (Ναυσικάα). Photius[1] quotes one line from the *Nausicaa*. This is all that remains of a play that went by either name,[2] as is clear from two passages in Eustathius. In his commentary on the *Odyssey* p. 1553, 63 he relates the anecdote that Sophocles was fond of playing ball, and that when he brought out the Πλύντριαι he wore the mask of Nausicaa playing ball and "made a great hit" (ἰσχυρῶς εὐδοκίμησεν). In his commentary on the *Iliad* p. 381, 10 Eustathius refers to the same incident, naming the play the *Nausicaa*.

The story which the poet used was clearly the one delightfully told in the Sixth Book of the *Odyssey* (VI, 110 ff.) in which the shipwrecked Odysseus lying in the bushes is awakened by the shouts of Nausicaa and her maidens as they play ball while the royal linen, which they had come to the shore to wash, is drying; how he makes himself known to them, wins the confidence of Nausicaa and is guided by her to the palace of her father.

Pearson suggests that the *Nausicaa* was an early play. If the anecdote of the ball playing of Sophocles is true, that in itself would be good evidence in support of his theory.

For the lost *Phaeacians* see p. 250.

[1] R. Reitzenstein, *Der Anfang des Lexikons Photios*, p. 120, l. 29.

[2] Pearson, *op. cit.*, II, pp. 92 ff.; Welcker, *op. cit.*, I, pp. 227 ff.; Séchan, *op. cit.*, pp. 167 ff.

LXIX

The Niobe

THERE are six references in the literature to the *Niobe* of Sophocles, but only one complete line from it has been preserved.[1] Four much-mutilated fragments, amounting in all to parts of thirty-nine lines, have been recovered from a papyrus which had been used as part of the lining of a mummy case, and although not positively identified, were thought by Blass to belong to the play.[2] He has been rather generally followed. Another small fragment published in the *Hibeh Papyri*[3] may possibly have belonged to it also. But two other papyrus fragments which have to do with the story of Niobe probably came from the *Tantalus* (see p. 268).

The story of Niobe is one of the most familiar in Greek mythology—her boast that she had more children than Leto, the subsequent slaughter of her sons by Apollo and her daughters by Artemis as punishment for her presumption, and finally her own transformation into a ledge of rock. The best-known account is probably that of Ovid (*Metamorphoses*, VI, 146 ff.), and the oldest that of Homer (*Iliad*, XXIV, 602 ff.). There are variants in the tale as told by different authors. One definite statement in regard to the *Niobe* of Sophocles is made by the scholiast on *Iliad* XXIV, 602, namely that Sophocles represented the children of Niobe as slain at Thebes and that she returned to Lydia.[4] Apollodorus[5] says that Apollo slew the sons while they were hunting on Mount Cithaeron, and that Artemis slew the daughters in their home. Pearson,[6] following Welcker and Robert, believes that in the play the daughters were slain on the stage.

The scene of the play was almost certainly laid at Thebes; but

[1] Pearson, *op. cit.*, II, pp. 94 ff.; Welcker, *op. cit.*, I, pp. 286 ff.
[2] Frags. 442–445. See Blass, *Rhein. Museum*, LV, pp. 96 ff.
[3] I, p. 44, No. 11.
[4] . . . Σοφοκλῆς τοὺς μὲν παῖδας ἐν Θήβαις ἀπολέσθαι, νοστῆσαι δὲ αὐτὴν εἰς Λυδίαν.
[5] *Bibl.* III, 5, 6.
[6] *Op. cit.*, II, pp. 96 f.

how the plot developed and how Niobe was transported to Lydia is far from clear. A ledge of rock on Mount Sipylus over which water trickled was identified in the local tradition as the weeping Niobe turned to stone.[1]

In 1935 Vitelly published a papyrus from Oxyrhynchus dating from the second century A.D. containing twenty-one lines from the lost *Niobe* of Aeschylus.[2]

LXX

The Odysseus Acanthoplex

THE Ὀδυσσεὺς Ἀκανθοπλήξ (*Odysseus smitten by the Fish-bone*) of Sophocles was a well-known tragedy dealing with the incidents leading up to the death of Odysseus.[3] Seven fragments, each consisting of a single line, or a little more than one line, and one of two words have survived, and there is about a line cited from the *Niptra*, which may have been another title for the play.[4]

The story which served as the basis for the plot was related at length in the *Telegonia* attributed to Eugammon of Cyrene. This work in two books was the latest poem in the Epic Cycle and dated from about 568 B.C. According to the brief summary of it by Proclus (*Chrestomathia*, p. 241, ed. Westphal) Telegonus, who was said to be the son of Odysseus by Circe, came to Ithaca in search of his father. He landed on the island and began plundering it, when Odysseus came out and attacked him and was slain by him. When he found out that he had killed his father,

[1] See e.g., Pausanias, I, 21, 3.

[2] *Papiri Greci e Latini*, XI, 1935, pp. 92 ff. See p. 192, n. 4.

[3] Pearson, *op. cit.*, II, pp. 105 ff.; Welcker, *op. cit.*, I, pp. 240 ff.; Séchan, *op. cit.* pp. 173 ff.

[4] It has been inferred from Cicero, *Tusc. Disp.*, II, 21, 48 f. that the *Niptra* of Pacuvius was adapted from the *Odysseus Acanthoplex* of Sophocles. The one extant quotation from the *Niptra* of Sophocles comes from Photius, *Lexicon*, p. 400, 5 (ed. Porson). See Pearson, *op. cit.* II, p. 105. For the *Niptra* of Pacuvius see Ribbeck, *op. cit.*, I, pp. 107 ff.

Telegonus, accompanied by Penelope and Telemachus, took the body to Circe, who made them all immortal. Then Telemachus married Circe, and Telegonus, Penelope.

The story is also told by Apollodorus (*Epit.* VII, 36 f.) who adds that the spear with which Telegonus slew Odysseus was tipped with the bone of a fish,[1] whence the name of the tragedy. It is needless to say that Homer knows nothing of Telegonus, or of the death of Odysseus by a spear tipped with a fish-bone, although in the *Odyssey* (XI, 134) Tiresias prophesies that death will come to him from the sea (ἐξ ἁλός). According to Hyginus (*Fab.* 127) an oracle had warned Odysseus that he would die at the hands of his son. He was, therefore, on his guard against Telemachus. Four of the extant fragments of the tragedy refer to Dodona, where the prophecy mentioned was evidently made. Odysseus no doubt went there while complying with the instructions of Tiresias to travel inland with an oar on his shoulder until he met people who did not know what an oar was. Two of the fragments (Nos. 453 and 454) seem to refer to this incident.

How Sophocles utilized this material can only be conjectured. If *Niptra* really was another title for the play one might imagine that a disguised Odysseus, perhaps on his return from Thesprotia, was identified through the washing of his feet, as in the Odyssey. But it is not at all clear how such an incident could be made of sufficient importance to justify *Niptra* as an alternative title. Neither is it clear what connection such a scene could have with the death of Odysseus at the hands of Telegonus. Our knowledge of the plot must, therefore, remain in this unsatisfactory state until we can obtain more light.

[1] The fish was the τρυγών, or sting-ray, the bones of which were used by South Sea islanders for the same purpose. For other references to the story see Frazer, *Apollodorus*, Vol. II, p. 303, n. 2. There are some differences in regard to the details.

LXXI

The Oecles

THERE are two brief references in the literature to a play of Sophocles entitled *Iocles*. As no such person is known, the word has been presumed to be corrupt and to stand for *Oecles* or *Iphicles*.[1] Both emendations were suggested by Brunck; but Pearson calls attention to the fact that the corruption Iocles for Oecles occurs in manuscripts of the *Suppliants*, and probably of the *Phoenissae*, of Euripides, and five times in manuscripts of Apollodorus. He concludes, therefore, that *Oecles* was the correct title. What the plot of the play was it is impossible to say. Oecles was the father of Amphiaraus and accompanied Heracles on his expedition to Troy, where he lost his life.[2]

LXXII

The Oeneus

IT IS very doubtful whether Sophocles ever wrote a play entitled *Oeneus*. Two passages are quoted by Pearson[3] which have some bearing on this question. One is from Philodemus (*de pietate* p. 22 G) where there seems to be a reference to Sophocles ἐν Οἰ [νεῖ] ; and the other from Hesychius (s. v. ἄλυτον) where the words Σοφοκλῆς ἰνεῖ occur. ἰνεῖ is, perhaps, for Οἰνεῖ. This is too slender evidence to establish the existence of an *Oeneus* by Sophocles, though the subject was well suited to tragedy, and the *Oeneus* of Euripides was well known.

In Volume VIII of the *Oxyrhynchus Papyri*[4] issued in 1911 A. S. Hunt publishes some twenty-five lines and thirty-five small fragments of a satyr drama in which Oeneus was evidently the principal character. His name is written in the margin of the papyrus and he carries on a dialogue with the chorus of satyrs

[1] Pearson, *op. cit.*, II, pp. 119 f. Welcker, *op. cit.*, I, p. 430 preferred *Iphicles*.
[2] Apollodorus, *Bibl.*, II, 5, 4.
[3] *Op. cit.*, II, p. 120 and Frags. 26 and 732.
[4] No. 1083, pp. 60 ff.

who have presented themselves as suitors for the hand of his daughter. Oeneus inquires as to their qualifications, and they duly set them forth. Oeneus is impressed, but at this moment sees some one approaching and wishes to question him. Here the large fragment of the papyrus breaks off. Whether the new-comer was Heracles, and how he was made to win Deianeira must be left to the imagination. In two of the small fragments the name Phoenix occurs, probably that of another character. Hunt suggests the possibility that we have here fragments of a lost satyr drama by Sophocles entitled *Oeneus*. The style would not exclude such an attribution, but the evidence is too unsatisfactory to permit a more positive statement.

LXXIII

The Oenomaus

THERE are five quotations in the literature from the *Oenomaus*, amounting to a total of about nine lines. In addition three lines are quoted by Stobaeus[1] as coming from a *Hippodamia* not otherwise known, but probably belonging to this play; and five lines (Frag. 474) quoted by Athenaeus (p. 564 b) without designation of the drama. The latter were spoken by Hippodamia in reference to the beauty of Pelops.[2]

The story of the chariot race between Oenomaus and Pelops was one of the most famous in Greek legend. It is told with some variants by different authors, notably by Apollodorus.[3] In brief it was this: Oenomaus, king of Pisa, had a very beautiful daughter Hippodamia, but he had been warned by an oracle that he would die at the hands of the man who married her. He therefore challenged each suitor to a chariot race and, as he passed his opponent, slew him; for the speed of his horses, given him by Ares, was too great for any of the suitors. He had thus

[1] *Florilegium*, XXVII, 6 (ed. Hense, Vol. III, p. 612, 1).

[2] Pearson, *op. cit.*, II, pp. 121 ff.; Welcker, *op. cit.*, I, pp. 352 ff.

[3] *Epit.*, II, 4 ff. For a list of the sources for the story see Frazer, *Apollodorus*, Vol. II, p. 157, n. 4.

slain thirteen of them, according to Pindar,[1] when Pelops with the winged horses which Poseidon gave him defeated him and won Hippodamia for his bride. There are some differences of detail as to how the victory was won, whether because Pelops enjoyed the favor of the gods, as Pindar states, or because of treachery on the part of Myrtilus, the charioteer of Oenomaus. One version has it that Pelops bribed him to remove the linchpins from the king's chariot or to substitute wax for them, thus causing the chariot to break down and so bring about the death of Oenomaus. According to other versions, Hippodamia fell in love with Pelops and begged Myrtilus to aid her; or Myrtilus was in love with Hippodamia, and Pelops later got rid of him by casting him into the sea. The race was from Pisa to Corinth, and according to some sources served as the foundation of the Olympic Games.

How Sophocles handled this material and what version of the story he followed cannot even be conjectured. If Fragment 474 really comes from the play, the love of Hippodamia for Pelops played a part in it. The story was also used by Euripides as the basis for his *Oenomaus*;[2] and in Roman times by Attius, who no doubt followed one or the other of the Greek tragedies. The chariot race was not only a favorite theme with poets, but with artists as well. Séchan[3] lists fourteen vase-paintings illustrating some portion of the story. The preparations for the start in the race formed the subject of the sculptures in the east pediment of the temple of Zeus at Olympia.

Demosthenes in the oration on the *Crown* (ch. 180) sneers at Aeschines for his poor acting of the part of Oenomaus at Collyte, and Hesychius[4] adds the information that the play was the *Oenomaus* of Sophocles. From this Pearson[5] infers that the *Oenomaus* was one of the most successful tragedies of the poet.

[1] *Ol.*, I, 79.

[2] Bates, *Euripides*, pp. 269 f.

[3] *Op. cit.*, pp. 450 ff.

[4] S. v. ἀρουραῖος Οἰνόμαος.

[5] *Op. cit.*, II, p. 125.

LXXIV

The Palamedes

FOUR fragments alone survive of the *Palamedes*, one a single line, one of four lines, two of one word each.[1]

Palamedes was one of the most famous of the heroes who took part in the expedition against Troy, and his fate most tragic. It was Palamedes who detected the fraud when Odysseus pretended madness in order to escape going to Troy.[2] It was he, too, who invented the games of draughts and dice to while away the time when the army was delayed at Aulis. He was generally accounted one of the wisest of the Greek leaders; but in spite of his knowledge his enemies were able to bring about his death. His story was told in the old epic poem the *Cypria*, and Pausanias (X, 31, 2), who refers to that poem as his authority, says that Palamedes while fishing was drowned through the machinations of Odysseus and Diomedes.

A more complicated plot against him is related by Hyginus (*Fab.* 105) as follows: Odysseus sent word to Agamemnon that he had dreamed that the site of the Greek camp should be changed for one day. Agamemnon believed him and, when the camp had been moved, Odysseus buried some Trojan gold where the tent of Palamedes had been. He then gave a letter to a Phrygian captive ordering him to carry it to Priam, but at the same time he sent a soldier to waylay the man and kill him. The next day the army returned to its former camp. The letter found on the Phrygian purported to be from Priam to Palamedes and mentioned the sum of gold buried by Odysseus where the tent of Palamedes had been. The spot was examined, the gold found, and Palamedes accused of treason. Then, in spite of his protestations of innocence, he was put to death. Socrates apparently had this story in mind when he compared his fate with that of Palamedes in the *Apology* (p. 41, b).

[1] Pearson, *op. cit.*, II, pp. 131 ff.; Welcker, *op. cit.*, I, pp. 129 ff.

[2] The *Mad Odysseus* of Sophocles had to do with this incident. See p. 232.

There are some variations in the narrative in different authors, as might be expected, but the story in its general outlines contains all the elements for a tragic plot. How Sophocles handled this material is unknown. It was used by Aeschylus and by Euripides,[1] both of whom wrote tragedies entitled *Palamedes.*

LXXV

The Pandora

THE satyr drama *Pandora* is quoted five times in all; four times under this title and once as Πανδώρα ἢ Σφυροκόποι.[2] One of the quotations consists of a single line, one of two lines, and the remaining three of one word each.[3] Nowhere is it mentioned as a satyr drama, but the title is sufficient evidence that it could have been nothing else, and this is confirmed by the fragments.

The plot evidently had to do with the making of Pandora, the first woman, by Hephaestus at the command of Zeus. Hesiod (*Works and Days*, 60–105 and *Theogony*, 570–589) tells the story, how Zeus determined to punish mankind after Prometheus had given them fire. He therefore ordered Hephaestus to mingle earth and water and make a beautiful woman. When the work was done she was named Pandora, because all the gods gave her gifts, and sent to Epimetheus. The latter had been warned by Prometheus not to accept any gift from Zeus; but he received Pandora, who brought woe upon mankind by removing the lid of the jar in which all human ills were confined. When she put the lid back Hope alone remained.

There is no word as to how the plot was constructed; but the first part of it can hardly have been concerned with anything else than the making of the image by Hephaestus, with the help of the satyrs who formed the chorus. So much may be inferred from the alternative title *Hammerers.* No doubt there was much

[1] See Bates, *Euripides*, pp. 271 f.
[2] Hesychius, s. v. κεχήλωμαι πόδας.
[3] Pearson, op. cit., II, pp. 135 ff.

delight and buffoonery on the part of the satyrs as the figure of the woman gradually took shape. The latter part of the play may have included the presentation of Pandora to Epimetheus, perhaps by Hephaestus and the satyrs, but the greater part of it may well have had to do with the creation of the image.[1] The story is one which would naturally lend itself to the boisterous fun characteristic of the action in a satyr drama.

LXXVI

The Peleus

TEN fragments of a *Peleus* by Sophocles survive. The longest consists of three lines, one has two short lines, six are single lines, and two are of one word each.[2] The fragment of three lines (Frag. 487) refers to the childish old age of Peleus, and this implies that the plot was concerned with the misfortunes of the aged man, and that it was probably not unlike the plot of the *Peleus* of Euripides.[3] Apparently the aged father of Achilles who had been driven from his kingdom by Acastus was living on the little island of Icus, north of Euboea. Neoptolemus on his way home from Troy had reached the land of the Molossians when he heard what had befallen his grandfather. He set out to assist him but was shipwrecked and lost nearly all his men. He found Peleus, however, living in a cave, overcame his enemies and rescued him. The outlines of the plot may have been something like this; but with the evidence which we have it is unsafe to attempt to reconstruct it in any detail; and it is not even clear where Sophocles laid the scene of the play. Dictys Cretensis (VI, 7–9) seems to have had the *Peleus* of Euripides in mind when he wrote the version of the story which he has preserved for us.

[1] See *Jour. of Hel. Studies*, XXI, pp. 1 ff.

[2] Pearson, *op. cit.*, II, pp. 140 ff.; Welcker, *op. cit.*, I, pp. 205 ff. Welcker would identify the *Peleus* with the *Phthiotides*.

[3] See Bates, *Euripides*, pp. 272 f.

It is worth noting that the second line of Fragment 487 is quoted with a slight change by Aristophanes in the *Knights* (line 1099); which is proof that the *Peleus* was produced before 424 B.C.

LXXVII

The Phaeacians

Two fragments, one of one word and one of three, are quoted from the lost *Phaeacians*.[1] Nothing at all is known of its plot. Welcker thought the play a sequel to the *Nausicaa*,[2] and that the plot was concerned with the latter part of the story told in Book Six of the *Odyssey*. This is a natural inference, though it cannot be proved. Pearson even suggested that it might have had to do with the adventures of the Argonauts in Phaeacia.[3] In the present state of the evidence nothing more can be said about it.

LXXVIII

The Phaedra

THERE are seventeen quotations extant from the *Phaedra* of Sophocles, amounting in all to about twenty-five lines.[4] Five of the fragments are single words, two are of two words, two are single lines, four consist of two lines each, two of three lines, one of four, and one of five. So far as can be judged from these fragments the plot was very similar to that of the extant *Hippolytus Crowned* of Euripides. There Phaedra, at Troezen, falls in love with Hippolytus, her husband's son by the Amazon Hippolyte. Her old nurse makes known her mistress's passion to the young man, who scorns her. Phaedra then hangs herself,

[1] Pearson, *op. cit.*, II, pp. 293 f.; Welcker, *op. cit.*, I, pp. 231 f.
[2] See p. 240.
[3] Apollonius Rhodius, *Argonautica*, IV, 982 ff.
[4] Pearson, *op. cit.*, II, pp. 294 ff.; Welcker, *op. cit.*, I, pp. 394 ff.

leaving a note for her husband accusing Hippolytus. When Theseus finds it he curses his son and calls upon Poseidon to fulfill one of the three promises he had once made him, and to destroy the youth. Hippolytus in all innocence is driving along the shore when a sea-monster frightens his horses, which run away, and he is thrown out of his chariot and killed. Theseus learns the truth when it is too late.

How far the plot of Sophocles differed from this there is no means of knowing. There are certain variants in the story as it has come down to us,[1] perhaps the most important of which is the one that makes Phaedra herself declare her passion. That seems to have been the case in the lost *Hippolytus Veiled* of Euripides[2] and in the *Hippolytus* or *Phaedra* of Seneca. There is not, however, sufficient evidence to prove that Sophocles in his *Phaedra* followed this version of the story. In fact, about all that can be inferred from the fragments agrees with the main outlines of the extant *Hippolytus* of Euripides.

LXXIX

The Philoctetes at Troy

BESIDES the extant *Philoctetes* Sophocles wrote another play *Philoctetes at Troy*, of which seven small fragments alone survive.[3] Three of these are single lines, one a line and a half, one of two words, and two of one word. With such meager remnants it is not possible to reconstruct the plot, but two of the fragments seem to refer to the sore with which the hero was afflicted, and two others perhaps refer to his healing. The play, therefore, apparently dealt with the curing of the ulcer on the leg of Philoctetes, and his subsequent exploits at Troy, probably ending with the slaying of Paris.

Presumably the scene of the tragedy was laid at Troy after the

[1] For the sources see Frazer, *Apollodorus*, Vol. II, p. 146, n. 1.
[2] See Bates, *Euripides*, pp. 249 f.
[3] Pearson, *op. cit.*, II, pp. 307 ff.; Welcker, *op. cit.*, I, pp. 138 f.

hero had been brought back from Lemnos. That is implied in the title. It was, therefore, in a way a sequel to the extant play. The story of the exploits of Philoctetes was found in the *Little Iliad*, which was evidently the source from which Sophocles drew his plot. It is told briefly by Proclus in his summary, and at greater length by Quintus of Smyrna, chiefly in the Ninth and Tenth Books of his *Posthomerica*.[1] It was briefly this:

When the Greeks learned that they could not take Troy without the aid of the arrows of Heracles a committee was sent to Lemnos, and Philoctetes, who had the arrows, was persuaded to return to Troy. After he had done so he was cured of his sore by Podalirius, the son of Asclepius, and restored to health. A great banquet was held at which Agamemnon presented him with splendid gifts and promised others when the city was taken. Philoctetes accepted them and forgave the chiefs for their harsh conduct towards him. The next day, bearing the arms of Heracles, he set forth for battle. His various exploits are related. At length he encounters Paris and shoots an arrow at him which just grazes him. A second arrow strikes Paris in the groin and he withdraws from battle mortally wounded. Whether Sophocles made use of the Oenone episode as related by Quintus it is impossible to tell. It may be that a messenger who came to announce the death of Paris told how he went to Oenone, the wife whom he had deserted for Helen, and begged her in vain to cure his wound. The subsequent exploits of Philoctetes are also related by Quintus. At first he opposed the device of the Wooden Horse, but afterwards became one of the heroes who concealed himself within it and so got into the city.

Just how Sophocles worked up this material into a plot for a tragedy is far from clear. There seems to be no one event to which the dramatic action would gradually lead unless it was the death of Paris. Even then it is not easy to see how a good tragic plot could be developed, or how the play ended. But one fact

[1] See especially IX, 461 ff. and X, 167 ff.

stands out, that it had to do with a sound, not an afflicted Philoctetes.

LXXX

The Phineus A and B

SOPHOCLES wrote two tragedies entitled *Phineus*, but meager fragments of them only have survived.[1] There is one reference to *Phineus A*, and two to *Phineus B*; and there are eight others simply to the *Phineus*. The longest quotation consists of two and a half lines, and there are three quotations of one line each. Two consist of two words, and five of one word. Very little information can be gathered from such scanty material. Fortunately Sophocles himself in a choral passage in the *Antigone*[2] gives a brief account of the early part of the story, namely that the sons of Phineus by his first wife were blinded by his second wife, who tore out their eyes with her shuttle. Here is clearly the main theme for a tragic plot. Sophocles does not tell us the motive for the blinding of the youths by their stepmother, nor does he say what had become of their mother.

The story of Phineus is told by various ancient authorities with many variants.[3] Thus according to Apollodorus,[4] Idaea,[5] the second wife, falsely accused the youths of making an attempt upon her virtue, and Phineus blinded them in consequence; for which he was himself later blinded by the Argonauts. But in an earlier passage[6] he gives another version in which he follows Apollonius Rhodius,[7] namely, that the Argo-

[1] Pearson, *op. cit.*, II, pp. 311 ff.; Welcker, *op. cit.*, I, pp. 329 ff.

[2] Lines 966 ff.

[3] See Frazer, *Apollodorus*, Vol. II, p. 106, n. 3; and Vol. I, p. 103, n. 3.

[4] *Bibl.* III, 15, 3.

[5] Called Eurytia in scholium to *Odyssey*, XII, 69; and Eidothea in scholium to *Antigone* 981.

[6] *Bibl.*, I, 9, 21.

[7] *Argonautica*, II, 178 ff.

nauts drove off the Harpies which were tormenting the blind old man. There would seem to be material for two good tragic plots in the story. The first would deal with the blinding of the sons of Phineus by their stepmother; and the second with his remorse and punishment until rescued by the Argonauts. What Sophocles made the cause of the blindness of Phineus, and whether he represented the sons as recovering their sight or not are points that cannot now be determined.

Sophocles wrote a third play, the *Tympanistae*,[1] on the same theme. Welcker tried to identify it with one of the two tragedies just mentioned, but his argument is not convincing.

Aeschylus is known to have written a *Phineus* brought out in 472 B.C. as the first play in the tetralogy which contained the *Persians*. Little is known about it, and it does not help us in the elucidation of our present problem.

LXXXI

The Phoenix

A SINGLE iambic trimeter line and two single words alone are quoted from the *Phoenix* of Sophocles.[2] Nothing can be inferred from them as to the nature of the plot. About forty-five lines are preserved from the *Phoenix* of Euripides[3] which was a famous play. The story upon which that tragedy was based is told by Apollodorus[4] and other writers. It is, in brief, this: that Phoenix, son of Amyntor, was tempted by his father's concubine, Phthia, and when he rejected her advances she falsely accused him to his father. Amyntor in a rage blinded Phoenix; but at a later time Peleus took him to Chiron, who cured him of his blindness. Still later he was made king of the Dolopians.

Whether Sophocles followed the same story in his tragedy there

[1] See p. 278.

[2] Pearson, *op. cit.*, II, pp. 320 ff.; Welcker, *op. cit.*, I, pp. 140 ff.

[3] See Bates, *Euripides*, pp. 281 f.

[4] *Bibl.*, III, 13, 8.

is no means of knowing. Pearson thinks that he did not; but that his plot was based upon a tale told in the Ninth Book of the *Iliad*.[1] According to that, Phoenix acknowledged his guilt, but declared he was urged to it by his mother. He was not blinded, but fled to Peleus and later accompanied Achilles to Troy.[2] Until further evidence is available the nature of the plot must be left unsettled.

It is not known whether the *Phoenix* of Sophocles preceded or followed that of Euripides.

LXXXII

The Phrixus

THE *Phrixus* is quoted three times, twice with single lines and once with a single word.[3] Nothing can be learned from these quotations about the plot. The general outlines of the myth with which Phrixus was concerned are familiar, and Sophocles used parts of it in his two plays entitled *Athamas* (see p. 181). It may be that he found the plot of his *Phrixus* in the earlier part of the story, as Welcker imagined.

From Hyginus[4] we learn that Demodice, wife of Cretheus, fell in love with Phrixus, son of Athamas; that he disregarded her, was falsely accused by her and, when he was about to be punished by Cretheus, was hidden by a cloud, rescued, and carried over the sea. At a later time, after his stay among the Colchians, he was brought back and Athamas convinced Cretheus of the young man's innocence. There are some variants in the story such as that which makes Demodice the stepmother of Phrixus.[5] With the evidence now available any attempt to suggest a plot for the tragedy can be nothing but conjecture.

[1] IX, ll. 447 ff.
[2] See Frazer, *Apollodorus*, Vol. II, p. 74, n. 2.
[3] Pearson, *op. cit.*, II, pp. 322, ff.; Welcker, *op. cit.*, I, pp. 317 ff.
[4] Hyginus, *Poet. Astron.*, II, 20.
[5] Pindar, *Pyth.*, IV, 162 and scholium.

LXXXIII

The Phrygians

THERE are extant two quotations from the *Phrygians* of Sophocles,[1] one of four lines to the effect that Ares likes to slay the noble and the brave; and the other a little more than a line in which the speaker commands others to stop celebrating a marriage with song. Without the context it is impossible to know what bearing these lines had on the plot. It has been conjectured that the play was about the same subject as the *Phrygians or Ransoming of Hector* of Aeschylus. In that case the second title shows that that tragedy was based on the incident related in the Twenty-fourth Book of the *Iliad*,[2] in which Priam goes to the tent of Achilles and ransoms the body of Hector. The conjecture is a natural one, but there is no means of knowing whether or not it is right. The subject does not seem well adapted to a tragic plot.

LXXXIV

The Phthiotides

THERE are three fragments with a total of four lines extant from the lost *Phthiotides*, or *Women of Phthia*, of Sophocles.[3] The title must refer to the chorus, but what the plot was, or what part the women may have had in it, it is impossible to say. In one of the fragments an older man is addressing a youth. In another one old man, apparently a slave, is addressing another old man. The third fragment refers to a trial for homicide. These hints are not enough to help us to recover the plot. One would naturally think of the Homeric Phthia and that the tragedy was somehow concerned with the story of Achilles. Campbell[4] suggested tentatively that it had to do with the

[1] Pearson, *op. cit.*, II, pp. 325 ff.; Welcker, *op. cit.*, I, pp. 135 f.
[2] XXIV, 468 ff.
[3] Pearson, *op. cit.*, II, pp. 305 ff.; Welcker, *op. cit.*, I, pp. 205 ff.
[4] *Sophocles*, II, p. 541, note.

education of Achilles. Welcker thought it might be another title for the *Peleus*, but Aristotle differentiates between the two plays. Pearson inclines towards Vater's suggestion that it was another title for the *Hermione*. From the evidence at present available nothing satisfactory can be determined.

The *Phthiotides* seems to have been a tragedy of some distinction in antiquity, for Aristotle[1] refers to it as an example of a play expressing character. He does not, to be sure, mention the name of the author, but there can be little doubt that it is the play of Sophocles which he had in mind.

LXXXV

The Polyxena

THE story of the sacrifice of Polyxena, daughter of Priam, at the tomb of Achilles after the fall of Troy is familiar from many sources.[2] It was told originally in the *Iliupersis*, as may be gathered from the brief notice of that poem preserved by Proclus (*Chrestomathia*, p. 240, ed. Westphal). It was the principal incident in the first part of the *Hecuba* of Euripides.[3] A few fragments of the *Polyxena* of Sophocles have come down to modern times. There is one of seven lines, one of three, one of two, and three are of one line each. Still another consists of but two words.[4]

The scene of the tragedy was laid on the shore near Troy after its fall, and the action apparently began with a quarrel between Agamemnon and Menelaus about sailing home. According to Proclus (p. 240) the epic poem *Nosti* began with an account of this quarrel, and this was very likely the source from which Sophocles drew. Fragment 522 seems to have been addressed by Agamemnon to Menelaus. The ghost of Achilles then

[1] *Poet.*, p. 1456a 1 ἡ δὲ ἠθική, οἷον αἱ Φθιώτιδες καὶ ὁ Πηλεύς.

[2] See Frazer, *Apollodorus*, Vol. II, p. 240, n. 1.

[3] See Bates, *Euripides*, pp. 91 ff.

[4] Pearson, *op. cit.*, II, pp. 161 ff.; Welcker, *op. cit.*, I, pp. 176 ff.

appeared and demanded the sacrifice of Polyxena at his tomb. This may be inferred from Fragment 523:

> Departing from the joyless, gloomy shores
> Of Acheron's haven and those barren streams
> Where shrill laments reëcho have I come.

The scene that followed may well have resembled that in the *Hecuba* of Euripides.[1] Polyxena was no doubt led away to her death, but whether voluntarily or not cannot be told. After this it may be conjectured that preparations for the departure were resumed and that Agamemnon left the stage for his ship.

LXXXVI

The Priam

Four single words, three of them from one passage in Pollux (VII, 118) are assigned to the *Priam* of Sophocles.[2] Nothing whatsoever is known about the plot, but it might be presumed to deal with the ransoming of Hector, as related in the Twenty-fourth Book of the *Iliad*. Aeschylus apparently used that episode in his *Phrygians or the Ransoming of Hector*. Welcker suggested that the slaying of Priam by Neoptolemus after the fall of Troy might have served for the plot of the tragedy; but in the absence of specific evidence no conclusion can be arrived at. A *Priam* is known to have been written by the tragic poet Philocles.[3]

LXXXVII

The Procris

One incomplete line quoted by Pollux (IX, 140) alone remains of the *Procris*.[4] The story is, however, familiar from several

[1] Lines 177–442.
[2] Pearson, *op. cit.*, II, pp. 169 f.; Welcker, *op. cit.*, I, pp. 157 f.
[3] Suidas, s. v. Φιλοκλῆς.
[4] Pearson, *op. cit.*, II, pp. 170 ff.; Welcker, *op. cit.*, I, pp. 388 ff.

sources, and its tragic ending might well serve for the climax of a tragedy. In its general outlines it is this: Cephalus and his wife Procris, daughter of Erechtheus, were deeply in love with each other. Cephalus was fond of hunting, and the Dawn ('Hώς) seeing him, fell in love with him; but he rejected her advances. She, however, declared that Procris was not faithful to him, and to test her Cephalus visited her in disguise. When he thought that his suspicions were confirmed he revealed himself to her. Procris had now become suspicious of him; for a servant had reported that when out hunting with his master he had heard him beg *νεφέλη*, that is, "cloud" to come. He was really calling for a cloud to relieve him from the heat of the sun; but the man thought he was calling some woman named Nephele. The next time, therefore, that Cephalus went hunting Procris followed him, and hearing his cry started to go forward. Perceiving a movement in the bushes and thinking it caused by a wild animal, Cephalus cast his dart, which always hit the mark it was aimed at, and so accidentally killed his wife. Later on Cephalus was tried for homicide before the court of the Areopagus.

There are several important variants in the story as told by different authors,[1] such as the eight years' absence from home on the part of Cephalus,[2] and the visit of Procris to Minos and the gifts she received from him;[3] but it is decidedly tragic and supplies good material for the dramatist. How Sophocles used it cannot now be told. The climax must have come with the death of Procris; and it is not unlikely that the play came to an end with the trial of Cephalus.

[1] For the sources see Frazer, *Apollodorus*, Vol. II, p. 103, n. 4.

[2] Scholium on *Odyssey*, XI, 321 on the authority of Pherecydes. *ἡ δὲ ἱστορία παρὰ Φερεκύδῃ ἐν τῇ ἑβδόμῃ.*

[3] See e.g., Apollodorus, *Bibl.*, III, 15, 1.

LXXXVIII

The Prophets or Polyidus

THERE are three references in the literature to the *Polyidus* of Sophocles, one a quotation of five lines, one of one line, and one of one word. Besides these there are seven quotations from the *Prophets* (Μάντεις), each of a single line or part of a line.[1] Two of these mention Polyidus by name, one calling him a seer. On the strength of these references Pearson argues, correctly I think, that the *Polyidus* of Sophocles and the *Prophets* were one and the same play.

The story upon which the plot was based is told in some detail by Apollodorus[2] and Hyginus.[3] It is this: The boy Glaucus, son of Minos and Pasiphaë, while at play fell into a great jar of honey and was drowned. When nobody could tell what had become of him Minos consulted the oracle of Apollo, or the Curetes, to find out where he was. In reply he was told that whoever could interpret the remarkable prodigy of a calf which changed color every four hours, being first white, then red, and then black, could find his son. This man proved to be the seer Polyidus, who likened the calf to a mulberry which is first white, then red, and then black. Three lines quoted by Photius (p. 45, 4) as coming from Sophocles but without naming the play (Frag. 395) apparently refer to this incident. Polyidus was then ordered to find Glaucus and at length did so. Minos then told him to restore the boy to life, and when he declared that he was unable to do it, ordered him to be shut up in a tomb with the dead body. While he was there a serpent approached the dead boy and he killed it. Another serpent entered the tomb and finding its mate dead hastened away. It soon returned with an herb which it placed on the dead snake and quickly restored it to life. Polyidus procured some of the herb, applied it to Glaucus and so brought him back to life. When this was made

[1] Pearson, *op. cit.*, II, pp. 56 ff.
[2] *Bibl.*, III, 3, 1.
[3] *Fab.*, 136.

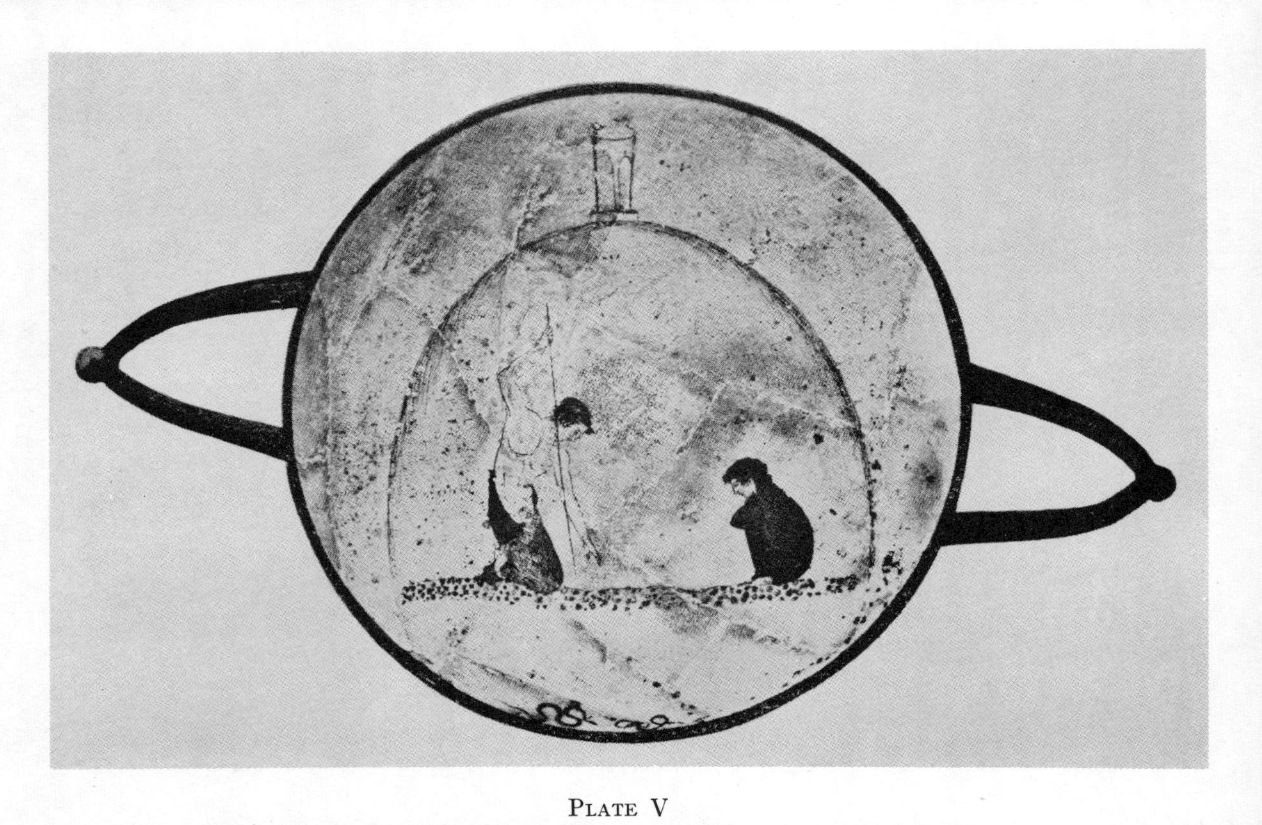

PLATE V

POLYIDUS IN TOMB SLAYING SERPENT; GLAUCUS FACING HIM

From a Cylix in the British Museum

known to the watchers outside the tomb Polyidus was released and given great rewards.

How Sophocles handled this material is unknown. Euripides also wrote a tragedy on the same subject called the *Polyidus*,[1] but the thirty lines of it which are preserved do not give any clear indication of the way in which the plot was constructed.

The general outlines of the story were known to the vase painters, for on a white cylix by Sotades in the British Museum Polyidus is represented inside the tomb in the act of slaying a serpent while the boy Glaucus squats near him. Their names are inscribed beside the figures (PLATE V).[2]

LXXXIX

The Salmoneus

THE *Salmoneus* is quoted five times, once being expressly designated as a satyr drama. The longest citation consists of three lines and refers to the game of cottabus. The others are a line and a half, a line, two words, and one word.[3] The plot cannot be recovered from these scraps.

Salmoneus is known as the brother of Sisyphus, Athamas, and Cretheus. Apollodorus[4] says of him that at first he lived in Thessaly, but afterwards removed to Elis, where he founded a city. He was arrogant, declared that he was Zeus and ordered sacrifices to be made to him. He dragged about dried hides and bronze kettles fastened to his chariot declaring that he was thundering. He also hurled lighted torches into the air, saying that he was sending forth lightning. Zeus struck him with a thunderbolt and destroyed him, together with his city and its people. So much for Apollodorus. There is no hint here of any association of satyrs with this madman. Perhaps they were

[1] Bates, *Euripides*, pp. 284 ff.
[2] *White Athenian Vases in the British Museum*, pl. XVI.
[3] Pearson, *op. cit.*, II, pp. 177 ff.
[4] *Bibl.*, I, 9, 7.

represented as being in his service. This would be in keeping with the practice followed by Sophocles in some of his other satyr plays.[1] One fragment (No. 540) mentions Carian goats, an uncomplimentary name which Salmoneus may have applied to the satyrs. Part of the fun may, perhaps, have been excited by the antics of the satyrs in their terror at the actions of their insane master.

XC

The Scyrians

THERE are nine references to the *Scyrians* (Σκύριοι) of Sophocles in the literature, five of them being single words, two single lines, one of six, and one of six and one half lines,[2] and in addition two papyrus fragments, one of six and the other of twenty-three broken lines.[3] The title is twice wrongly given by Hesychius as Σκύριαι.

The subject of this tragedy has been much discussed. The *Scyrians* of Euripides was concerned with the story of the concealment of the young Achilles by Thetis among the daughters of Lycomedes on the island of Scyros to prevent him from taking part in the expedition against Troy. This is made certain by a papyrus in Florence which gives the first line of the play and a summary of the plot.[4] Odysseus found him out by exhibiting beautiful arms which led the disguised youth to reveal

[1] E.g., in the *Amycus*, the *Cedalion*, and the *Pandora*.

[2] Pearson, *op. cit.*, II, pp. 191 ff.; Welcker, *op. cit.*, I, pp. 102 ff.; Séchan, *op. cit.*, pp. 185 ff.

[3] *Ox. Pap.*, XVII, 1927, No. 2077. They are proved to belong to this play, as three of the broken lines agree with three lines of Frag. 555, quoted by Stobaeus as coming from the *Scyrians* of Sophocles. See R. Pfeiffer, *Philologus*, LXXXVIII, 1933, pp. 1 ff.

[4] The summary breaks off after sixteen lines. The papyrus also contains twenty-five lines on the plot of the *Rhesus* and eight lines from an account of the *Rhadamanthys*. See C. Gallovatti, *Rivista di Filologia*, 1933, pp. 177 ff.; and A. Körte, *Hermes*, LXIX, 1934, pp. 1 ff.

his identity. Achilles among the maidens of Scyros was the subject of a famous painting by Polygnotus in the north wing of the Propylaea at Athens.[1]

On the other hand it has been shown with considerable certainty that Sophocles followed the story that made Odysseus and Phoenix go to Scyros to bring back with them to Troy Neoptolemus, the son of Achilles, when it was found that the city could not be taken without his aid. One of the longer fragments (No. 557), as Pearson[2] and others have thought, points to this. It may be translated as follows:

> But if by weeping one could cure his ills
> And by his tears raise up the dead again
> Why, tears would be a greater prize than gold.
> But now, my aged friend, this cannot be,
> To bring to light one hidden in the tomb.
> If tears could aught avail, my father, too,
> Would have come back to life.

These words were probably spoken by Neoptolemus to Phoenix.

R. Pfeiffer[3] calls attention to the fact that about 450 B.C. the departure of Neoptolemus from Scyros became a subject for the painters of red-figured vases, and he thinks this due to the influence of the *Scyrians* of Sophocles.

XCI

The Scythians

THE *Scythians* is quoted seven times, but in two places the exact words of the quotation are not given. Of the remaining citations one has three defective lines, one one line, and three are single words.[4] Little can be gathered from them except that the play had to do with the Argonautic expedition. Pearson presents

[1] Pausanias, I, 22, 6.
[2] *Op. cit.*, II, p. 192.
[3] *Op. cit.*, p. 14.
[4] Pearson, *op. cit.*, II, pp. 185 ff.; Welcker, *op. cit.*, I, pp. 337 ff.

succinctly the argument that the slaying of Apsertus, brother of Medea, in Scythia was the incident about which the plot was constructed. This may well have been the case. In the *Argonautica* of Apollonius Rhodius (IV, 454 ff.) we are told that Medea induced Apsertus, who was leading the pursuing Colchians, to come ashore on an island in the Ister where Jason ambushed and killed him. His followers were then afraid to go back to Aeetes, and settled in that locality. This does not accord with the more familiar story that Apsertus was a boy, that he was carried off by Jason and Medea, slain on shipboard and his dismembered body cast overboard to delay the pursuers; but it is better suited to the stage and gives a possible reason for the title. More than this cannot be inferred from the evidence available.

Sophocles also made use of the history of Medea in the *Colchian Women*, in the *Sorcerers*, and probably in the *Aegeus*. The story of the Argonautic expedition was one familiar to the Greeks both in their literature and in their art. In the Anaceum at Athens there was a famous painting of it by Micon. Whether this had any influence upon Sophocles in suggesting to him the subject for his tragedy there is no way of knowing.

XCII

The Shepherds

TWENTY-FIVE fragments, two doubtfully, may be assigned to the *Shepherds* (Ποιμένες). Eight of these consist of single lines; one has two lines and one three, the others consist of either one or two words.[1]

The plot had to do with the first arrival of the Greeks in Trojan territory. Apparently a shepherd saw the expedition advancing along the shore[2] early in the morning and reported it. The

[1] Pearson, *op. cit.*, II, pp. 147 ff.; Welcker, *op. cit.*, I, pp. 113 ff.

[2] Cp. Frag. 502, ἐωθινὸς γάρ, πρίν τιν' αὐλιτῶν ὁρᾶν,
θαλλὸν χιμαίραις προσφέρων νεοσπάδα
εἶδον στρατὸν στείχοντα παραλίαν πέτραν.

Greeks landed and were attacked by the Trojans with stones. These seem to have been the Shepherds who formed the chorus. Protesilaus, the first Greek to land, slew several of them before Hector hastened from the city and killed him. Thus the prophecy of Thetis, who warned Achilles that the first man to land would die, was fulfilled. Later on Achilles slew Cycnus, the son of Poseidon, by hitting him on the head with a stone. The Trojans then fled to Troy and the siege began.[1] These incidents were related in the *Cypria* and were undoubtedly included in the play. How they were worked into a tragic plot by Sophocles must be left to conjecture.

XCIII

The Sinon

THE *Sinon* is cited three times by Hesychius, but each citation gives but a single word.[2] The story of Sinon is well known from various sources. It was taken from the *Iliupersis* and is related at length by Quintus of Smyrna in his *Posthomerica*.[3] It is this:

When Epeus had built the Wooden Horse and all was ready, Odysseus called for a volunteer to go with it and mislead the Trojans. Sinon offered himself for the task. The Greek fleet sailed away and the Trojans found the Horse with Sinon near by. He pretended that the Greeks had left for home and that Odysseus had advised that he be sacrificed before they sailed. He had, however, saved himself by clinging to the feet of the Horse, and the Greeks had been obliged to leave him. The Trojans tortured him and cut off his nose and ears, but he stood by his story. When the great Horse had been dragged into the city the Trojans held high festival and, after they were overcome by wine, Sinon lighted a torch as a signal to the fleet at Tenedos to

[1] See Apollodorus, *Epit.*, III, 29–32.
[2] Pearson, *op. cit.*, II, pp. 181 ff.; Welcker, *op. cit.*, I, p. 157.
[3] XII, ll. 243 ff.; XIII, ll. 23 ff.; XIV, ll. 107 ff.

return. Then he gave the word to the warriors inside the Horse to come out. This they did and seized the gates. After the fall of the city Sinon was loaded with honors for his work.

This then, is the story which Sophocles used. How he constructed a tragic plot out of it is unknown.

XCIV

The Sisyphus

Two words quoted by Hesychius[1] alone testify to a *Sisyphus* by Sophocles, but there is no good reason to doubt the existence of such a play.[2] What it was about can only be conjectured, for the stories current about Sisyphus furnished the dramatist with abundant material with which to work. That the offense for which he was punished in Hades was one of impiety seems clear, although there are different statements as to what this offense was supposed to be. According to Pherecydes,[3] Zeus sent Death to punish Sisyphus, but the latter put Death in chains. He was, however, released by Ares and carried Sisyphus away to the Lower World. But even then the wily king was not conquered, for before departing he told his wife Merope to omit all funeral rites in his honor. The divinities thus failed to receive their due honors, and when they complained he persuaded Persephone to let him go back to punish his wife for her dereliction. Once in the upper world he refused to return to Hades until he was dragged off by force. This part of the story may well have been included in the play, but whether it was a tragedy or a satyr drama cannot be determined. Aeschylus is known to have written a satyr drama about Sisyphus, and possibly a tragedy.[4] The satyr drama *Sisyphus* sometimes wrongly attributed to Euripides was probably written by Critias.[5]

[1] S. v. ζεῦγος τριπάρθενον.

[2] Pearson, *op. cit.*, II, pp. 184 f.; Welcker, *op. cit.*, I, pp. 402 f.

[3] Quoted by scholiast on *Iliad*, VI, 153.

[4] See Smyth, *Aeschylus*, II, p. 457.

[5] Bates, *Euripides*, p. 16.

XCV

The Sorcerers

THE *Sorcerers* (Ῥιζοτόμοι) dealt with one of the famous incidents in the career of Medea—the device by which she caused the death of Pelias. There are but three fragments of the play left, but one of these has seven lines and one six. The third consists of three words.[1] The longest quotation comes from Macrobius[2] who distinctly says that in the Ῥιζοτόμοι Sophocles represented Medea cutting the deadly plants and extracting the poisonous sap from them. The title probably came from the chorus, who may be imagined as helping Medea gather the herbs for her magic rites; though the possibility must be acknowledged that they may have been called Sorcerers who assisted the daughters of Pelias in their unfortunate experiment. Welcker's suggestion that the play set forth the devices by which Medea persuaded the daughters of Pelias to kill their father in the belief that they were making him young again is reasonable.

The story is familiar. During the absence of Jason on the Argonautic Expedition Pelias treated his family with great cruelty, causing the death of his father, mother, and young brother. When Jason returned from his voyage Medea determined to help him punish the wicked Pelias. She explained to the latter's family that his youth could be brought back again by means of magic rites. In proof of her assertion she cut up an aged ram, boiled it and made it young again. The daughters were convinced and tried the same experiment upon their father disastrously. While the experiment was going on Medea signaled to the Argonauts by means of a lighted torch on the roof of the palace, and they seized the building. Afterwards Jason and Medea retired to Corinth.

The death of Pelias must have been the crisis in the tragedy, as it presumably was in the *Peliades*[3] of Euripides. The play

[1] Pearson, *op. cit.*, II, pp. 172 ff.; Welcker, *op. cit.*, I, pp. 340 ff.

[2] *Saturnalia*, V, 19, 8.

[3] See Bates, *Euripides*, pp. 273 ff.

may have come to an end with the departure of Jason and Medea for Corinth.

Welcker identified the *Sorcerers* with the *Pelias* which is cited once; but Pearson[1] points out that that reference is more likely to one of the tragedies entitled *Tyro*.

XCVI

The Tantalus

A SINGLE iambic trimeter line is the only fragment definitely stated as coming from the *Tantalus*;[2] but a manuscript of Stobaeus[3] gives two and a half lines of a play which it calls *ταντᾶ*. There would seem to be little doubt that the *Tantalus* was the tragedy meant. In addition there are two badly mutilated fragments of papyrus of twelve and ten lines respectively[4] which have been much discussed.[5] Blass, for example, attributed them to the *Niobe* of Sophocles; while Wecklein thought they came from the *Niobe* of Aeschylus, to which tragedy Reinhardt would also assign them. Pearson agrees with Blass that Sophocles was the author, but concludes that they belonged to the *Tantalus*, not the *Niobe*. Tantalus seems to be the speaker,[6] and the scene to be laid in Lydia. This would point to the *Tantalus*; but a satisfactory conclusion cannot be obtained from the evidence available.

When it comes to the plot there is little that can be said. Pearson's suggestion that it was concerned with the theft of the golden dog of Zeus and its consequences seems a reasonable conjecture. Pandareos deposited the dog for safe keeping with Tantalus, who perjured himself in order to retain it; but Hermes

[1] *Op. cit.*, II, p. 274, note on Frag. 648.

[2] Pearson, *op. cit.*, II, pp. 209 ff.

[3] *Florilegium*, IV, 53, 1 (p. 1097, 1, ed. Hense).

[4] *Ox. Pap.*, II, pp. 23 ff., No. 213.

[5] See Pearson, *op. cit.*, II, pp. 97 f.; also p. 211, note on Frag. 574; and Reinhardt, *Hermes*, LXIX, 1934, pp. 250 ff.

[6] Reinhardt thinks that the speaker was Amphion.

recovered it and Tantalus was punished by being buried under Mount Sipylus. His city was destroyed by an earthquake, to which there may be an allusion in one of the papyrus fragments.[1] No more satisfactory account of this tragedy can now be given.

XCVII

The Telephus

THE references to the *Telephus* are so scanty that there has been a difference of opinion as to whether it was a tragedy or a satyr drama. Welcker[2] even thought that it was not a separate play, but another name for the *Mysians*. This is now known to be a mistake. One word only is preserved from it;[3] but the existence of a *Telephus* by Sophocles is supported by a Rhodian inscription dating from the fourth or third century B.C.[4] It records a victory in Rhodes with certain plays of Sophocles, one of which is called σατυρικὸν Τηλεφ. The last letter is, to be sure, defective, and it has been suggested that the word might be restored Τηλέ [γονον] though there is no evidence for such a play by Sophocles. The restoration Τήλε[φον] is, however, confirmed by another inscription found in 1929, where there is mention of a *Telepheia* by Sophocles. This has already been discussed in the account of the *Aleadae*. *Telepheia* can hardly mean anything else than a tetralogy dealing with the Telephus story. The *Telephus* would then be a satyr drama completing the tetralogy in which the *Aleadae*, the *Mysians*, and the *Muster of the Achaeans* may have made up the trilogy of tragedies preceding it.

Previous to the discovery of the inscription near Vari, various scholars had argued that the *Telephus* was a satyr drama; and Pearson had pointed out how suitable the mountains of Arcadia

[1] Frag. 575, l. 2.

[2] *Op. cit.*, I, pp. 414 ff.

[3] See Hesychius, s. v. ἀείφορος, and Pearson, *op. cit.*, II, pp. 220 f.

[4] See p. 211 where the inscription is quoted.

were for the setting of a satyr play. Unfortunately nothing certain can be learned as to its plot.

XCVIII

The Tereus

THE *Tereus* is better represented by fragments than most of the lost plays of Sophocles. It is quoted by name thirteen times, and two other passages may be assigned to it with considerable probability. Of the fragments definitely stated to have come from it, one is of twelve lines, one of six, two of five, one of four, two of two, and four are single lines. In addition two are single words.[1]

The story, to which there are numerous references in both Greek and Latin writers, is familiar. In brief it is this: Procne, daughter of Pandion king of Athens, was married to a Thracian, Tereus. She wished her sister Philomela to visit her, and Tereus went to Athens in order to escort her to Thrace. He, however, violated Philomela, and to conceal his crime cut out her tongue; but she by means of embroidery made her misfortune known to Procne. The two women then revenged themselves upon Tereus by slaying his son Itys and serving his cooked flesh to his father. After Tereus had eaten of it they told him the truth and fled. He pursued them, but all three were transformed into birds, Tereus into a hoopoe, Procne into a nightingale, and Philomela into a swallow. As might be supposed, there are variants in this story as told by different authors.

Whether the *Tereus* of Sophocles had any peculiar features it is impossible to tell from the extant fragments. So far as any inference can be drawn from them they seem to confirm the familiar tale; but Aristotle in the *Poetics*[2] speaks of the recognition scene in the play being brought about by the voice of the

[1] Pearson, *op. cit.*, II, pp. 221 ff.; Welcker, *op. cit.*, I, pp. 374 ff.
[2] *Poet.*, p. 1454 b 36 f. καὶ ἐν τῷ Σοφοκλέους Τηρεῖ ἡ τῆς κερκίδος φωνή.

shuttle. C. R. Post[1] makes the interesting suggestion that Sophocles may have represented a strong-minded Procne and a weaker Philomela, somewhat as he portrayed Antigone and Ismene, and Electra and Chrysothemis. There is, however, no way of knowing whether or not this was the case. Aristophanes refers to the play in his *Birds*.[2]

XCIX

The Teucer

THERE are three quotations from the *Teucer* extant, one of four lines, one of a line and a half, and one of two words.[3] In addition there are various allusions which may with great probability be referred to the play. From these it can be determined that the scene was laid in Salamis and that the plot was concerned with the return home of Teucer and the anger of his father Telamon that he should have come back without his brother Ajax. It may have reached a climax with the banishment of Teucer from Salamis and his departure to found Salamis in Cyprus.

The *Teucer* is quoted by Aristophanes in the *Clouds* (l. 583) according to the scholiast on that passage; and it was apparently followed closely by Pacuvius in his *Teucer*, which was a famous play among the Romans. Twenty-one short fragments of the latter tragedy remain,[4] but it would hardly be safe to claim any one of them as a translation of a line of Sophocles. Cicero was evidently a great admirer of it.

[1] *Harv. Stud. in Class. Philol.*, XXXIII, p. 51.
[2] Cp. l. 100 and scholium on 281.
[3] Pearson, *op. cit.*, II, pp. 214 ff.; Welcker, *op. cit.*, I, pp. 191 ff.
[4] Ribbeck, *op. cit.*, I, pp. 116 ff.

C

The Thamyras

THE *Thamyras* is another tragedy better represented by extant fragments than many of the lost plays of Sophocles. It is quoted by name seven times and there are two other passages, one of four lines and one of two, which almost certainly belong to it.[1] We have, then, all told about fourteen lines of the play preserved, a rather pitiful amount, it must be confessed, when one thinks of the whole tragedy.

The way in which the poet developed his plot is unknown, though the outlines of the story upon which it was based are familiar. Thamyras, or Thamyris as he is better known,[2] was a king of Thrace who attained such preëminence in song that he either challenged the Muses to a musical contest,[3] or boasted his superiority to them.[4] The result in either case was that he was deprived of his sight and of his power of song as well, and destroyed his lyre.

The scene of the tragedy seems to have been laid by Sophocles near Mount Athos in Thrace. That is implied in Fragment 237. Another fragment (No. 244), though it does not bear the name of the *Thamyras*, speaks of the broken lyre,

> He broke the lyre's gold-wrought arm,
> He broke the music of its strings.

The steps by which the poet led up to the crisis in the plot can only be imagined.

Thamyras after his punishment is not unfamiliar in Greek art. Thus Pausanias (IX, 30, 2) says that in the grove of the Muses on Mount Helicon there was a statue of Thamyras blind and

[1] Pearson, *op. cit.*, I, pp. 176 ff.; Welcker, *op. cit.*, I, pp. 419 ff.; Séchan, *op. cit.*, pp. 193 ff.

[2] Thamyras is said to have been the Attic form of the word, see Pearson, *op. cit.*, I, p. 179.

[3] See Euripides, *Rhesus*, 923 ff.

[4] Homer, *Iliad*, II, 597 ff.

PLATE VI

THE BLIND THAMYRAS THROWS AWAY HIS BROKEN LYRE

From a Hydria in the Ashmolean Museum, Oxford

holding a broken lyre; and in the great painting of Polygnotus in the Lesche of the Cnidians at Delphi the artist represented Thamyras in Hades as a blind man with long hair and beard, seated, with a broken lyre at his feet.[1] The story was also familiar to the Attic vase painters (PLATE VI). The tragedy, then, had to do with the reversal in the fortunes of the singer from good to bad. Sophocles himself, as already noted,[2] is said to have played the lyre in this play.

CI

The Theseus

SUIDAS quotes the word *ὄμπνιον* in the sense of *μέγα, πολύ, ηὐξημένον* as being used by Sophocles in the *Theseus*.[3] There is no other reference to this play, and no hint as to what part of the story of the Attic hero the poet made the subject of his drama. Euripides wrote a *Theseus*[4] in which the slaying of the Minotaur seems to have had an important part. This may also have been true of the *Theseus* of Sophocles; but in the absence of definite information it is idle to speculate as to its plot.

CII

The Thyestes

THE number of tragedies written by Sophocles dealing with the story of Thyestes has long been a matter of dispute. There are in the literature fifteen references to a *Thyestes* simply; one to a *First Thyestes* (ἐκ τοῦ α' Θυέστου); two to a *Second Thyestes* (e.g., Σοφοκλῆς Θυέστῃ δευτέρῳ, Hesychius, s.v. *ἠγόμην*); and five to a *Thyestes at Sicyon*. Besides these there has more recently

[1] Pausanias, X, 30, 8.
[2] See p. 5.
[3] Pearson, *op. cit.*, I, pp. 184 f.
[4] Bates, *Euripides*, pp. 301 f.

come to light a papyrus in which there is mention of a *Third Thyestes* (Θυέστου τρίτου Σοφοκλέους). There is also one reference to an *Atreus* (see p. 183).

The story of Thyestes is a story of horrible crimes and equally horrible punishments.[1] The more important incidents in it are these: He seduced Aërope, the wife of his brother Atreus; by her help he got possession of the golden lamb of Atreus and so became king; Atreus invited him to a banquet and served him as food the flesh of his own children; he became by his own daughter, Pelopia, the father of Aegisthus who avenged him by killing Atreus and later Agamemnon. Finally there is the suicide of Pelopia when she discovered who the father of her son, Aegisthus, was.

It would seem to be clear that the *Thyestes at Sicyon* dealt with the story of the incest of Thyestes and Pelopia and its tragic results, for it was at Sicyon that the scene of that crime was laid. But the mention of a first and second *Thyestes* shows that Sophocles must have written at least one tragedy which had to do with the earlier part of the story. Pearson[2] thought the play referred to as the *First Thyestes* was really the *Atreus*, and that Sophocles wrote only one other play on the subject. That explanation now seems untenable. In *Aegyptus* for 1921 (pp. 281 ff.) H. I. Bell discusses a papyrus dating from the middle of the second century A.D. which contains a bookseller's account. It records payments made for the copying of manuscripts. In lines 19 and 20 of the first column occurs the entry: "For copying the *Plutus* of Aristophanes and —— and the third *Thyestes* of Sophocles, 12 drachmas."[3] This would seem to settle the question of the number of tragedies by Sophocles concerned with the Thyestes story. The first may have been rightly called the *Atreus*, as Pearson thought; the second would also have to do

[1] See Apollodorus, *Epit.*, II, 10 ff.; Hyginus, *Fab.* 87 and 88.

[2] *Op. cit.*, I, pp. 91 ff. For other discussions of the subject see Welcker, *op. cit.*, I, pp. 366 ff.; Petersen, *Die Attische Tragödie*, pp. 617 ff.; Séchan, *op. cit.*, pp. 199 ff.

[3] The papyrus reads, ὑ]πὲρ γράπτων Πλούτου 'Αριστοφάνους καὶ.[. . .]ύρου καὶ Θυέστου τρίτου Σοφοκλέ(ους)(δραχμὰς) ιβ'.

with the earlier part of the story and probably include the banquet; and the *Thyestes at Sicyon* (Θυέστης ὁ ἐν Σικυῶνι or Θυέστης Σικυώνιος) would then be the third. There is no evidence as to the way in which the poet developed his plot in any of these plays. Apart from single words the quotations from all of them together amount to but twenty-two lines.

Euripides wrote a *Thyestes*,[1] as did the Roman poet Ennius.[2]

CIII

The Triptolemus

THERE are twenty-one fragments of the *Triptolemus* preserved, but they are all very short. The longest consists of three lines, nine are single lines, and the others are of one, two, or three words.[3] Pliny records the fact that it was brought out 145 years before the death of Alexander the Great, that is, in 468 B.C.[4] It is thus seen to have been one of the earliest of the plays of Sophocles. The fragments themselves confirm this early date, for they show the influence of Aeschylus upon the author. One of them in fact (Frag. 597) is clearly an imitation of line 815 of the *Prometheus Bound.*

The plot of the play cannot be reconstructed from the existing fragments, though it can be inferred that the scene was laid at Eleusis. The journey of Triptolemus over the earth in a chariot drawn by winged serpents, (FIG. 4) spreading among mankind knowledge of cultivating grain, had an important place in it. Demeter was naturally one of the principal characters. There would appear to be little material here for a tragic plot; but the poet would have a good opportunity to glorify Attica as the land from which knowledge of the cultivation of the soil

[1] Bates, *Euripides*, pp. 302 f.

[2] Ribbeck, *op. cit.*, I, pp. 57 ff.

[3] Pearson, *op. cit.*, II, pp. 239 ff.; Welcker, *op. cit.*, I, pp. 299 ff.

[4] *Nat. Hist.*, XVIII, 65. His words are ....*ante mortem eius* (i.e., of Alexander) *annis fere CXLV*.

FIGURE 4.—TRIPTOLEMUS IN WINGED SERPENT CAR. DEMETER, CELEUS, PERSEPHONE AND HIPPOTHOÖN STANDING BY.

From a Vase in Vienna

spread to other countries. The number of fragments preserved is evidence that readers had not lost interest in it in late Greek times.

Pearson thinks that the departure of Triptolemus on his mission formed the conclusion of the play, and that the earlier part included the arrival of Demeter at Eleusis and her unsuccessful attempt to make the son of Celeus immortal. This is conjecture, but it may be correct. The play was evidently largely narrative in character. It shows the simple nature of the plots with which the young Sophocles began his career as a dramatist. Contrary to his later practice he made the characters divine or semi-divine beings.

CIV

The Troilus

EIGHTEEN quotations have come down from the *Troilus*, one consisting of two lines, three of one line, and the rest of either one or two words.[1] They give very little information about the play, and there is nothing in them to suggest that there was in it any variation from the usual story. This was briefly that the boy Troilus, son of Priam, while exercising his horses was ambushed and slain by Achilles. According to Apollodorus[2] this happened at the sanctuary of Thymbraean Apollo, and the scholiast on *Iliad* XXIV, 257[3] explicitly states that Sophocles laid the scene of the killing there. The story was told in the *Cypria*,[4] which the dramatist probably used as his source.

The death of Troilus must have been the most important event in the plot, and the action must have led up to it. Otherwise the title would be hard to understand. But whether it was

[1] Pearson, *op. cit.*, II, pp. 253 ff.; Welcker, *op. cit.*, I, pp. 124 ff.

[2] *Epit.*, III, 32.

[3] He says ἐντεῦθεν Σοφοκλῆς ἐν Τρωίλῳ φησὶν αὐτὸν λοχηθῆναι ὑπὸ Ἀχιλλέως ἵππους γυμνάζοντα παρὰ τὸ Θυμβραῖον καὶ ἀποθανεῖν.

[4] Proclus, *Chrest.*, p. 236, l. 17, ed. Westphal.

represented as coming about as the result of a chance encounter, or was deliberately planned, is another matter. The First Vatican Mythographer says that if Troilus reached the age of twenty Troy could not be taken.[1] This may have been the story that Sophocles followed. It would give a motive for the ambuscade and the slaughter of the youth. The statement of Dictys Cretensis[2] that Troilus was taken prisoner and slain in cold blood by order of Achilles is hardly suited to tragedy.

The death of Troilus at the hands of Achilles was a favorite subject with the painters of Greek vases.

CV

The Tympanistae

THE *Tympanistae*, or *Tambourine Players*, is quoted by name no fewer than nine times, but the quotations are all short. One consists of three lines, two of one line, and the rest are single words.[3] It is not surprising that no help can be had from them for reconstructing the plot, and in fact we should have no clue as to what the play was about if it were not for a statement made by the scholiast on the *Antigone*. In a note on line 981 he says that in the *Tympanistae* Sophocles mentioned the marriage of Phineus to Idaea, daughter of Dardanus, called by some authorities Eidothea, sister of Cadmus. This would seem to connect the play definitely with the story of Phineus, about whom Sophocles is known to have written two tragedies (see p. 253). Welcker thought the *Tympanistae* a revision of one of them, and G. Wolff[4] tried to identify it with the first *Phineus*. The fact that it is cited so many times under the name *Tympanistae* seems to prove that this was not an alternative title, but designated a separate tragedy.

[1] 210. *Cui* (i.e., Troilo) *dictum erat quod si ad annos XX pervenisset Troia everti non potuisset.*

[2] *Bellum Troianum*, IV, 9.

[3] Pearson, *op. cit.*, II, pp. 262 ff.; Welcker, *op. cit.*, I, pp. 329 ff.

[4] *Philologus*, XXVIII, pp. 343 f.

The title must have been taken from the chorus, who were evidently represented as engaged in some kind of orgiastic celebration. This might be taken to imply that the scene was laid in Thrace, the home of Dionysiac worship, but with the evidence now available it is idle to speculate upon how a group of tambourine players would fit in with any part of the story of Phineus.

CVI

The Tyndareus

Two passages are quoted from the *Tyndareus*,[1] one of six lines in which the poet moralizes on the instability of human fortune, and the other a single line saying that the eye grows dim with age. Little can be conjectured about a tragic plot from two such passages. Welcker[2] thought that Tyndareus was not a title, but a character in the *Aletes*, and that the longer of the two fragments came from that tragedy; but the fact that it is quoted twice[3] as the name of a play is strong evidence against that conjecture.

Tyndareus was not distinctly a tragic character. According to Apollodorus[4] he was driven from Lacedaemon by Hippocoön, but afterwards returned and became king. Perhaps the plot was concerned with this part of his history. He was more famous for his children Clytaemnestra, Helen, and the Dioscuri. That fact, however, is of no help to us in finding a clue to the plot.

[1] Pearson, *op. cit.*, II, pp. 268 ff.

[2] *Op. cit.*, I, pp. 216 f.

[3] By Stobaeus (IV, p. 928, 5, ed. Hense) and by Photius, *Lexicon*, ed. Reitzenstein, p. 89, l. 20.

[4] *Bibl.*, III, 10, 5.

CVII

The Tyro A and B

SOPHOCLES wrote two tragedies on the story of Tyro,[1] as is proved by references which have come down in the literature. There is one clear reference to *Tyro A*, which is, perhaps, also named in two other passages in which the text is corrupt. There are four references to *Tyro B*. Besides these, twelve quotations are said simply to have been taken from the *Tyro* of Sophocles, without further designation; and, in addition, there are three passages which do not name the play, but which can, nevertheless, be assigned to it with some probability. Besides the mutilated papyrus fragment mentioned below, about twenty-seven lines of the tragedy are known. One of the quotations is ten lines long, one three, and the others two lines or less each. Fifty-eight badly mutilated lines on papyrus from wrappings of a mummy found at Hibeh[2] and dating from 280 to 240 B.C. were assigned to the *Tyro* of Sophocles by Blass. There is also a possible reference to one of the two plays in the *Epitrepontes* of Menander (ll. 108–116).

The story of Tyro was, in brief, this. She was the daughter of Salmoneus, king of Elis. Before her marriage to Cretheus, her father's brother, she had borne twin sons to Poseidon. These she had exposed with tokens in a small boat. One of the boys, subsequently called Pelias, was stepped on by a horse and disfigured; the other was given the name Neleus. They were brought up by the keeper of the horses. All this time Tyro was being badly treated by her stepmother, Sidero. Her beautiful hair was cut off and she was otherwise abused. When Pelias and Neleus grew to manhood they met Tyro, were recognized by her, either by means of the boat in which they had been exposed, or by tokens, and avenged her by slaying Sidero. These are the main outlines of the story, but there are many variants

[1] Pearson, *op. cit.*, II, pp. 270 ff.; Welcker, *op. cit.*, I, pp. 312 ff.
[2] *Hibeh Papyri*, I, pp. 17 ff.

in it.[1] Aristotle[2] distinctly says that the recognition in the *Tyro* came about through the boat. There can be little doubt that he is referring to the *Tyro* of Sophocles, though he does not mention the author; and he does not indicate which of the two plays he has in mind. In fact it is difficult to see how two good plots could be developed from the myth as we know it. Welcker thought that the second *Tyro* was merely a revision of the first; but this is not the natural inference one would draw from the references to it. It is possible that there was more to the earlier part of the story than now appears, and that the first *Tyro* had to do with that. The papyrus fragment is so badly mutilated that little can be made out of it except that there seems to be a reference to a bad dream. Tyro's marriage to Cretheus may well have been represented as occurring after her rescue.

Hyginus (*Fab.* 60) says that Salmoneus and Sisyphus were brothers but enemies; that when Sisyphus asked the oracle how he might kill an enemy Apollo replied that if he had sons by his niece Tyro they would avenge him. The children were born; but Tyro, learning of the oracle, killed them to save her father. There is, however, no evidence to connect this story with Sophocles.

[1] For a discussion of the myth see Engelmann, *Archäologische Studien zu den Tragikern*, pp. 40 ff.; Séchan, *op. cit.*, pp. 219 ff.; and Picard-Cambridge in Powell, *New Chapters in the History of Greek Literature*, 3d Series, pp. 104 f.

[2] *Poet.*, p. 1454b 25 . . . οἷον ἐν τῇ Τυροῖ διὰ τῆς σκαφῆς.

Appendix

THE PAPYRI

Sophocles is not as well represented as Euripides in the Greek papyri brought to light in Egypt in modern times, although in a few cases important additions to our knowledge of his drama have come from that source. A list of the papyri so far published is given below. The amount of the text preserved, the date of the papyrus, the place where it was found when that is known, and the place of publication are stated. Three papyri which cannot be definitely proved to be the work of Sophocles, although they have been claimed for him, are included in the list with a question mark. No attempt has been made to give the bibliography of any fragment. The volumes of the *Oxyrhynchus Papyri* are designated by the abbreviation *Ox. Pap.*

1. *Ajax*, lines 51–66; 266–276; 291–307. *Ox. Pap.* XVII, pp. 129 ff. No. 2093. From Oxyrhynchus. Date late second or early third century A.D.

2. *Ajax*, lines 694–705; 753–764. *Ox. Pap.* XIII, pp. 162 f. No. 1615. From Oxyrhynchus. Date early fourth century A.D.

3. *Antigone*, lines 242–246, badly mutilated. *Ox. Pap.* VI, pp. 181 f. No. 875. From Oxyrhynchus. Date early second century A.D.

4. *Electra*, lines 993–1007. *Ox. Pap.* IV, pp. 138 f. No. 693. From Oxyrhynchus. Date third century A.D.

5. *Eurypylus*, 107 fragments, most of them small; about 200 lines in all and 40 nearly complete. *Ox. Pap.* IX, pp. 86 ff. No. 1175 and XVII, pp. 74 ff. From Oxyrhynchus. Date late second century A.D. Diehl, *Supplementum Sophocleum*, pp. 21 ff.

6. *Ichneutae*, about 400 lines and numerous small fragments. *Ox. Pap.* IX, pp. 30 ff. No. 1174 and XVII, pp. 72 ff. From Oxyrhynchus. Date late second century A.D. Diehl, *Supplementum Sophocleum*, pp. 3 ff.

7. *Inachus*, about 60 broken lines. *Tebtunis Papyri*, III, Pt. 1, pp. 3 ff. No. 692. From Tebtunis. Date second century B.C.

8. *Muster of the Achaeans*, 24 lines and a few words. *Berliner Klassikertexte*, V, 2, pp. 64 ff. No. P. 9908. Date second century A.D. Diehl, *Supplementum Sophocleum*, pp. 29 f.

9. *Niobe* (?). Four fragments badly mutilated. *Greek Papyri*, II, pp. 14 ff. From Oxyrhynchus. Date third century B.C.

10. *Oedipus at Colonus*, lines 136–145. *Michigan Papyri*, III, p. 23. No. 140. Provenance unknown. Date second or third century A.D.

11. *Oedipus Tyrannus*, lines 178–190 with scholia, badly mutilated. *Papiri Greci e Latini*, XI, 1935, pp. 69 f. From Oxyrhynchus. Date second century A.D.

12. *Oedipus Tyrannus*, lines 375–385; 429–441. *Ox. Pap.* I, pp. 47 ff. No. 22. From Oxyrhynchus. Date fifth century A.D.

13. *Oedipus Tyrannus*, lines 688–697; 708–710; 731–740; 751–753; 775–777; 779–784; 819–827; 1304–1310; 1351–1358 badly mutilated. *Ox. Pap.* XI, pp. 121 ff. No. 1369. From Oxyrhynchus. Date fifth century A.D.

14. *Oeneus* (?). 37 fragments, one of 20 lines, one of 8, the others small. *Ox. Pap.* VIII, pp. 60 ff. No. 1083. From Oxyrhynchus. Date second century A.D.

15. *Scyrians*. Two fragments, one of 6 and the other of 23 broken lines. *Ox. Pap.* XVII, pp. 30 ff. No. 2077. From Oxyrhynchus. Date late second century A.D.

16. *Tantalus* (?). Two fragments, one of 12 and the other of 10 lines. *Ox. Pap.* II, pp. 23 ff. No. 213. From Oxyrhynchus. Date early second century A.D.

17. *Trachiniae*, lines 12–21; 37–39; 275–283; 289–292; 301–303; 360–365; 370–387; 532–535; 576–581; 602–606; 744; 763–764; 781–797; 851–855; 873–878; 1064–1073; 1131–1147; 1253–1257; 1274–1276. Badly mutilated. *Ox. Pap.* XV, pp. 172 ff. No. 1805. From Oxyrhynchus. Date late second century A.D.

INDEX